World Mythology

World Mythology

Human Desires, Wishes, Fears, and Foibles

DAVID SEAL and SHARON K. SMITH

WIPF & STOCK · Eugene, Oregon

WORLD MYTHOLOGY
Human Desires, Wishes, Fears, and Foibles

Copyright © 2021 David Seal and Sharon K. Smith. All rights reserved. Except for brief quotations in critical publications or reviews, no part of this book may be reproduced in any manner without prior written permission from the publisher. Write: Permissions, Wipf and Stock Publishers, 199 W. 8th Ave., Suite 3, Eugene, OR 97401.

Wipf & Stock
An Imprint of Wipf and Stock Publishers
199 W. 8th Ave., Suite 3
Eugene, OR 97401

www.wipfandstock.com

PAPERBACK ISBN: 978-1-7252-6800-5
HARDCOVER ISBN: 978-1-7252-6801-2
EBOOK ISBN: 978-1-7252-6802-9

08/09/21

Scripture quotations are from New Revised Standard Version Bible, copyright © 1989 National Council of the Churches of Christ in the United States of America. Used by permission. All rights reserved worldwide.

Contents

Preface | ix
Abbreviations | xi
Acknowledgments | xiii

1   How to Read a Myth | 1

PART 1: NATURE AND HUMAN NATURE MYTHS

2   **Vasalisa.** Russian | 12
     Baba Yaga, the Wicked Witch of Russia, Shows Her Softer Side

3   **How Thomas Connolly Met the Banshee.** Irish | 18
     What Is This Screaming Old Hag in the Mist?

4   **Chi Li Slays the Serpent.** Chinese | 22
     You Think Daughters Aren't as Valuable as Sons? Ha! Meet the Dragon Slayer!

5   *The Epic of Gilgamesh.* Sumerian/Babylonian | 26
     Enki Was My Best Friend, and He Just Had to Die.

6   *Penthesileia.* Greek | 32
     The Original Wonder Woman

7   *Hymn to Hermes.* Greek | 39
     Family Drama

PART 2: MORAL INSTRUCTION MYTHS

8   **The Trickster.** Native American | 45
     Mocking the Medicine Man

9   *Oedipus the King.* Greek | 51
     Freud Had It Wrong: Oedipus Didn't *Want* to Kill His Dad and Marry His Mom, It Just Happened That Way.

10 **Moni-Mambu and Anansi.** African | 57
    Arachnid Antics

11 **Myths of Filial Piety.** Asian | 62
    Ninja Filial Piety

12 *Sir Gawain and the Green Knight.* British | 68
    Green and Gallant Knights

13 **The King, the Pigeon, and the Hawk.** East Indian | 77
    Animal Rights and Wrongs

14 **The** *Aeneid.* Roman | 81
    Rome Wasn't Built in a Day. Here's How Long It Really Took.

15 *Antigone.* Greek | 91
    C'mon, King Creon. May I Please Bury My Brother?

16 **The** *Odyssey.* Greek | 96
    Cyclops and Sirens and Sun Gods, Oh My!

17 **The Boy who Was Kind to Animals.** Tibetan | 108
    The Vegetarian Boy Who Sits on a Pink Shell Throne

18 **The Old Woman Who Was Kind to Insects.** Inuit | 112
    What's This about Marrying a Blowfly?

19 **The Tale of the Orphan and the Old Woman.** African | 116
    I Prefer to Vomit Gold and Jewels Rather than Toads and Vipers, Thank You.

20 **Sedna.** Inuit | 120
    What Kind of a Dad Would Chop Off His Daughter's Fingers?

PART 3: CREATION MYTHS

21 **Genesis.** Ancient Hebrew | 125
    The Start of Something New

22 *Popol Vuh.* Mayan | 131
    Word Power

23 *Völuspá* **Part 1, Creation.** Norse | 135
    From Chaos to Calm

24 *Creation of the Titans and Gods.* Greek | 142
    Let's Not Eat Our Offspring, Dad.

25 **The Emergence.** Native American | 147
    From Bugs to People in Five Worlds

26 **Creation of the Universe and Ife.** African | 152
    A Cat Just Isn't Enough Company for a God. Gods Need People.

27 **Creation.** Egyptian | 156
    From Nun to Nut

28 **Pangu.** Chinese | 160
    His Decaying Body Became the Earth. And I Thought I Had Big Bones.

29 **Creation.** Mongolian | 163
    Why Do Cats and Dogs Have Fur and We Don't?

30 *Rangi and Papa.* Polynesian | 167
    Tawhiri-Matea Is Mad because His Parents Separated.

PART 4: END OF THE WORLD AND AFTERLIFE MYTHS

31 **Revelation.** Middle Eastern | 171
    Then I Saw a Great White Throne.

32 *Völuspá* **Part 2, Ragnarok.** Norse | 175
    Mistletoe Mayhem

33 **Afterlife.** Persian | 181
    A Narrow Bridge

34 **The Moon and Death.** Australian | 185
    The First Astronomers

35 **Pele, Goddess of the Volcano.** Hawaiian | 189
    Temper, Temper, Temper! Jealousy Causes Massive Lava Flows.

Bibliography | 195

Index | 205

Preface

A MYTH IS A story with an eternal truth.

When I took Brad Hick's mythology class several years ago, I appreciated how he related each myth to our modern day. Regardless of when it was first told, and regardless of whether or not it was based on fact, myths all contain kernels of truth that resonate through the ages.

Since I have been teaching mythology, I have used Brad's approach to focus on the human connection. David Seal and I wrote this book so that students and others interested in myth would be able to explore questions and answers that the ancients and moderns have asked and tried to resolve. We have made our primary focus the timeless truths, instead of the geographic region where the myth originated. The book is divided into three sections: myths about human nature, myths designed to teach morality, and myths about our origins and ends. We hope you enjoy reading about human desires, wishes, fears, and foibles as you connect with these stories.

Sharon Smith
Howell, Michigan

Abbreviations

BCE	Before the Common Era
CE	Common Era
ch.	chapter(s)
Dan	Daniel
ed(s).	editor(s)
et al.	et alia
Exod	Exodus
Gen	Genesis
Isa	Isaiah
l.	line(s)
Mal	Malachi
n.p.	no page number
NRSV	New Revised Standard Version
Rev	Revelation
trans.	translator
vol.	volume

Acknowledgments

THE AUTHORS WISH TO thank Dr. Rebecca Abbott at Wipf and Stock for her outstanding job as copyeditor.

1

How to Read a Myth

INTRODUCTION

MANY FACTORS CAN MAKE myths difficult to appreciate and understand. Mythology comes to us from the past and from people of diverse worldviews, cultures, and languages. Myths are also a specific genre of literature, having their own rules of formulation and interpretation. In addition, in mythology, there is the reality of the absent author, where the myths are listened to and read by people like you and me, who are not able to contact the author (or authors), to ask questions or to get clarification about the meaning of his or her composition. All these factors and others can make the task of appreciating and understanding myths difficult. This chapter attempts to provide a foundation that will help mitigate the various degrees of separation that prevent you from enjoying and comprehending myths from around the world.

Initially, we will provide a working definition of myth. Though many exist, we can settle on certain common features. Second, we will give an overview of creation myths. Most cultures have a myth describing the earth's origin. Third, we will provide an overview of the nature of oral cultures. Many, if not all, myths were originally enjoyed by a person hearing them performed out loud, together with other listeners, rather than reading them silently to themselves. Oral literature differs in many ways from written literature. Fourth, we will summarize the various functions myths had in their original contexts. Finally, regardless of the distance that separates us from understanding the various world myths, we will acknowledge that there are familiar human experiences expressed in these stories. The world's mythologies reflect human curiosities, wishes, desires, fears, foibles, and concerns. We want to encourage you to discover these commonalities that bind together a culturally diverse humanity.

CHARACTERISTICS OF A MYTH

To read a myth effectively, one needs to know the nature of the literature. A survey of the many books on mythology will reveal that there is no one definition of myth. William Doty devotes two entire chapters to defining myth. Doty lists the following attributes:[1]

1. A mythological corpus consists of a complex network of myths that are culturally important to the people that composed and preserved them. Myths are a communal possession; they have obtained currency because of their acceptance by a community.[2] Over an extended period, a group has endorsed certain stories which address some of the larger questions about human life.

2. The myths portray a world where the characters, including deities and other supernatural beings,[3] are treated as having the same visibility as anything else you might consider as existing. Even the physical world in myths—rivers, streams, woods, mountains, and the very earth itself—is alive with the divine presence. In short, myths deal with a numinous order of reality behind the appearances of the phenomenal world. Furthermore, the transcendent figures of the mythical world are represented as taking part in activities on a cosmic scale, which

---

1. Doty, *Mythography*, 33. For clarification, where necessary, I have elaborated on them.

2. Dulles, "Symbol, Myth," 8.

3. The names of the gods and supernatural beings can be confusing. They make much more sense when one understands their linguistic derivations. J. F. Bierlein provides helpful illustrations: "Wotan, the German form of the name of the god known as Odin in Norse mythology, is reminiscent of the modern German word wüten, meaning 'to rage.' One of the names of the Greek god Phoebus, means 'the shining one,' a reference to his role as sun-god" (*Parallel Myths*, 9). As you encounter the odd and confusing names of deities in the myths, research them to understand their origin.

exert a permanent causal influence on earthly happenings.[4] When myth is employed, it presupposes that humanity has learned to make some distinction between the natural and transcendent realm. Only when this insight has been achieved, does humanity "look to the actions of the gods as offering an explanation of what is experienced in the world."[5] Notably, these gods or forces are depicted as if they were persons, or at least they are portrayed using personal terms.[6] As John Oswalt claims, "Mythical descriptions of the gods invariably depict them as human in every respect, only more so. They are strong; they are weak; they are good; they are bad; they are trustworthy; they are fickle."[7] Consequently, myths generally tend to have a low view of the gods. As you read a myth, look for examples of this characteristic. Often the gods even fear death and are helpless to do anything about it. Further, myth is almost always polytheistic. There are many different forces in the world, and there is usually a god for each one.[8]

3. Likewise, there is a uniformly low view of humanity in myth.[9] Humans are often created to serve the gods, and, to a large degree, their creation was an afterthought. This relatively low view of humans is the case in the Norse creation myth, where only a small percentage of the myth discusses humanity. In addition, humans have no real control over their destinies. Choice appears to be an illusion.

4. Myths are conveyed in story form, employing graphic imagery and metaphorical and symbolic language.[10] Graphic imagery is important because it demands and receives a greater amount of processing time

---

4. Dulles, "Symbol, Myth," 9.
5. Dulles, "Symbol, Myth," 8.
6. Dulles, "Symbol, Myth," 8–9.

7. Oswalt, *Bible among the Myths*, 45. One reason for this continuity, especially between the human and divine realms, is that the only way for the mythmaker to explain the particular characteristics of the invisible world is to suppose that the invisible world takes the same shape as the visible one. The mythmaker reasons from the given visible realm to the divine invisible realm (Oswalt, *Bible among the Myths*, 50).

8. Oswalt, *Bible among the Myths*, 57.
9. Oswalt, *Bible among the Myths*, 59.

10. Leland Ryken defines a symbol "as an image that stands for something in addition to is literal meaning. It is more laden with meaning than simply the connotations of the straight image" (Ryken, *Dictionary of Biblical Imagery*, xiv). In most cases, symbolism emerges as a shared language in a culture. In other words, it will be extremely rare for an author to create a symbol for a single occasion.

by listeners, and thus, it will be more memorable.[11] Storytellers often utilized image-based techniques to evoke an audience's "visualization" of the text. Metaphors are important devices for helping people understand something unfamiliar; they teach by generating connections that would otherwise remain undetectable by the listener or reader. The presence of metaphors in a text might suggest that the author wanted to clarify a topic or to teach his audience content that he felt would require a comparison to foster comprehension of the topic. Myths also employ symbols, which function more effectively to describe reality, because some things elude a precise description or definition.

5. Myths are often expressed in emotional language to both convince the original audience of their relevance and to lead listeners to participate in them.[12] Emotions foster empathy with the characters of the tale. Participation by listeners becomes empathetic identification.

Not all these components of myth noted above will be self-evident in every myth you read. However, knowing them will help prepare you for the elements you might encounter as you read and try to comprehend this genre of literature.

CREATION MYTHS

The subject matter of myths helps a culture to understand their surrounding universe, its history, and arrangement, and explain humanity's place in it. Consequently, most cultures have a myth that explains the world's origin or a creation myth. Creation myths can be categorized by certain characteristics, which we will summarize in this section.

---

11. Minchen, *Homer*, 134.

12. Plato's character Ion, a performer, stated about his oral performance of Homeric epic: "For I will tell you without reserve: when I relate a tale of woe, my eyes are filled with tears; and when it is of fear or awe, my hair stands on end with terror, and my heart leaps" (Plato, *Ion* 535c, in *Statesman. Philebus. Ion,* 427). Further on the same page, Ion notes the reaction of the crowd to his emotional performance: "... for I look down upon them from the platform and see them at such moments crying and turning awestruck eyes upon me and yielding to the amazement of my tale. For I have to pay the closest attention to them; since, if I set them crying, I shall laugh myself because of the money I take, but if they laugh, I myself shall cry because of the money I lose."

Creation myths are grouped according to their symbolic structure. They include creation from nothing, creation from chaos, creation from a cosmic egg, creation from world parents, creation through emergence, and creation through the agency of an earth diver.[13]

Creation from nothing is seen in Hebrew, Polynesian, and Egyptian cultures, among others. The deity brings forth creation from nothing as a deliberate act. In several cultures, this deity is symbolized as a sky deity.[14]

Creation from chaos is seen in several Near Eastern and Indian myths. There is primordial chaos in some form, whether it is water or a swirling mass of substance, and this is held at bay by some sort of monster, such as a serpent which withholds some life-giving force such as water or sun. Some myths of creation from chaos start as a constant state of change, so that nothing can be distinguishable. Creation emerges from this flux, and, in some cases, chaos is never completely overcome.

Creation from a cosmic egg is seen in Polynesian, African, India, and Greek myths. The egg is a symbol of fertility, and incubation occurs to produce a time-ordered creation.[15]

Some myths feature creation from primordial world parents, who are often completely indifferent. The offspring may appear unintentionally and tend to be alienated from their parents. Tension occurs when the offspring become agents of separation, and it is the offspring who are the archetypes for later humans.[16]

Emergence creation myths tend to be a progressive development, symbolic of gestation. Maturation takes place gradually, typically in different levels of the underground, "Mother Earth." When beings are fully developed, they emerge as humans in the daylight.

Finally, earth-diver creation myths consist of an animal that dives into primordial waters to bring up a small rock or bit of earth from which more land can come forth. These myths are common in North American native cultures.

These ancient stories come from cultures that were predominantly oral. This aspect of culture influenced the myths and gave them an additional set of characteristics. Next, we will briefly explain the oral features of myths.

13. Long, "Cosmogony," 1987.
14. Long, "Cosmogony," 1987.
15. Long, "Cosmogony," 1988.
16. Long, "Cosmogony," 1988.

MYTHS AND THE NATURE OF ORAL CULTURES

In many ancient cultures, going to the marketplace involved not only buying goods, but also attending lawsuits, participating in philosophical dialogues, or listening to the performance of songs, myths, or other narratives.[17] Societies where news, information, and entertainment are predominantly conveyed orally are called oral cultures. Another term typically used to describe cultures of this nature is "aural," which means of or relating to the ear or to the sense of hearing. Oral cultures enjoy media of all forms primarily through the ears, rather than by reading with the eyes. Many of the myths were composed at a time when writing had not been invented, or it was not widely used for literary purposes. The stories at some point were written down, but the texts that we now have still contain traces of their oral composition. The aim of this section is to acquaint you with some of the predominate oral characteristics of mythologies and suggest techniques to help you understand them better.

Several features are common to oral performances, including myths. First, when performed out loud, the recipient is guided in the myth's interpretation by the person reciting the story in front of them. By contrast, when literature is read privately, readers must make their own interpretation of the words on the page. The listeners are directed in the interpretation of the myth as they experience the reader's facial expressions, voice inflection, posture, and body language. A myth teller would sit, stand, or a combination of both, surrounded by listeners, and recount a tale. It was never just a recitation. The voice was raised or lowered—used as a means of dramatization. The tale was acted out with body gestures, even when the storyteller was sitting.

Second, orally performed myths can serve to establish a feeling of group identity. When a myth is heard collectively, the experience is shared, and joy, melancholy, fear, or aggression is contagious among the participants. Not only are listeners linked to each other collectively by those hearing the recitation of a myth, but they are also connected to their ancestors, the subjects of the myths. When experiencing the performance, the audience members feel that their own world is a continuation of that of their heroic ancestors and that they contribute to keeping the heroes alive by

---

17. Jensen, "Performance," 45.

hearing of their great deeds.[18] The performance reactivates the events of former times.

Third, oral compositions often work differently from purely literary works. Myths show particularly elaborate uses of oral devices; some were developed to help illiterate performers remember a long narrative as a memory device. The performance of an oral storyteller or poet is not only judged on his or her ability to entertain and hold the interest of his or her audience, but success would be judged on his or her memory. Thus, oral storytellers might recite long lists of names and places to demonstrate their mastery of memory. For example, in the first book of the Greek myth *Posthomerica*, the author catalogs the elaborate names of the twelve Amazonian warriors who accompany Penthesileia into battle against the Argives—names that the audience would have noticed if improperly cited.[19] While we might perceive the long list as distracting, boring, and cumbersome, the ancients would have viewed the feat with pleasure and been impressed by it, in the same manner that the performance of any athletic achievement would strike modern day spectators.

Fourth, in oral cultures, where most individuals heard sacred myths rather than read them, it was advantageous for the storyteller to repeat things in the same way or in a similar manner two or three times. Authors of histories and narratives used repetition to communicate the central message and the main points of the whole story. Repetition attracts us like a steady music beat. In oral communication, repetition creates a sense of rhythm, increases listener attention, and highlights an author's emphasis, while also making the content more memorable. Repetition serves to focus the attention of the reader, and, at the same time, it was pleasing to the ear for a culture that listened to the text.[20] For example, in the ancient epic *Gilgamesh*, the character whose name is the title of the myth has a series of three dreams, each more ominous than the last. Not only does this repetition provide mounting suspense, but the sequence of dreams gives the myth teller an opportunity to develop the relationship of Gilgamesh to his faithful companion Enkidu, who gives more and more implausible interpretations of the dreams.

18. Jensen, "Performance," 48.

19. "The companions were Clonie, Evandre, Polemusa, Derinoe, Antandre, Bremusa, and Harmothoe with eyes of dark luster, and Hippothoe, Antibrote, Alcibie, Derimacheia, and finally, Thermodosa glorying in her spear" (lines 42–46, Dyce, *Select Translations*, 5–6).

20. Exum, "Aspects of Symmetry," 12.

In mythology, the spoken word has great power. It is through the spoken word that God created the world in Genesis (Gen 1:1–31). In Persian mythology, the utterance of only one word by Ahura Mazda (the good god) casts Ahriman (the bad god) into hell. As myths were shared out loud by storytellers, the power of the spoken work continued to be revered and appreciated.

THE FUNCTIONS OF MYTHS

Myths had several different functions, including to entertain, to excite, and to delight their listeners. However, myths were seldom only a form of entertainment; myths served multiple purposes at one time. Readers of myths today should know that the goals of the myth tellers are likely very foreign, and knowledge of their various purposes will help you understand them more intelligently.

One function of myths was to teach moral lessons. Myths were told to shape personal ethics and form admirable behavior. There was a spectrum of values and codes that a society wanted to be understood and embraced by their population. Didactic myths convey lessons to help prevent the decline of the social order and the decay of moral responsibility. Values conveyed by myths may relate ideals for social interaction (e.g., family structure), ideals for rulers and kings towards their subjects, and the expected relational interactions between humans and their gods. Morals, values, and social codes were often expressed by repeatedly praising exemplary individuals and stressing their good behavior or by constantly rejecting poor models and behavior. People would identify with the heroes, take them as their models, and learn from their misfortune or success.[21]

Second, myths may also teach cosmic lessons, explaining some feature of life or the cosmos. This is illustrated in the Greek myth *Hermes,* which explains the origin of the art of kindling fire with sticks. Cosmic or creation myths can describe the origin of the world. Many creation myths explain why things are as they are now. This function of myths is related to the human fear of chaos. Chaos destroys our security, and security is perhaps the greatest of all human longings. In order to gain security, the first task is to have some sense of intellectual order. This can be achieved, in part, if we can explain why things are as they are. This also gives the feeling that we know how to relate to the thing explained. Further, the most profound

---

21. Jensen, "Performance," 48.

How to Read a Myth

questions of life are the ones that give rise to creation myths: Who are we? Why are we here? What is the purpose of our lives and our deaths? How should we understand our place in the world, in time and space? These issues are addressed most directly in creation myths.

Cosmic myths can also explain how the natural world functions. These myths explain such things as why plants and animals look or behave the way they do or why there is day and night, why there are natural disasters and why there are seasons. In responding to the change of seasons, it is noteworthy that many of the world's nature mythologies are stories about a harvest deity who spends part of the year in the underworld, thereby explaining the cycle of the seasons.

Third, myths may justify a political situation, reflect belief systems, or authorize and validate a group's social customs and institutions. These are called charter myths. For example, a myth might justify political privileges that nobles claimed or account for why only certain members of a group like that of priests had the right to perform certain rituals. Charter myths might also narrate the founding of cities and the establishment of laws, customs, and dynasties (royal families). In this function, myth serves as the "glue" that binds societies together and as the basis of identity for communities, tribes, and nations.

Fourth, a myth may explain a ritual or festival, providing either an etiology[22] for it or a verbal counterpart to what goes on in the ritual. A ritual is an act or series of acts designed to bring people into contact with higher spiritual powers. In such cases, the myth may be perceived not as an event of the distant past, but as happening now in ritual space. Sometimes myths of culture heroes impart sacred knowledge by teaching people how to perform rituals and ceremonies. This is demonstrated in the *Hymn to Hermes* as Hermes carries out the twelve-part sacrifice to the twelve Olympian gods. In a myth featuring the White Buffalo Woman of the Lakota people, this mythical figure instructs the people in the proper use of the sacred pipe for prayer, for the marriage ceremony, and for the rituals that attend a death.[23] One major function of ritual myths is explain how to maintain order over chaos.[24] Again, because of humanity's fear of chaos and disorder, ritual myths explain the ways to prevent chaos and give people a sense that they have some control over it. So, some myths describe what is to be done

---

22. Etiology is the study of causes or origins.
23. Stookey, *Thematic Guide*, 53–54.
24. Oswalt, *Bible among the Myths*, 49.

in the case of drought or pestilence that threatens to destroy the source of human sustenance. A ritual does not merely repeat the ritual acts that came before it, but is linked to it and continues them, either at fixed periods or otherwise.

MYTHS OFTEN EMBODY UNIVERSAL HUMAN EXPERIENCES

Contrary to what we might think, mythology, even though ancient and from diverse cultures and widespread geographical places, has an uncanny ability to embody universal human experiences—and, if viewed in a certain way, is as up-to-date as the daily news. J. F. Bierlein says, "Myth is an eternal mirror in which we see ourselves. Myth has something to say to everyone, as it has something to say about everyone."[25] Understanding myths can help us to understand ourselves. To help explain how myths can have contemporary and personal relevance, Bierlein again is helpful.[26] He claims that myths are a road map of the human experience common to us all, and they speak to us as finite creatures (finite in both knowledge and existence), estranged from God and/or some transcendent other, living out a process of becoming, making choices, living in societies and families, and finding our identity and place in the cosmos. *World Mythology* will focus predominately on how myths reflect human curiosities, wishes, desires, fears, foibles, and concerns. For example, the curiosity about the earth's origin, the fear of death, the value of friendship, the pain of betrayal, and the cost of maintaining one's principles, are just some of the topics that universally appear in mythology. By discerning the underlying similarities and threads in the world's myths and traditions, we better understand our shared humanity, while honoring the diverse ways human beings live and make meaning of their experience.

CONCLUSION

Myth is a genre of literature having its own characteristics. Rather than providing a definition of myth, we have listed its characteristics, which will prepare you for what will be encountered in the various myths you read. In

---

25. Bierlein, *Parallel Myths*, xiii.
26. Bierlein, *Living Myths*, 3–4.

addition, because myths come from oral cultures, we have listed features that may still be present in the written form of the myth. Look for these oral traces as you read. It will also be advantageous, as you read, for you to consider the various potential functions myths had in their original setting. Lastly, myths reveal the way others have worked at addressing the big questions of life and how they reconciled the opposing forces at work in human experience. While reading, determine how the stories cohere with your worldview, values, and approach to navigating your own life's journey.

2

Vasalisa. Russian
Baba Yaga, the Wicked Witch of Russia, Shows Her Softer Side

HISTORICAL AND THEMATIC OVERVIEW

For a Russian rural population that could not read, folktales were a source of entertainment for all social classes. These tales have strongly influenced Russian literature and the arts, including authors and composers such as Fyodor Dostoevsky, Peter Tchaikovsky, and Leo Tolstoy.[1] Despite their influence and appeal, not everyone has appreciated their value. The medieval Russian church considered folktales evil and diligently sought to suppress them. Under the Soviet Union, such tales were criticized as being backward and harmful, and were rewritten to reflect current social problems and Soviet ideology.[2] After the 1970s, the government no longer controlled the study of these old stories, and they have since flourished and have been reexamined, published, and studied.

There are many stories in Russia, Poland, and the Baltic countries that tell of Vasalisa, sometimes referred to as Wassilissa the Wise. In her fascinating work *Women who Run with the Wolves*, Clarissa Pinkola Estés

---

1. Arant, "Folklore," 507.
2. Arant, "Folklore," 508.

reports that there is evidence of this tale that predates classical Greek culture.[3] Specifically, references to Baba Yaga stem back to the horse-goddess cults. In Russian folklore, she is known as the Life/Death/Life Goddess.

Baba Yaga was portrayed as either a witch or an ogress, living in darkness away from humanity.[4] Typically, in Russian folklore, Baba Yaga is depicted as either a child-eating hag or a wise old woman. In this story, she is both. Her macabre dwelling is found deep in the woods. An abundance of human bones and skulls surround her dwelling, and her hut is supported by the legs of a chicken.

As in many of the Western European and Russian folktales, in this story, the heroine leaves home and must carry out several different tasks while encountering obstacles; she accomplishes the tasks and is successful at the end.[5]

This tale speaks of the power of the instinctual intuition. In Estés's version, the myth starts with, "Once there was, and once there was not...," alerting the reader that this story takes place in a world where things are not as they seem. The story ends abruptly, returning the reader to reality.

MYTH SUMMARY: VASALISA[6]

Once there was, and once there was not, a young mother who lay dying, with her young daughter and husband beside her. The mother desired to give her daughter Vasalisa a final gift and parting advice. She called to Vasalisa and gave her a tiny doll dressed just like her daughter, with red boots, a white apron, black skirt, and a vest embroidered with colored thread. Vasalisa's mother instructed her, "Here are my last words, beloved. Should you lose your way or be in need of help, ask this doll what to do. You'll receive assistance. Keep the doll with you always. Do not tell anyone about her. Feed her when she is hungry. This is my mother's promise to you, my blessing on you, dear daughter."

She died shortly thereafter and, after a long period of mourning, the father married a widow with two daughters. But they were not as polite and kind as they initially seemed; rather, they were cruel and, when alone

---

3. Estés, *Women Who Run*, 71.
4. Gimbutas, "Baba Yaga," 727.
5. Arant, "Folklore," 509.
6. Myth summary from Estés, *Women Who Run*, 71–77.

with Vasalisa, they tormented her. But Vasalisa, being innocent and kind, thrived anyway. One day the stepmother and stepsisters decided to get rid of Vasalisa permanently. They let the fire die down and plotted to send Vasalisa in the forest to Baba Yaga the witch to beg for fire, believing that Baba Yaga would kill and eat her.

Vasalisa returned home from working and foraging that evening and noticed there was no fire. "Where is the fire?" she inquired.

"You stupid child," said the stepmother, "Obviously we have no fire. And I can't go out into the woods because I am old. My daughters can't go because they're afraid. So you are the only one who can go out into the forest to find Baba Yaga and get a coal to start our fire again."

Vasalisa set out through the scary forest, frightened and unsure, but touching the doll her mother gave her brought her comfort. At every fork in the road, Vasalisa consulted the doll, who told her which way to turn. She fed the doll some of her bread. Suddenly a man in white on a white horse galloped by, and it became daylight. Another man on a red horse passed, and the sun rose. Vasalisa continued to walk until she reached a hut, a strange dwelling with a fence made of glowing skulls and bones. The house sat atop a huge yellow chicken leg that walked around by itself, with bolts made of human fingers and toes. A rider in all black passed, and it became night.

Vasalisa consulted the doll, asking if this is the house. The doll indicated that it was. Baba Yaga descended upon Vasalisa and shouted, "What do you want?" Baba Yaga was an ugly old woman with greasy hair and warty skin. She rode in a cauldron.

"Grandmother, I come for fire. My house is cold. . .my people will die. . .I need fire," Vasalisa humbly asked.

Baba Yaga snapped, "Oh yesssss, I know you, and your people. Well, you useless child. . .you let the fire go out. That's an ill-advised thing to do. And besides, what makes you think I should give you the flame?"

Vasalisa consulted her doll and quickly replied, "Because I asked."

Baba Yaga purred, "You're lucky, that is the right answer."

Vasalisa felt very lucky that she had given the right answer.

Baba Yaga insisted that Vasalisa complete some tasks before she would help and threatened Vasalisa with death if she did them incorrectly. Baba Yaga ordered her to clean the house, sweep, do the laundry, separate mildewed corn from good, and see that everything was in order.

"I will be back to inspect your work later. If it is not done, *you* will be my feast," sneered Baba Yaga.

Vasalisa consulted her doll. The doll assured Vasalisa that she would be able to complete the tasks. Vasalisa, much relieved, ate a little, fed her doll, but was so fatigued, she fell asleep. The doll completed the tasks while Vasalisa was asleep, and when Baba Yaga returned, she could find no fault. Baba Yaga commanded her servants to grind the corn, and three pair of hands appeared in midair. The corn flew like golden snow. Baba Yaga ordered Vasalisa to continue working and directed her to a pile of dirt. "In that pile of dirt are many poppy seeds, millions of poppy seeds. And I want, in the morning, to have one pile of poppy seeds and one pile of dirt all separated out from each other. Do you understand?"

Vasalisa almost fainted. "Oh my, how am I going to do all that?" She reached into her pocket, and the doll whispered, "Don't worry, I will take care of it." That night Vasalisa desperately tried to separate the dirt and seeds. After a time, the doll said to her, "Sleep now. All will be well."

Again, the doll accomplished the tasks, and when the old woman returned home, she bid her servants to press oil from the poppy seeds. Again, pairs of hands appeared to do her bidding. Vasalisa asked about the three horsemen. Baba Yaga reminded her that too much knowledge makes a person old too soon. Baba Yaga would say only that the horsemen are "my day," "my rising sun," and "my night." Vasalisa wanted to ask more, but the doll jumped up and down inside her pocket, and Vasalisa realized she should say no more. Baba Yaga asked how she became so wise, and Vasalisa replied, "By the blessing of my mother."

"Blessing?" screeched Baba Yaga. "We need no blessing, be on your way." Baba Yaga pushed her out and gave her a fiery skull on a stick to take home. Vasalisa started to thank Baba Yaga, but again the doll jumped up and down in her pocket, so she left. She ran home, following the directions given by the doll. At one point Vasalisa became frightened and thought about leaving the skull, but the skull itself spoke to her and calmed her. Vasalisa finally arrived home. Her stepmother and stepsisters ran to her, saying they had been without fire since she had left, and no matter how hard they tried to start one, it always went out.

Vasalisa entered the house feeling triumphant, having survived the dangerous journey. But the skull watched the stepmother and stepsisters, and by morning, they were burned to tiny cinders.

COMMENTARY

This is a story of maturation.[7] Vasalisa endures the death of her mother, mistreatment by her stepfamily, and a forced exile where she faces a series of difficult tasks which test her. She returns to her home with new insights, confidence, and maturity.

The story is replete with symbolism from start to finish. One of the first things the reader may notice is the recurrence of the colors red, white, and black. The doll is wearing these colors, which match exactly what Vasalisa is wearing. Even the men on horseback come with the same colors. In ancient times, these colors symbolized the ancient colors of birth (red), life (white), and death (black).[8]

Another important symbol is the use of the doll, which has a long history of symbolism in many cultures, from Paleolithic and Neolithic times to the present. Dolls are used in rituals and rites and are symbolically considered infused with life. In this story, the doll and Vasalisa are firmly bonded through her mother's blessing and command, representing intuition passed down from one generation to the next. The doll, which is really Vasalisa's inner guidance, steers her through the forest and gives her insight when dealing with Baba Yaga. Intuition which is not fed and used atrophies like an unused muscle, but Vasalisa trusts and uses her intuition. Vasalisa feeds the doll—feeds her intuition—and listens to the counsel of the doll, which saves her.

Her intuition guides her when Vasalisa is asked to separate the mildewed corn from the good corn and the poppy seeds from the dirt. These are tasks which require fine distinctions. The sorting requires skill beyond what Vasalisa thinks she has, but the doll does it while Vasalisa sleeps. This is often how intuition works in one's subconscious; the distinctions are made while one is not even conscious of the sorting, until one becomes conscious of the results.

The housekeeping tasks assigned to Vasalisa are also symbolic. She is told to do the laundry. In the old country, one must go to the river to wash clothes, the same place where ritualistic ablutions are made.[9] Doing Baba Yaga's laundry is a symbol of cleansing and purification of the soul. In handling, the "laundry" is brought to consciousness. In laundering, it

---

7. Scielzo, "Analysis of Bába Yagá," 171.
8. Estés, *Women Who Run*, 98.
9. Estés, *Women Who Run*, 91.

is cleansed, renewed, and purified.[10] Vasalisa is also assigned to sweep. Sweeping is symbolic of keeping order within one's mind, carving out a place free from distractions.

The skull with the fiery light is symbolic of ancestors, where in ancient cultures it was believed that the "timeless knowledge of the old ones" lives on in the bones, particularly the skull.[11] Baba Yaga gives Vasalisa the fiery skull, the ancestral knowledge, to carry with her as she returns home.

QUESTIONS FOR REFLECTION: THE HUMAN DIMENSION

1. Provide an example of when you have experienced maturation through trials.
2. Why do you think it was considered important to pass on the concept of intuition? Do you think that, today, intuition is given much thought or respect?
3. When have you relied on intuition? How might listening to our intuition aid us today?
4. Name two childhood fairy tales that contain symbols such as dolls, colors for life/death, healing, or another concept.
5. How have you experienced "doing laundry" of the mind?

QUESTIONS FOR REFLECTION: CRITICAL ANALYSIS

1. Why do you think folktales endure, despite attempts to suppress them?
2. What one story have you heard that features a character similar to Baba Yaga?
3. Consider the concept of a fiery skull. How else may this be symbolic?
4. Consider the beginning ("Once there was, and once there was not...") and abrupt end of this story. What might you conclude about this way of presenting the story?

---

10. Estés, *Women Who Run*, 91.
11. Estés, *Women Who Run*, 102.

3

How Thomas Connolly Met the Banshee. Irish

What Is This Screaming Old Hag in the Mist?

HISTORICAL AND THEMATIC OVERVIEW

THE ICONIC BANSHEE HAS worked her way into modern idioms. Many people have heard the phrase, "he/she screamed like a banshee," even if they do not know what a banshee is. The term refers to a supernatural harbinger of death that dates centuries back in Ireland, as recognizable as leprechaun lore. The banshee is an otherworldly woman, a female fairy figure of folklore that foretells death. She usually appears as a keening woman. Banshees do not cause death, but rather forewarn of impending death. Originally known as *bean sidhe* (fairy woman), the phrase was conflated into "banshee."

A banshee was most often heard at midnight, dawn, or dusk, times most closely associated with supernatural activity.[1] The dimming light heightens imagination and supernatural interpretations of events. Typically, a banshee is said to be heard near the home of a dying person, close to an unusual natural formation such as a rock, tree, cave, or crevice. Bodies of

---

1. Lysaght, "Banshee," 97.

water are also common places where one might hear this purported death messenger.

The physical description of a banshee varies widely, from an attractive young woman to an old hag. Generally speaking, she is portrayed as an old woman in loose clothing, combing her long hair. She keens and wrings her hands and is heard by either the relatives of the person to die or by neighbors.

Sometimes the banshee is said to have been kidnapped by fairies, and sometimes she is said to be a fallen angel; a human woman who upon her death becomes a death messenger herself, due to some past misdeed or violence once wreaked upon her; or a guardian angel who is giving notice of death. Many times, the banshee is linked with a particular family, where the same banshee wails before the death of various family members through the generations.[2] Having a family banshee was often seen as a status symbol, and high-ranking families boasted of their own banshees.[3]

The following Irish folktale, recounted by the poet William Butler Yeats (1865–1939), is typical of the many stories involving a banshee.

MYTH SUMMARY: HOW THOMAS CONNOLLY MET THE BANSHEE[4]

I was going home from work one day in the dusk o' the evening. I had a mile or so to go where I was lodgin' with a decent widder woman, Biddy Maguire. It was a lonesome road I had to travel, and I came nigh upon where a brudge used be, with white mist steamin' up out o' the water all around it.

Often as I'd passed by the place before, it seemed strange to me, and I began to feel a cold wind blowin' through the hollow o' me heart. I put a bold face on it an' I made a struggle to set one leg afore the other, until I came to the rise o' the brudge. And there, God be good to us! In a cantle o' the wall I seen an old woman.

I pitied the old creature an' I up an' sez to her, "That's a cold lodgin' for ye, ma'am." She no more took notice o' me than if I hadn't let a word out o' me, so I sez to her again, "Eh, ma'am, is there anyt'ing the matther wid ye?" I made to touch her shoulder on'y somethin' stopped me. Her hair! The

---

2. Lysaght, *Banshee*, 53.
3. MacKillop, "Banshee," 34.
4. Myth summary from Yeats, ed., *Irish Fairy and Folk Tales*, 109–112.

likes of it I never seen on mortal woman, young or old, before nor since. The first squint I got of it, I thought it silvery gray, but when I got up beside her, I saw it was a sort of an Iscariot color, an' a shine out of it like floss silk.

I made a step back from her an' said, "The Lord be between us an' harm," an' wid that I blessed meself. The word wasn't out o' me mouth afore she turned her face on me. 'Twas the awfulest apparition ever I seen—as pale as a corpse, an' two eyes sewn in wid red thread, as blue as two forget-me-nots, an' as cold as the moon in a bog hole of a frosty night, an' a dead-an'-alive look that sent a cold shiver through the marra o' me bones.

'Twas then I began to suspect what she was, an' I made a great struggle to get me two legs into a trot. How I brought meself home that same night the Lord in heaven only knows, but I must ha' tumbled against the door, where I lay in a dead swoon for mostly an hour, and the first I knew was Mrs. Maguire stannin' over me with a jorum o' punch she was pourin' down me throat. So by degrees I began to come to a little; an' that's the way I met the banshee! "But how did you know it was really the banshee after all?" asked Mister Harry.

I knew the apparition of well her enough, but 'twas confirmed by a circumstance that occurred the same time. There was a Mister O'Nales was come on a visit to the place in the neighborhood, a royal old Irish family—an' the banshee was heard keening round the house that same night, be more than one that was in it, sure enough he was found dead in his bed the next mornin'. So, if it wasn't the banshee I seen that time, I'd like to know what else it could a' been.

COMMENTARY

This story contains the usual characteristics associated with a banshee encounter: twilight, a woman at an unusual rock formation, her noticeable hair, and a death that night. Traces of these same characteristics can be seen dating back to medieval Irish literature, where the deaths of noble families were announced by lamenting female figures.[5] Stories of banshees were not present before the seventeenth century.[6] However, it is likely that this tradition has its origins even further back in a patron goddess whose purpose was to foretell and announce death.[7]

5. Lysaught, "Banshee," 96.
6. MacKillop, "Banshee," 33.
7. Lysaught, "Banshee," 96.

The mythology was reinforced in medieval times. Funerals would have a "keener," often professional, who would sing sad songs at the graveside. Eventually, the layers of stories surrounding funerary practices, as well as impending death, developed into a harbinger figure, the banshee.

It is not surprising that the banshee developed, given the fascination and horror that humans feel with regard to imminent death. Death is inevitable, but there is a special fascination with the days surrounding death and particularly with any perceived indicators that death may be near. When a friend or acquaintance dies, people tend to remember every detail about the last time they saw that person alive. Humans tend to look for patterns in sounds, sights, and circumstances, and even when these are mere coincidence, the tendency is to attach these to an omen. Given the fascinations humans have for events surrounding death, it is little wonder that the myth of the banshee developed as a way of coping with the macabre.

QUESTIONS FOR REFLECTION: THE HUMAN DIMENSION

1. Keening developed as a way of coping with grief. Why do you think this is?
2. Do you have clear recollection of the events surrounding a death of a family member or friend? Were there special signs that you recall? Why do you think these memories tend to be particularly strong?

QUESTIONS FOR REFLECTION: CRITICAL ANALYSIS

1. What may be the significance of the banshee's hair color in this story?
2. What metaphors were used in the narration? Comment on how they add to the story.

4

Chi Li Slays the Serpent. Chinese
You Think Daughters Aren't as Valuable as Sons? Ha! Meet the Dragon Slayer!

HISTORICAL AND THEMATIC OVERVIEW

THE SERPENT OR DRAGON theme is common in Chinese mythology, dating back to the Xia, a people who dominated northern China from about 2000 to 1500 BCE.[1] The Xia worshipped the snake, which eventually evolved into a dragon and became an iconic symbol in Chinese art. While dragons are common in world mythology, Chinese mythology uniquely views dragons as necessary for cosmic rhythm. Dragons are associated with the water and rain necessary for agricultural life, and ancient Chinese dragon figures were designed to elicit rainfall.

Dragons generally were believed to bring wealth and happiness, yet there were dragon slayers in Chinese mythology, such as Emperors Yu and Chuan-hin.[2] In the story of Chi Li, as in many others, the dragon required a yearly human sacrifice in order to ensure success and good crops.

The tale of Chi Li most likely originated prior to the Ch'in dynasty of 227–21 BCE. The emperor of this dynasty destroyed all books unrelated to

---

1. "Chinese Mythology," 2:232.
2. Grottanelli, "Dragons," 4:2433.

practical matters such as farming and medicine. However, this story and other forms of literature were kept alive by the scholarly class and then recast to become acceptable when writings were again allowed. This tale gives an indication of the status of women during this time period in China, yet it successfully challenges common assumptions.

The three religious traditions of Confucianism, Taoism, and Buddhism play a significant role in Chinese mythology. It has been speculated that this myth arose as a commentary on the rigidity of Taoism, over and against the more circumspect Confucianism.

MYTH SUMMARY: CHI LI SLAYS THE SERPENT[3]

A huge dragon reigned in the Yun Mountains of China. It was a dangerous dragon who ate travelers and magistrates traveling on business. The locals tried to assuage the dragon by offering sheep and oxen, but the dragon demanded human sacrifice on the eight month each year, the sacrifice of a young maiden.

For nine years, the magistrates chose girls whose fathers were criminals or young girls who themselves were slaves, thus considered expendable. The magistrates would bind the girl and leave her in a temple near the dragon's lair.

In the tenth year of this practice, a young girl named Chi Li decided to volunteer herself to be the sacrifice. Chi Li was the youngest of six daughters, and as such, she considered herself expendable, just another mouth to feed. Sons were most desirable in China, and her family was impoverished. When Chi Li told her parents of her plan, they objected strenuously, stating, "We will never consent to that, Chi! We love and honor every one of our daughters." Her parents refused to agree, but Chi Li secretly approached the magistrates. They were relieved to have a volunteer and readily agreed. She asked to bring a serpent hound, a sword to confront the dragon, and the freedom to make use of them. The magistrates agreed.

On the appointed day, Chi Li was left at the dragon's cave with her dog, sword, and the freedom to make use of them. She also brought along some rice balls that she sweetened with malt sugar. She knew she would likely die, but thought to herself that perhaps the gods would look with favor on those who help themselves. Chi Li bravely approached the cave and left the rice balls at the mouth of the cave. The serpent smelled the balls and glided out

---

3. Myth summary from Rosenberg, *World Mythology*, 331–333.

toward them. Chi Li experienced a moment of intense fear, until she told herself, "The child of terror is certain death! So push fear from your heart, and force your mind to think only of the task at hand!"

The serpent was so entranced with the rice balls that it did not notice Chi Li. She unleashed the hound, who ran for the throat of the serpent. Chi Li stabbed the serpent's head and neck, called off her dog, and retreated to the temple. The dragon thrashed wildly and slowly died. Chi Li emerged and entered the dragon's cave, where she encountered the bones of the maidens from the nine previous years. She collected their skulls and commented that it is a shame that they died because of fear. Chi Li returned down the mountain and was met by the magistrates, who had viewed the entire scene from afar. She was triumphantly escorted by those same officials who had first brought her up the mountain.

The news of Chi Li's sacrifice and bravery reached the king. The king was so impressed that he brought her entire family to the royal palace, where Chi Li became his queen, her father became an important magistrate, and her mother and sisters became wealthy.

COMMENTARY

In a society where males were highly prized and females were often discarded, this story stands as a stark corrective. In her offer to sacrifice herself, Chi Li reminds her parents that wealthier families would have killed their infant daughters because they created a burden. She believes this would ease their lives and give her meaningless life a purpose. Her parents refuse to accept societal norms and insist that they love and cherish each of their six daughters. Chi Li insists despite their objections. She demonstrates her intelligence by requesting a sword and dog and by bringing rice balls. In killing the dragon, she becomes the female heroine that outwits the dragon and achieves something the male magistrates in power could not. The story serves to demonstrate the value of those whom society may originally deem worthless.

Chi Li's heroic qualities are presented as a model for all people. She is selfless, foremost, as she has put her own self-interests behind that of her family and community. She shows compassion toward her family, believing them to be better off without the added expense of a sixth daughter. She is determined to continue, even when her parents attempt to dissuade her. Chi Li is brave and calls upon her inner strength when confronted with the

Chi Li Slays the Serpent. Chinese

terror of the dragon. She is strong, wielding a sword and stabbing a dragon. Many of the best characteristics of a hero are demonstrated in Chi Li.

QUESTIONS FOR REFLECTION: THE HUMAN DIMENSION

1. Reflect on other societies, including your own. What type of people are devalued? What stories do you know that tell of a devalued person who became a hero?
2. Chi Li exhibited intelligence, bravery, determination, and strength. What qualities do you consider heroic? Why?

QUESTIONS FOR REFLECTION: CRITICAL ANALYSIS

1. Point out the ironies in this story.
2. Do you think that the myth's conclusion where Chi Li becomes a queen is appropriate? What might be a more satisfying ending that would reinforce the theme of the value of women?

5

The Epic of Gilgamesh.
Sumerian/Babylonian
Enki Was My Best Friend, and He Just Had to Die.

HISTORICAL AND THEMATIC OVERVIEW

On a November day in London in 1872, Assistant Curator George Smith of the British Museum was attempting to translate clay tablet fragments excavated some twenty-five years earlier. George Smith was too junior in status to even be allotted a lantern for his work, but there was enough daylight on this particular day for Smith to begin to decipher the clay fragments spread out on the table before him. At one point, he became so deliriously excited that he arose and began to throw off some of his clothes.[1] For in amongst receipts for grain and oxen, petitions to officials, contracts, and various other records, Smith decoded a parallel to the Noah flood story found in the biblical book of Genesis. This fragment was part of a fascinating narrative known as *The Epic of Gilgamesh*. The discovery created no small stir among scholars of both myth and the Bible, as the epic predates Genesis by about fifteen hundred years. It is the earliest known written story.

---

1. Damrosch, *Buried Book*, 12.

The Epic of Gilgamesh. Sumer/Babylonian

The Epic of Gilgamesh had been lost for over two thousand years until Smith translated the cuneiform fragments. Twenty-five years before Smith, British archaeologist Austen Henry Layard unearthed the broken pieces from some enormous mounds of dirt in what had been the Mesopotamian city of Nineveh, now in Iraq. These tablets were shipped to London until they could be translated but remained in storage for a quarter-century. Smith was the first to decode parts of the epic. *The Epic of Gilgamesh* originated in the cradle of civilization, the Mesopotamian Valley, around 2750 to 2500 BCE.[2] *Gilgamesh* evolved in several stages, from an early cycle of songs in Sumerian to an Akkadian epic written in around 1800 BCE to a final, expansive version written in around 1200. Mesopotamian tradition attributes the authorship to the scribe Sinleqqiunninni (alternatively Sin-leqe-unnini), a legendary poet, priest, or professional scholar. The most completely preserved version of the epic is divided into twelve tablets written in Akkadian cuneiform. As is typical of most myths, the story was based on a kernel of truth, in this case, the historical King Gilgamesh of the Sumerian city of Uruk (oo-RUEK). The myth chronicles Gilgamesh's quest to find meaning in life and death. The epic was surely told in part to entertain, whether in royal courts, in private houses, around the campfires of desert caravans, or on long sea voyages. However, the myth has value and purpose beyond mere entertainment. Its human drama makes it relevant to people in every era.

The central character in the epic is the powerful yet immature King Gilgamesh, who at first is self-absorbed, abusive, and dissatisfied with his life. As the story continues, Gilgamesh engages in a series of struggles and adventures. Interwoven in the tale are themes of friendship and pleasure, devotion, challenge to find one's way, the fierce determination to overcome adversity, grief over death, and longing for immortality. The narrative ends as Gilgamesh gains maturity, empathy, and acceptance of his lot as a mortal. Gilgamesh fails in his attempt to become immortal; nevertheless, he discovers that his very struggle gives his life meaning.

MYTH SUMMARY: THE EPIC OF GILGAMESH

The narrative begins by describing the strong walls of the city of Uruk, walls constructed by King Gilgamesh. Gilgamesh was one-third human (his father's side) and two-thirds divine (his mother was said to be the

---

2. Carnagie et al., eds. "Epic of Gilgamesh," 5:61–72.

goddess Ninsun). Gilgamesh was handsome, strong, and intelligent, yet an unprincipled and formidable bully. With no regard for decent behavior, he brutally interfered in the lives of his citizens, exploiting both men and women by forcing men into labor and demanding conjugal rights to brides on their wedding nights. The citizens of Uruk cried out to the gods for relief from this tyrannical king. In response, the gods created a wild man named Enkidu (EN-key-doo), who would be as strong and powerful and fearless as Gilgamesh. After a brief struggle, Gilgamesh and his equal Enkidu became friends and embarked on a series of adventures. The goddess of fertility Ishtar noticed Gilgamesh and asked him to marry her, but he refused, knowing how she treated other men. Spurned, Ishtar implored her parents to send the Bull of Heaven to destroy Uruk and its king. Gilgamesh and Enkidu killed the bull, and in retribution for this act, Enkidu was sentenced to a slow death by the gods. The death of his closest friend caused Gilgamesh so much grief and anguish that he decided to go on a quest to find meaning in life. He sought out Utnapishtim, the Noah-like figure who survived a flood by building a boat and who was later granted immortality by the gods. Gilgamesh asked for immortality but failed the test Utnapishtim gave him. This and a series of encounters left Gilgamesh physically and emotionally bereft. Nevertheless, this unsuccessful pursuit of immortality resulted in Gilgamesh's maturity and understanding of his life's purpose. He was repeatedly told of the benefits of mortality and came to accept that this was his lot. The epic concludes back at the city of Uruk with another boastful description of the strength of the city walls.

COMMENTARY

Because of the human drama, which is contemporary for every century and culture, *The Epic of Gilgamesh* is one of the most intensely studied ancient stories. Gilgamesh's striving to find his place in the world and his angst over mortality—his own and his friend's—are universal experiences. Not only does Gilgamesh grapple with difficult life questions, he experiences deep friendship, adventure, and the desire to achieve and leave a legacy. In short, his life mirrors common human experiences.

    A prevailing theme that spans the epic is Gilgamesh's struggle to find his place in the world. At the beginning of the epic, King Gilgamesh is arrogant and abusive, wielding his power wherever he wants. Although he is at the top of the socio-economic hierarchy, Gilgamesh's life lacks meaning.

The Epic of Gilgamesh. Sumer/Babylonian

Gilgamesh longs to make his mark in the world, and the epic begins with some extensive descriptions of the city walls Gilgamesh built. But building strong walls does not satisfy Gilgamesh's longing for meaning. He seeks to find meaning through adventure, to establish himself, to "leave behind me a name that endures," and he and Enkidu travel to kill the giant Humbaba. They succeed, and Ishtar, noticing Gilgamesh's beauty, asks for his hand in marriage. Annual fertility rites would often feature the king having public sex with the high priestess of Ishtar. This act was believed to result in a bountiful harvest.[3] In exchange for the overflowing fields, the king would have to surrender his identity, his very soul, to Ishtar. For Gilgamesh, losing his identity is the equivalence of death and impermanence, the very thing the king most fears. It is no wonder that he flat out refuses her advances.

Gilgamesh has been on adventures, he has saved his people by killing the Bull of Heaven who was sent to destroy them, he has made and lost a close friend, and he is still searching. Like a politician who has reached the highest office in the land and then wants the world, Gilgamesh remains filled with dissatisfaction. He has had everything, and yet he longs for meaning. What brings meaning in life? How can he ensure that he will not be forgotten? Gilgamesh embarks on a quest to answer these questions. The alewife Siduri suggests that he live it up, enjoy life to the fullest. That will allow him to stop ruminating on death and grief. Again, it is not enough. Gilgamesh decides to seek eternal life. That too fails, and the quest is not enough. It is only through the reflection of his struggle and failure that Gilgamesh realizes his growth and finally finds meaning.

Facing death is another predominate theme in the epic. With Enkidu's death, Gilgamesh experiences a distinct and intimate loss. Like many who face the death of a loved one, Gilgamesh appears to be in denial as he spends six days and nights by his friend's body. When he finally accepts that Enkidu is dead, Gilgamesh turns his fear inward and wonders what will become of him. He is afraid and uncertain, in stark contrast to the brash and fearless king at the start of the epic. He asks again and again the questions that one usually asks when facing death. In an attempt to conquer this fear, Gilgamesh seeks immortality. And yet his appeal to Utnapishtim fails, and he sees that "death inhabits my room." Finally, Gilgamesh tries yet another tack to gain immortality with the plant that promises youth and strength. This too fails. Gilgamesh hits rock bottom. He is a scruffy, miserable, grieving version of his former self.

3. King, *Ancient Epic*, 23.

At his lowest point, Gilgamesh is washed and renewed. He then reverses course, and toward the end of the epic, he is regaining status as he comes to terms with his struggles. He returns to Uruk to become a beloved king. He may not have eternal life, but he has the love and respect of his subjects and family.

While the themes of finding life's meaning, fear, and ultimate acceptance of death are central to the epic, not all of the epic is ruminating on death. The epic explores the concept of close friendship. Gilgamesh is described as a fearless warrior with no equal. He finally finds a friend in Enkidu. Apart, they are incomplete; together, they experience mutual fulfillment. Once bonded, the two are inseparable, faithful friends, compatriots in battle.

Another theme examined in the epic is the interplay between nature and civilization. Enkidu is a wild man, unfamiliar with women, knowing nothing of cultivation; he is eventually tamed by a temple priestess who uses sexual charm. Gilgamesh is a supremely civilized man, semi-divine, builder of the mighty walls of Uruk, master of all he surveys. Enkidu represents humanity at its most raw; Gilgamesh represents the height of civilization. The two join forces to battle Humbaba, evil guardian of the forest. By asserting themselves against the forces of nature, they hope to overcome their perishable, human nature by achieving fame and lasting recognition for their exploits.

QUESTIONS FOR REFLECTION: THE HUMAN DIMENSION

1. Most people have a fear of death when confronting it head-on. We humans are among the only animals that (as far as we know) live with the knowledge of our impending death. Since the death rate is one per capita, all who live to an age of reason must come to terms with this or else live in denial. How have you observed people deal with the reality of their own mortality?

2. To grow through struggle is a nearly universal human experience. Gilgamesh's struggle leads him to grow into a new mindset of compassion. Where have you experienced or seen struggle leading to growth?

3. How does the interplay of nature and civilization manifest itself today?

The Epic of Gilgamesh. Sumer/Babylonian

4. In your opinion, is the lesson of this myth a satisfying answer to death? Why or why not?
5. Literature often features the topic of friendship. Yet, paradoxically, authors often kill the friend; the friend almost inevitably dies. Why might this be? Why do poems, novels, and short stories end on the battlefield, the grave, the pyre, or at the memorial service?

QUESTIONS FOR REFLECTION: CRITICAL ANALYSIS

1. The epic opens with an introduction to King Gilgamesh of Uruk, who was known for having built the city's famous walls made of baked bricks and for having written tales of his many adventures on tablets. Baked bricks were used only for top-quality work. Unbaked mud bricks were more commonly used.[4] As you read the prologue, think about the function of city walls. What was the function of walls for a city?
2. The Sumerian worldview was shaped by the constant and unpredictable flooding of the Tigris and Euphrates, which was both destructive for crops and beneficial for soil fertility. The Sumerians also were subject to foreign invasion. How might flooding and threat of invasion have shaped their stories and their worldview? How might it shape their view of how to lead one's life?
3. Why do you think the author boasts about the strength of the city of Uruk?
4. Some view the quest of Gilgamesh as a failure. After all, Gilgamesh does not conquer death. As Enkidu died, so he must die. No immortality of the kind Utnapishtim enjoys is possible for him. Others contend that, in a profound way, Gilgamesh is "healed" in the quest. Which view do you find valid?
5. Some have called the epic a story of "learning to face reality," a story of "growing up." Trace the development of Gilgamesh from child to mature adult.

---

4. Dalley, trans., *Myths from Mesopotamia,* 126.

6

Penthesileia. Greek
The Original Wonder Woman

HISTORICAL AND THEMATIC OVERVIEW

> Long ago, in olden times, this earth thundered with the pounding of horses' hooves. In that long-ago age, women decorated themselves and sat on their horses. They would instantly saddle their horses, grab their lances and daggers, and ride forth with their menfolk to meet the enemy in battle. The women of that time not only comforted their loving men with their hands but could stand by their sides as well and cut out an enemy's heart with their swift, sharp swords. Still, they were able to harbor great love in their hearts.[1]

This narrative, from the ancient Northwest Caucasian peoples, is part of a legend known as *Lady Nart Sana*. It describes a band of women warriors who were Eurasian nomads from Scythian and Amazonian territories (now southern Russia).[2] These women were first encountered by Greeks

---

1. Colarusso, ed. and trans., *Nart Sagas*, 129–130.

2. For the Greeks, "Scythia" represented an extensive cultural zone of very many loosely connected nomadic and seminomadic ethnic and language groups that encompassed a great strip of territory extending from Thrace, the Black Sea, and northern Anatolia across the Caucasus Mountains to the Caspian Sea and eastward to Central and Inner Asia (Mayor, *Amazons*, 35).

who sailed the Black Sea in the seventh century BCE.[3] Several Greek myths feature Amazonian female warriors, whose fighting skills matched those of men.[4]

Greek heroic females are also featured in myths. For example, Atalanta was a female who pursued typically male ventures. Legend says she was abandoned by her father when she was born, because he had wanted a son. Atalanta was nursed by a she-bear and later discovered by some hunters who raised her as their own. She grew up learning how to survive in the wilderness, where she sharpened her hunting skills. As an adult, she participated in the Calydonian boar hunt and was first to strike the beast with her weapon.[5]

The heroic exploits of Amazonian women took on mythical proportions, but their characters and actions arose from a historical reality—warrior cultures of the steppes, where nomadic men and women lived in equality at a level almost unthinkable for ancient Greeks. Recent discoveries help to elucidate the historical reality that stands behind Greek myths featuring Amazonian warriors. Archaeologists have unearthed Scythian graves containing battle-scarred skeletons of women, even some with arrowheads still embedded in their remains.[6] The gravesites also contain the female fighters' weapons and horses. As expert horse riders, their lifetime on horseback is evident in the bowed legs seen in their skeletal remains.[7] Scientific bone analysis proves that these women rode, hunted, and engaged in combat in the very regions where Greco-Roman mythographers and historians once located the "Amazons."[8] From modern bioarchaeological methods, it is known that in the Amazon cemetery populations, armed females represent as many as thirty-seven percent of the burials.[9]

In the third century CE, the Greek historian Quintus of Smyrna drew on the *Aethiopis*,[10] one of the lost Trojan War epics from the eighth/seventh century BCE, to retell the story of the Amazon warrior Penthesileia

---

3. Mayor, *Amazons*, 18.

4. Some other Greek myths featuring Amazonian female warriors are those of Hippolyte and Antiope.

5. For the account of the boar hunt, see Ovid, *Metamorphoses*, 7.260-437.

6. Mayor, *Amazons*, 18-19.

7. Mayor, *Amazons*, 65.

8. Mayor, *Amazons*, 20, 63.

9. Mayor, *Amazons*, 64.

10. The ancient work *Aethiopis* survives only in fragments.

(Pen·the·SIL·ee·a) who came to the aid of Troy to battle the Greek champion Achilles. The storyline picks up after the death of Hektor at the end of the *Iliad*. It is recounted in Quintus's work, which has usually been known by the Latin title *Posthomerica*.

MYTH SUMMARY: PENTHESILEIA

Penthesileia opens at the funeral of Hektor, who had been killed by the Greek warrior Achilles. After Hektor's death, the Trojans were too frightened of Achilles to leave the protection of their city's walls.

The description of mourning and fear is followed by the arrival of Penthesileia and her glamorous army. Each of her noble companions was radiant in beauty and possessed a battle-hardened appearance. The queen of the Amazons and her band of female warriors were welcomed by the Trojans as their savior from the Greeks. Penthesileia's motivation for war was in part an attempt to remove the shame she felt for causing the accidental death of her sister, Hippolyte.

> Came Penthesileia, clothed in the beauty of the immortals.
> She was eager to engage in war,
> And wanted also to stop the reproach of shame
> From all her kin for her grievous deed.
> Though by accident, it caused her ceaseless grief.
> While aiming at the mountain stag,
> She had slain Hippolyte, her dear sister. (lines 19–25)[11]

Penthesileia promised deeds surpassing mortal strength, vowing to slay Achilles. King Priam of Troy welcomed her with mixed feelings, "like a man who has only partly recovered from blindness" (lines 73–79). The Amazon warrior enjoyed a reception and was entertained and lavished with gifts in a manner more suitable for celebrating victory. However, Andromache, Hektor's widow, was not so celebratory and optimistic, as she pointed out Penthesileia's inferiority to Hektor.

> Fool! She did not know how
> Achilles was untouchable in the fight.
> When Andromache, the daughter of Eetion,

---

11. All quotations of the Amazonian myth are from Dyce, *Select Translations*, 3–38. The language has been updated, and certain parts have been replaced with more recent scholarly translations. The significant changes will be noted. Line numbering roughly follows Quintus Smyrnaeus's *Trojan Epic*.

> Heard her so proudly boasting,
> She said to herself: "Ah wretch!
> What fatal impulse fires your mind to boast so foolishly?
> You are no match for Achilles.
> He will soon exult over your pale corpse,
> Defiled with gory dust." (lines 96–104)

Priam prayed publicly to Zeus for Penthesileia's success and for relief from the war. Trojan hopes appeared justified by the Amazon's initial success in battle. She displayed military prowess and excessive self-confidence.

> Where are your mighty now? Where is Achilles, and where is the son
> Of Tydeus? Where is Ajax? You say that these are powerful in the fight
> Yet they will not face the fury of my arm, fearing I will send them to the land of dead.
> After these arrogant words she leapt upon the Argives[12]
> Killing many men, now with her axe,
> And now her lance,
> While her dashing horse carried her ready bow,
> And quiver, should need occur
> In the bloody fight for her to use her bow
> And painful arrows. (lines 332–340)

Meanwhile, in Troy, war-lust seized the Trojan women. They were roused to eagerness to join the battle, but they were restrained by Theano's argument that, unlike the Amazons, they had no training in warfare, and there was no desperate need for them to leave their proper sphere as women.

> The Trojan dames inspired each other on.
> And seizing deadly arms,
> They cast their baskets and wool aside.
> Those women would have died beside their slaughtered friends,
> If prudent Theano had not checked their rush,
> With her words of wisdom:
> "Why do you desire to toil and strain in battle's fearful tumult?
> You have never been in battle.
> In ignorance you rush forward without thinking,
> Your strength can never be the same as the Danaans
> Who are trained in fighting.

---

12. Argos is a term often used in a general way to refer to the ancient Greeks who assaulted the city of Troy during the Trojan War. An Argive is a resident of the city of Argos.

> Amazons have enjoyed fighting, riding steeds, and doing all the work of men
> From childhood. The spirit of the war-god thrills them through.
> They do not fall short of men in anything.
> Their labor-hardened frames make their hearts great
> For all achievement. Their knees are never faint, and they don't tremble.
> Rumor has it that Penthesileia is a daughter of the mighty god of war.
> Therefore, no woman may compare with her in prowess. (lines 445–462)

Initial success for Penthesileia on the battlefield was quickly replaced by defeat as soon as the famed Achilles and Ajax entered the field. She was all too easy prey for them. The first spear that she threw was shattered by Achilles's shield. She threw a second, which simply hit Ajax's silver greave. Ajax left Achilles to deal with her alone. After telling Penthesileia that she would follow the fate of Hektor and other victims, Achilles severely wounded her in the chest with his spear. Dark red blood gushed forth from the wound, causing her hand to drop her weighty axe. While she debated whether to resist or beg for mercy, Achilles impaled both heroine and steed together "like someone hastily preparing a meal, skewering two bits of flesh on a spit placed over a hot fire" (lines 612–613). Struck dead, Penthesileia fell gracefully forward like a tall fir tree.

When the dead Amazon's helmet was removed, both Achilles and the other Greeks were amazed by her beauty. Achilles expressed regret that she was not his bride. His grief for Penthesileia prompted fellow Greek warrior Thersites to insult him for giving way to lust for a female enemy. Achilles struck him dead with his fist, which produced approval from the Greeks.

The myth ends with proper funerals and burials for the fallen. With the Greeks' cooperation, the Trojans burned and buried the dead Amazons, giving Penthesileia the honor of sharing a royal tomb.

COMMENTARY

In the major myths about Greeks against female Amazon fighters, despite their bravery, erotic appeal, and prowess, the women are almost always killed or captured.[13] No aspect of Scythian culture unsettled the Greeks more than the status of women. Greeks expected strict division of male and female roles.[14]

---

13. Mayor, *Amazons*, 31.
14. Mayor, *Amazons*, 36–37.

Penthesileia. Greek

In the ancient world, horseback riding equalized many differences between males and females. A skilled archer-horsewoman could hold her own against men in battle.[15] At a young age, girls and boys "learned to balance, relax, and move with the horse, guiding it with voice and body movements, without reins."[16] Horses can sense the heart rate, breathing, and body movement of the rider, leading them to adjust appropriately.[17] In the hands of expert archers, Scythian bows could shoot arrows extraordinary distances. A fourth century BCE inscription at Olbia (northern Black Sea) pays tribute to an archer for shooting an arrow nearly seventeen hundred feet.[18]

QUESTIONS FOR REFLECTION: THE HUMAN DIMENSION

1. Several theories have been proposed to explain why, in the Greek myths, the Amazonian warriors are either killed or captured. Some of these theories are: 1) Amazons exist in order to be defeated, because they have no history, no future, and the heroic warrior status to which they aspire is impossible; 2) Amazons threatened the Greek masculine ego; 3) Greek heroes crush foes, male and female alike; 4) Amazon female warriors served as figures justifying gender inequality or expressing fears of female rebellion against male oppression; 5) Amazons were enemies of civilization; 6) Amazons served as political stand-ins for inferior barbarians; 7) Amazons were an expression of xenophobia, showing the inferiority of foreigners. Using evidence from the myth, what function(s) do you think the myths of Amazonian warriors served for the Greeks? You may offer theories not mentioned above.

2. Do you think *Penthesileia* elevates or lowers the status of women? Support your answer from the myth.

---

15. Mayor, *Amazons,* 170–171.
16. Mayor, *Amazons,* 174.
17. Mayor, *Amazons,* 174–175.
18. Mayor, *Amazons,* 210–211.

QUESTIONS FOR REFLECTION: CRITICAL ANALYSIS

1. The numerous similes in this myth have been classified under four very broad categories:[19] 1) animals, or hunters and animals; 2) celestial elements, the sea, trees, plants, and crops; 3) myths or gods; and 4) other similes. Similes help sustain interest, emphasize a motif, express vividness or emotive intent, are informative or ornamental, provide relief, or provoke suspense. The simile can also be used to open a section or stanza or to end one section of the myth. If you can obtain a full copy of *Penthesileia*, identify a simile in the myth from each category above and describe its function.

2. Identify one example of each of the components of mythology as explained in the chapter "How to Read a Myth."

---

19. Maciver, *Quintus Smyrnaeus*, 127–128.

7

Hymn to Hermes. Greek
Family Drama

HISTORICAL AND THEMATIC OVERVIEW

THE MYTHICAL FOURTH HOMERIC *Hymn to Hermes* (HUR-meez) was one of a group of thirty-four songs. Thirty-three of the songs honor the gods and goddesses of the ancient Greek pantheon, while one is addressed to "hosts." They are called "Homeric" because, in antiquity, it was often assumed that they were composed by Homer, the poet who composed the *Iliad* and *Odyssey*. However, modern scholars have dated most of the hymns to 700 to 500 BCE and consider them to be the work of a range of anonymous poets.[1] The hymns narrate the birth of the god or goddess and/or describe important events in the gods' and goddesses' lives.

The *Hymn to Hermes* tells of the god's birth and the experiences leading up to the establishment of his place in the pantheon. Hermes employs whatever methods necessary to obtain his goal: theft, deception, magic, lies, persuasion, and force. This will be illustrated later in the myth. His

---

1. Rayor, *Homeric Hymns*, 2.

strategies illuminate Hermes's various functions as god of commerce, inventions, skillful use of language,[2] luck, music, thieves, travel, boundaries, and herds.[3]

The poet's literary skill is put on display in numerous ways throughout the hymn. For example, at one point in the myth, the poet describes each step as Hermes crafts the lyre, carving out the tortoise's flesh and fastening both vegetal and animal structures to the shell. He then covers the shell with cowhide and stretches seven cords. Finally, he tests his invention by plucking each chord with a pick. This detail allows the listening audience to visualize in their mind the construction of the lyre.[4] Using various animal parts in the instrument's construction, the lyre is portrayed as becoming a "hybrid" animal. The god's art is his "ability to mix different elements of nature together into a single, sublimated whole."[5]

MYTH SUMMARY: HYMN TO HERMES

The god Hermes is the son of Zeus and of a nymph named Maia. The hymn recounts how Hermes was born in a cave and how, immediately after his birth, he scrambled out of the cave to begin a day of mischief. First, he met a tortoise outside the cave. Hermes lured her inside by telling her it was safer there. Once inside, Hermes gutted the tortoise and used her shell to create the world's first lyre. His second adventure involved ingeniously stealing fifty of his half-brother Apollo's cows, steering them backward, so they would be difficult to track down.

> When he had leapt from his mother's heavenly womb,
> he did not lie long in his holy cradle,
> but he sprang up to seek out Apollo's cattle.[6]
> But as he stepped over the threshold of the high-roofed cave,
> he found a tortoise there and gained endless delight.
> For it was Hermes who first made the tortoise a singer.

---

2. See Tzifopoulos, "Hermes and Apollo at Onchestos," who notes several instances of Hermes's skillful use of proverbs.

3. Rayor, *Homeric Hymns*, 114.

4. Marco, "Hermes the Craftsman," 7.

5. Marco, "Hermes the Craftsman," 8–9.

6. All citations of the *Hymn to Hermes* are adapted from Hesiod and Homer, *Hesiod, Homeric Hymns*, 363–405. The language has been updated and certain parts have been replaced with more scholarly translations. Significant changes will be noted. Line numbering roughly follows Rayor's *Homeric Hymns*.

Hymn to Hermes. Greek

> The creature fell in his way
> at the courtyard gate, where it was
> feeding on the rich grass before the dwelling and waddling along.
> When he saw it, the luck-bringing son of Zeus laughed and said:
> "An omen of great luck for me so soon! I do not mind this.[7]
> Hello, my lovely lady-friend,[8]
> beating time to the dance, dinner companion. Dear tortoise who lives in the mountains,
> where did you get that fine toy, that dappled shell that you wear?
> But I will take you in, you shall help me, and I will do you no disgrace,
> though first you must profit me." (lines 20–35)

After stealing the cattle, Hermes slaughtered two heifers, roasted the meat, divided it into twelve portions, and then offered them to the gods. Finally, Hermes disguised every trace of the fire before he returned to Maia's cave, and then he pretended to be asleep.

Soon Apollo was out looking for his cattle. He tracked them as far as Maia's cave. While Hermes was inside pretending to be asleep, Apollo threatened to throw him into the underworld unless he provided the location of the cattle. Hermes claimed innocence, saying sleep and warm milk are all he had been thinking about. Besides, he added, it would be embarrassing for Apollo if the other gods heard that an infant had been able to steal his cows. Finally, the two half-brothers agreed to take the matter to Olympus and let their father Zeus be the judge.

> Hermes cuddled himself up when he saw the Far-shooter (Apollo).
> He squeezed head and hands and feet together in a small space,
> like a freshly bathed child seeking sweet sleep,
> though in truth he was wide awake, and he kept his lyre under his arm.
> But the son of Leto was aware and failed not to perceive
> the beautiful mountain-nymph and her dear son,
> albeit a little child wrapped up in his deceitful trickeries. (lines 238–244)[9]

---

7. The phrase "not mind this" is from Rayor, *Homeric Hymns*, 115.

8. Hermes addresses the tortoise as if she were a paid female companion (Rayor, *Homeric Hymns*, 114). The phrase "Hello, my lovely lady-friend," is from Rayor, *Homeric Hymns*, 56.

9. The phrase "wrapped up in his deceitful trickeries" is from Rayor, *Homeric Hymns*, 133.

Apollo presented his accusation to Zeus, which Hermes quickly rebutted. Hermes protested without lying to Zeus; he told a half-truth.[10] He did not drive the cows to his house; instead, he hid them in the cave. He did not walk over his threshold; instead, he turned into mist and slipped in through the keyhole. Hermes, god of tricky language, knew that only the literal meaning of an oath bound the one making an oath.

> But Hermes on his part answered and said,
> pointing at the son of Kronos, the lord of all the gods:
> "Zeus, my father, indeed I will speak truth to you,
> for I am truthful, and I cannot tell a lie.
> He came to our house at sunrise today
> looking for his shambling cows.
> He brought no witnesses with him nor any of the blessed gods who
>   had seen the theft,
> but with great violence ordered me to confess,
> threatening to throw me into wide Tartarus.
> For he is blooming with youth and love's glory,
> while I was born but yesterday—as he too knows—
> nor am I a cattle thief, a sturdy fellow.
> Believe my tale for you claim to be my own father.
> I did not drive his cows to my house—so may I prosper—
> nor did I cross the threshold. I speak the truth. (lines 365–379)

Fortunately for Hermes, his father laughed at his cleverness. Still, Zeus ordered him to take Apollo to the cows at once. When they reached the byre where he had hidden the cows, Hermes distracted his brother by showing him the tortoise-shell lyre he had made earlier. He played the lyre and sang to Apollo. Apollo was delighted by the music and was appeased when Hermes gave the lyre to him as a gift. Apollo, in turn, gave Hermes the whip used to drive the cattle, officially making Hermes a cattle herder.

The hymn closes with Zeus naming Hermes's honors, including being the "appointed messenger" to Hades, the underworld. It would be Hermes who would lead the dead to their final home.

> And Zeus decreed that Hermes should be lord over all birds of
>   omen and fierce lions, and boars with gleaming tusks, and over
>   dogs and all flocks
> that the wide earth nourishes, and over all sheep.
> He only should be the appointed messenger to Hades,[11]

---

10. Rayor, *Homeric Hymns*, 116.
11. Hermes is the guide of souls on their journey to and from the Underworld.

who, though he takes no gift, shall give Hermes no mean prize.
Thus, the lord Apollo showed his kindness for the Son of Maia
by all manner of friendship and the son of Kronos gave him grace besides.
He consorts with all mortals and immortals.
At times he helps them, but continually throughout the dark night he tricks humanity. (lines 569–578)

COMMENTARY

While the *Hymn to Hermes* contains elements of sibling rivalry and reconciliation, it is primarily a story about coming of age.[12] As a poem of this nature, it likely served to assist young men in their transition from childhood to adulthood. Hermes, as a younger and less powerful brother, uses deceit to make a place for himself among the gods. By the end of the hymn, he is recognized by Zeus, accepted by his brother, and assured of his own share of honors and powers.

The myth functioned on a performative level. As the myth is heard, adolescent males would be drawn into the struggles that Hermes must negotiate and overcome to be accepted into the company of the elders. By identifying with Hermes, the audience presumably would find encouragement and hope and perhaps even emulate the young god's tactics in their own struggle for acceptance into the adult world.[13]

As a didactic myth for young males, Hermes also provides religious education by recounting an appropriate and orderly model for remembering, honoring, and praising the gods in song (lines 429–438) and the proper way to offer them sacrifices (lines 120–129). In addition, the myth emphasizes the correct way for humans to seek the divine will, which is through the god Apollo (lines 533–549).[14]

QUESTIONS FOR REFLECTION: THE HUMAN DIMENSION

1. Hermes's place in the Greek pantheon was not a result of his actions. He was guilty of stealing the cows. None of his divine interlocutors

---

12. Johnston, "Myth, Festival, and Poet," 122.
13. Gordley, *Teaching through Song*, 52–53.
14. Gordley, *Teaching through Song*, 51.

is deceived by Hermes's lies. Nevertheless, they judge him successful. On what is his success based? As a story that might have functioned to illustrate to Greek youth the rite-of-passage from adolescence into adulthood, is Hermes's achievement, which is based on lies and deception, a good model for Greek youth to follow? Why or why not?

2. What do you like or dislike about this myth? Explain your answer.

3. The story of siblings, either in harmony or in rivalry, represents a part of human existence. Describe how you can relate to the relationships, bonds, and experiences between the siblings in this myth.

QUESTIONS FOR REFLECTION: CRITICAL ANALYSIS

1. Few can fail to notice that this hymn is extremely humorous. Identify some comic elements in the myth.

2. The Greek god Hermes displays a diversity of his roles in this hymn. He is portrayed as a precocious semi-divine child, a thief, and many others. Name three other roles he plays.

3. Is this primarily a story about a rite of passage, sibling rivalry, reconciliation, or something else? Explain your answer from citations in the myth.

8

The Trickster. Native American
Mocking the Medicine Man

HISTORICAL AND THEMATIC OVERVIEW

THE NATIVE AMERICAN FELT powerless against the gods who made the earth—the forces of nature which he or she could not understand or control.[1] One community figure who could assist in overcoming this feeling of helplessness was the shaman or medicine man. The shaman was the religious go-to expert, "society's first 'professional' (combining the modern roles of doctor, priest, psychologist, medium, and perhaps philosopher and theologian as well as actor)."[2] The shaman and those who followed him sought to win the blessings of the spiritual beings who controlled nature. The shaman employed the aid of other spirits who assisted him in doing what he could not do with his own strength. Shamans went on mystical journeys into the land of the spirits to discover the cause of poor weather and poor hunting. Shamans also acted as doctors, curing individuals from

---

1. Native Americans were for the most part polytheistic. Their religions reflected their cultural practices. The Pueblo people, whose primary means of subsistence relied on agriculture, tended to believe in sprits associated with planting and harvesting. The Siouan-speaking tribes of the Great Plains, whose subsistence was based on hunting and gathering, associated their religious practices with animals (Lauter, *Heath Anthology*, 1:4).

2. Ricketts, "Shaman and Trickster," 87.

illnesses. In their journeys to the otherworld, shamans learned what people must do to set things right with the spirits who were offended and who were responsible for the bad conditions or illnesses afflicting the community.[3]

But there was another way by which the Native American pursued mastery of the unknown, which was without an intermediary—directly by conquest. He or she could rise above powerlessness before the gods and nature through strength alone, through his or her own natural powers of mind and body. The trickster figure in Native American mythology embodies this approach as one who struggled alone against the supernatural. He viewed the gods and spirit world as his enemies to be defeated. The shaman had respect for the supernatural powers and was humble before them. He bowed down to the powers, worshiped them, tried to appease them, and win their aid and cooperation so that they became his powers. On the other hand, the trickster hero of the Native American myths, while he was a believer in the supernatural, was not a worshiper.[4] He was anti-god, and he was determined to destroy the gods, even though he knew they possessed powers he did not have.[5]

The Native American mythmakers were influenced by the animal life they saw around him. In the tragedies of the forest, they saw the weaker, smaller creatures escape the larger ones only by cunning. Thus, depending on the tribe, the trickster is a Coyote, Raven, Mink, Blue Jay, or Hare. In these myths, we see the trickster as a figure fighting alone against a universe of hostile, spiritual powers and vanquishing a supernatural being by virtue of his cleverness. Sometimes the creature was a "cannibal monster," which probably means that it represents disease or famine or baleful influences in general which afflicted humanity.[6] The trickster, unwilling to humble himself, tries only to imitate the shaman's powers.[7] The trickster also tries to imitate various animals whose powers are not his own. His blundering efforts to do what the animals (who are in some way superior to him) do, are a mockery of the shamans.[8]

Like other indigenous people, the Native Americans valued their oratorical skills. Audiences understood the stories through the myth teller's

---

3. Ricketts, "Shaman and Trickster," 90.
4. Ricketts, "North American Indian," 339.
5. Ricketts, "North American Indian," 339.
6. Ricketts, "North American Indian," 336.
7. Ricketts, "North American Indian," 339.
8. Ricketts, "North American Indian," 338.

slight variation of similar incidents in the tale or through varied rhythm.[9] Listeners responded to characters when the myth teller changed his voice volume or pitch or even paused in silence. Thus, myth telling could resemble dramatic performances as the speaker would enact scenes, often adopting different voices and gestures for different characters. At times, the myth teller would create a sacred space from which he or she performed, such as when the Navajo speaker told a story inside a sand-painted circle within a dwelling referred to as a hogan.[10]

MYTH SUMMARY: INKTONMI STEALS SUMMER[11]

The earth was covered with snow. So the trickster Inktonmi was hired by supernatural beings to secure summer for the people. Summer was kept in a bag tied to a pole on the medicine man's lodge. Inktonmi stationed animal helpers, one behind another. Fox stole the summer and passed it on to his animal associates, who escaped while Inktonmi engaged the medicine man in conversation. Inktonmi joined his comrades and created summer by opening the bag. A council was convened to decide the length of the winter. Frog proposed six months, and Inktonmi protested. But then Inktonmi felt bad and agreed to a six-month winter.

MYTH SUMMARY: HOW COYOTE STOLE FIRE[12]

Long ago, people were hungry and unhappy. They were cold. The only fire in the world was on a mountaintop, watched by three Skookums. The Skookums guarded the fire carefully. People might steal it and become as strong as they were. Coyote wanted humans to be warm and happy. One day, he crept to the mountain top and watched the Skookums. He watched all day and all night. They thought he was only a skulking coyote. Coyote saw that one Skookum always sat by the fire. When one went into the tepee, another came out and sat by the fire. Only when the dawn wind arose was there a chance to steal fire. Then Skookum, shivering, hurried into the tepee. She called, "Sister, sister, get up and watch the fire." But the sister was

---

9. Wiget and Justice, "Native American Oral Literatures," 1:20.
10. Lauter, *Heath Anthology*, 1:4.
11. Adapted from Radin, *American Indian Mythology*, 97.
12. Judson, *Myths and Legends*, 40–41.

slow. Coyote went down the mountainside and called a great council of the animals. He knew that if he stole fire, the Skookums would chase him. Coyote said the other animals must help him. Again, Coyote skulked to the mountaintop. The Skookums saw only a coyote shivering in the bushes. When the dawn wind rose, the Skookum on guard called, "Sister, sister, get up and watch the fire." But the sister was slow. Then Coyote seized the fire and jumped down the mountainside. Quickly, Skookum followed him. She caught the tip of his tail in her hand. Therefore, it is white, even to this day. But Coyote reached Wolf. Wolf seized the fire and leaped down the mountain. Skookum chased Wolf. But Wolf reached Squirrel. Squirrel seized the fire and leaped from branch to branch down the mountain. The fire was so hot it burned the back of his neck. You can see the black spot there, even to this day. The fire was so hot that it made Squirrel's tail curl up over his back. Skookum chased Squirrel. But Squirrel reached Frog. Frog took the coals of fire in his mouth and hopped away. Skookum chased Frog. She caught his tail in her hand. Frog jumped away, but Skookum kept the tail. That is why frogs have no tail, even to this day. Soon Skookum caught up with Frog again. To save the fire, Frog spit it out on Wood. Wood swallowed it. Skookum did not know how to get the fire out of Wood. But Coyote did. Coyote showed the Native Americans how to get fire out of wood by rubbing two dry sticks together, as they do even to this day.

COMMENTARY

The trickster figure frequently engages in socially unacceptable acts to call attention to the illogic of certain cultural patterns. The trickster's questionable behavior and "actions cast doubt upon both the motives and methods used by medicine men, thus urging the audience to distinguish between the *role* a person plays in society and the *character* of the person in the role."[13] Both scandalous and instructive, trickster stories ultimately draw attention to cultural traditions and provide useful and necessary correctives to unchecked cultural practices.[14]

Because the trickster succeeded in his perilous conflicts with nature and her gods, the Native Americans believed they could succeed in their battles; he was their model.[15] Like the trickster, wit, cunning, and brute

---

13. Wiget, "Creation/Emergence Accounts," 1:26.
14. Wiget, "Creation/Emergence Accounts," 1:26.
15. Ricketts, "North American Indian," 336.

force were sufficient for humanity to cope successfully with all the natural problems they encountered.[16]

The earliest and most typical kind of trickster hero myth is that of the theft of fire.[17] This theme, which is regarded generally as one of the world's oldest myths, becomes the pattern for a whole series of tales of theft: theft of the sun, of water, of fish, of game animals, of acorns.[18] The structure of the myth consists of: 1) the journey of the trickster hero (alone or accompanied by others) to the place where some substance vitally needed by humanity is being kept by a superior being; 2) the outwitting of the superior being by some device of cunning or deceit on the part of the trickster, who is admittedly weaker; and 3) the trickster's successful theft of the valuable commodity, often resulting in some permanent injury to himself or the world.

QUESTIONS FOR REFLECTION: THE HUMAN DIMENSION

1. Mac Linscott Ricketts states, "Cannot a human being respond to the experience of a superior being by challenging it, by demanding that it yield up its secrets to him, by commanding it to submit to his own powerfulness, and thus be no longer mysterious and other?"[19] Do you agree with Ricketts? Why or why not?
2. Can you think of contemporary models that function in the same capacity as the Native American trickster, as he challenges unchecked cultural practices and traditions?
3. Respond to the following quotation concerning trickster myths: "As a people that have so much to weep about as we Indians, we also need laughter to survive."[20]

---

16. Ricketts, "Shaman and Trickster," 92.
17. Ricketts, "North American Indian," 334.
18. Ricketts, "North American Indian," 334.
19. Ricketts, "North American Indian," 345.
20. Erdoes and Ortiz, *American Indian Trickster*, xxi.

QUESTIONS FOR REFLECTION: CRITICAL ANALYSIS

1. Taking into consideration the brief description of the oral performance practices of Native Americans, select one of the above myths and create an annotated script for an oral performance.

2. What do we miss when we read a myth, as opposed to hearing it performed or recited? Is it like the difference between reading a play and seeing it?

9

Oedipus the King. Greek
Freud Had It Wrong: Oedipus Didn't *Want* to Kill His Dad and Marry His Mom, It Just Happened That Way.

HISTORICAL AND THEMATIC OVERVIEW

SIGMUND FREUD COINED THE phrase "the Oedipal complex" to describe his theory about young children's sexualized idealization of their parents. Freud theorized that young boys subconsciously desire to kill their fathers and marry their mothers. In Sophocles's version, while Oedipus did indeed kill his father and marry his mother, he consciously desired the opposite. In fact, in order to ensure that the prophesy did not come true, Oedipus worked very hard *not* to kill his father and marry his mother.

The playwright Sophocles was born into a wealthy family and had numerous opportunities for education and culture. He began composing at age sixteen and, twelve years later, he bested the popular playwright Aeschylus in a competition. He received honors and awards on nearly all his plays, although of the one hundred twenty-three plays he wrote, only seven survive. *Oedipus the King* is the first of a trilogy, with *Oedipus at Colonus* and *Antigone* completing the series of tragedies. *Oedipus the King* is considered the best of the three and is often said to be the finest of any of the Greek tragedies. While it is highly lauded today and has been for centuries, when originally published, *Oedipus the King* received second place in competition.

In this play, Sophocles addresses the issues of fate and reversal of fortune. *Oedipus the King* is not original to Sophocles. Various versions of the myth had been circulating in ancient Greece and had been the subject of other playwrights. Sophocles's fresh perspective and unique contribution was to cast Oedipus in the place of an investigator who discovered his own awful truth.[1] In other versions, the truth was revealed by a deity.

This play takes place in Thebes in the thirteenth century BCE. Thebes had been an important and successful city. However, a series of invasions and destruction had devastated the city. Central to the plot is the idea that unfortunate circumstances are dictated by forces outside of one's control.

MYTH SUMMARY: OEDIPUS THE KING[2]

King Laius, the former king of Thebes, had been killed by robbers. The citizens of Thebes begged Oedipus, the new King of Thebes, for relief from a plague. Oedipus had already sent his brother Creon to consult with the gods through an oracle to determine what they might do to alleviate the plague. When his brother Creon returned, the verdict from the gods was that the city was suffering because the murderer of the former king Laius was living in Thebes. Oedipus vowed to find the killer and save the city. He consulted with the blind prophet Tiresias, who professed to know the truth, but insisted it is better for all if the truth remained unspoken. This angered Oedipus, and he pushed Tiresias to speak. Tiresias did so, saying,

> Blind who now has eyes, beggar who now is rich, he will grope his way toward a foreign soil, a stick tapping before him step by step. Revealed at last, brother and father both to the children he embraces, to his mother son and husband both—he sowed the loins his father sowed, he spilled his father's blood![3]

Tiresias was referring to a two-fold prophesy which stated that the son of King Laius would kill him, and this same son would also marry his own mother. Upon hearing this, Oedipus scorned and mocked Tiresias

---

1 Korovessis, "Oedipus the King," *Ancient Times*, 308.

2. Myth summary from various translations.

3. Sophocles, *Oedipus the King*, 185.

and ordered him to leave. Then Oedipus charged his brother Creon with treason, insisting that he be killed. The Chorus, which represents a kind of public opinion in Sophocles's plays, entreated Oedipus to reconsider, but to no avail. Queen Jocasta, who was the widow of Laius and now Oedipus's wife, also entered the conversation, assuring her husband that the prophecy of old had never come to pass. In fact, Laius and Jocasta had taken steps to ensure it would not happen. They had given away their infant son to a servant to take into the wilderness, bind his feet, and let him die of exposure on the side of a mountain. And, Jocasta reminds Oedipus, Laius was actually killed years later, not by his son, but by "strangers, thieves, at a place where three roads meet."[4]

Hearing this created anxiety in Oedipus, who asked for further details from a shepherd who had been a witness to the massacre. Rather than alleviate his fears, hearing the story retold from the shepherd only created more anxiety in Oedipus. Oedipus remembered being at the crossroads, where he had encountered and killed an entourage. He poured out his fear to Jocasta, as he recalled his own passage through the very crossroads where Laius had died.

Oedipus had believed his parents to be King Polybus and Queen Merope of Corinth. He heard the oracle that he would kill his father and marry his mother, so he left them in Corinth to ensure it would never come true. As he was fleeing Corinth, he encountered a group of men on the crossroads at Phocis. Neither group would yield, and in a fit of rage, Oedipus killed them all. Afterwards, he continued to Thebes, where he encountered the Sphinx, a mythical creature with the body of a lion. Everyone who passed by the Sphinx had to answer the riddle, and if they answered wrong, they were eaten. No one from Thebes was able to figure out the riddle, "What goes on four feet in the morning, two feet at noon, and three feet in the evening?" Oedipus correctly answered, "A human." In the morning of one's life, a person crawls. As an adult, at noon, the person walks. In the evening of one's life, a person uses a cane. The Sphinx was bested and died, and the Thebans were elated that Oedipus had solved the riddle. As a reward, he was offered the hand in marriage of their newly widowed queen, making him king.

Oedipus recognized the scenario that the shepherd and Jocasta related. He held out hope that it was thieves who killed Laius. While waiting

---

4. Sophocles, *Oedipus the King*, 201.

for confirmation from the sole surviving witness, a shepherd, King Polybus died, and the Corinthians sent word, asking Oedipus to be their king.

Oedipus was strangely buoyed by the news that his father was dead, relieved to know he would not be the one to kill him. He worried, however, that his mother Queen Merope was still alive; therefore, the second part of the prophecy may yet come true. In an attempt to console Oedipus, the messenger revealed that he was the one who found Oedipus as a baby and gave him to King Polybus and Queen Merope, who had had no children. Oedipus became more desperate and asked for details, but the messenger replied that it was another shepherd who discovered the baby with bound ankles. That very shepherd was on his way to the palace. As it turns out, that second shepherd was the one who had witnessed King Laius's murder.

Jocasta realized the implications of this and begged Oedipus not to pursue this further. But Oedipus insisted that he must know the truth. Jocasta yelled out that Oedipus was doomed and ran out of the palace. The second shepherd confirmed what Oedipus all along had suspected. The shepherd had not done the bidding of King Laius and had not left the infant to die in the wilderness; rather, he gave him away to King Polybus and Queen Merope in the hopes that he would have a chance to live. This unwittingly played into the oracle's prophesy. The terrible truth dawned on Oedipus. He had indeed killed his father, his true father Laius, and he had married his own mother, Jocasta. Oedipus cried out that he had been "revealed at last" and ran away. The Chorus entered to sing about the cruel nature of fate. A messenger arrived and told of Jocasta's suicide by hanging and gave a graphic depiction of Oedipus gouging out his own eyes with Jocasta's brooches, ensuring that the last sight he saw was of his wife and mother hanging from a noose.

Finally, a blind Oedipus, led by attendants, begged his brother King Creon to banish him. Creon replied that Oedipus was no longer the one to make such decisions, and Creon would be awaiting a decision from the gods. Creon took pity on Oedipus and sent for his daughters Antigone and Ismene, and Oedipus was led away to exile. The final haunting words of the Chorus are:

> Look ye, countrymen and Thebans, this Oedipus the great, he who knew the Sphinx's riddle and was mightiest in our state. Who of all our townsmen gazed not on his fame with envious eyes? Now, in a what sea of troubles sunk and overwhelmed he lives! Therefore

wait to see life's ending ere thou count one mortal blest; wait till free from pain and sorrow he has gained his final rest.[5]

COMMENTARY

At the time Sophocles authored this play, there was a revival of intellectualism in Greece. Socrates had critiqued religion from a rationalist viewpoint, and the Sophists also had begun to scrutinize religion.[6] This revival of intellectualism, along with an increasing wariness of seers who sold oracles for profit, caused the general public to begin to question religion. Did the gods exist? Could they ordain the future?

In his play, Sophocles may appear at first to take the position that prophesies are indeed valid and that only the gods are privy to foreknowledge. Humans appear unable to change prophesy, as the gods know all. However, the case could also be made that it was not prophesy that fated Oedipus, but his own unrelenting search for the truth, no matter how terrible. His pursual of the truth led to Jocasta's suicide and his blinding of his own eyes.

The audience would have found Oedipus a tragic figure who did not deserve the suffering that was inflicted upon him. The oracles, then, made the gods appear capricious and indifferent to human suffering. If what the gods ordain is unalterable, there appears to be little meaning to human life. Sophocles likely did not intend to satisfactorily answer the questions of the role of the gods, freedom of choice, and fate, but rather intended to open the discussion.

Fate is a theme commonly seen in Greek tragedy. Fate refers to the belief that humans have little control over some aspects of life but must submit to the will of the gods or another unseen force. In this play, Sophocles addresses fate in a unique way. Each character has freedom to act, yet the very choices they make play into fate. For example, Oedipus kills the entourage at the crossroads, and he does so because he is angry over who has the right of way. In letting his temper get the best of him, he unknowingly kills his father. Also, his unrelenting pursuit of the truth, as noble as it is, causes him to realize the horror of his actions. He gouges out his own eyes,

---

5. Sophocles, *Oedipus Triology*, 58.
6. Korovessis, "Oedipus the King," *Ancient Times,* 306.

fulfilling Tiresias's prophesy that he would be blind. If he had simply let it go, he could have lived out his life.

The narrative moves toward a continual delaying action in which no irony is undeveloped.[7] The audience observes as Oedipus gradually uncovers pieces of the truth, despite Jocasta's objections. Oedipus's life is driven by the oracles, by divine will, and by his own determination to find the truth. It ends tragically as a reminder that someone who appears to have everything, really only loses everything. We realize Oedipus's fate could be ours.

QUESTIONS FOR REFLECTION: THE HUMAN DIMENSION

1. Why is reversal of fortune a universal anxiety?
2. Oedipus has an experience at an actual crossroads. What are his options? What does he choose to do? Why? What might this teach us about our human tendencies?
3. Are you the type of person who prefers to handle the truth or a person who thinks ignorance of truth is bliss?[8]
4. What may be the advantages and disadvantages of believing in fate?

QUESTIONS FOR REFLECTION: CRITICAL ANALYSIS

1. What stands out to you about Jocasta? How does she handle (or not handle) the stress of finding the truth? How is she a reflection upon human nature?[9]
2. Referring to this play, what might you conclude about fate and free will?
3. What is the role of Tiresias? Would a modern-day Tiresias be welcomed in our society? Why or why not?

---

7. Scodel, "Hidden God," 62.

8. Bradley Hicks, discussion question from Humanities 160 course, Lansing Community College.

9. Bradley Hicks, discussion question from Humanities 160 course, Lansing Community College.

10

Moni-Mambu and Anansi. African Arachnid Antics

HISTORICAL AND THEMATIC OVERVIEW

THE TRICKSTER IS A figure who appears in mythology all over the world. In these myths, the trickster can represent primal creativity (e.g., bringing gifts essential to human culture, such as showing people how to extract fire from wood) or pathological destructiveness, childish innocence, and self-absorption. His physical character and qualities, as well as his outrageous actions, make the audience laugh at his ridiculous antics.[1] Trickster tales often have a moral or didactic dimension. Tricksters exemplify the consequences of thoughtless or disobedient behavior. By acting irresponsibly, the trickster helps model responsibility.[2]

Africa is richly endowed with trickster tales. The figures themselves are often animals or insects—the tortoise, the hare, the spider. With few exceptions, these animals are portrayed as thinking and acting like human beings in a human setting. This is sometimes brought out by the terminology, like the personal prefix added to a lion, Mr. Lion.[3] In other cases, the animals display human-like qualities, such as when a spider is described

1. Mphande, *Oral Literature*, 143.
2. Vecsey, "Exception Who Proves," 161.
3. Finnegan, *Oral Literature*, 381–382.

as taking off his cap, gown, and trousers. Trickster animals are also shown displaying "human faults and virtues, somewhat removed and detached from reality through being presented in the guise of animals, but nevertheless with an indirect relation to observed human action."[4] However, the fact that they are still animals is not altogether removed. Human foibles, weaknesses, virtues and strengths, ridiculous and appealing qualities, can be expressed less painfully and less directly by being disguised in animal characters.[5]

Anansi is a trickster spider of Akan origin. "Akan" denotes a West African ethnolinguistic group comprised of, among others, the Akuapem, Akyem, Baule, Asante, Brong, and Fante peoples.[6] Anansi has no sense of community. He is a loner. However, as Anansi wreaks havoc, the tales portray a very well-ordered society going on around him. While he is scheming and stealing and violating the rules, the other characters in the tales are, in contrast, team players. They are cooperating and being obedient. As Anansi threatens the social order, the other characters uphold it, reaffirming the importance of faith in the structures of the community.[7]

From the sixteenth century onward, Anansi tales came with Asante slaves across the Atlantic Ocean and into the Caribbean.[8] In Jamaica, the small, wily, and tricky Anansi, cheats, pits his wits against, and outdoes the larger and more powerful beasts like Tiger.[9] He does so using a host of ingenious tricks. In slave captivity and conflict, Anansi took on different roles and functions.[10] Anansi came to be a representative of the Jamaican slaves' human condition on the plantations.[11]

---

4. Finnegan, *Oral Literature*, 385.
5. Finnegan, *Oral Literature*, 386.
6. Marshall, "Anansi, Eshu, and Legba," 171.
7. Marshall, "Anansi, Eshu, and Legba," 179.
8. Marshall, "Anansi, Eshu, and Legba," 180.
9. Finnegan, *Oral Literature*, 379.
10. While Anansi is the name given to the trickster spider by the Ashanti and related Akan peoples of West Africa, he is known by many other names. In Jamaica, the mischievous arachnid has the name Annancy or Anancy.
11. Marshall, "Anansi, Eshu, and Legba," 180.

MYTH SUMMARY: MONI-MAMBU[12]

An example of a trickster myth that is both humorous and didactic in nature is the African story of Moni-Mambu. One day, during Moni-Mambu's travels, he came upon a village where a hospitable woman invited him to "eat some peanut stew she had simmering with her children for lunch." Moni-Mambu responded, "Can I really go and have the peanut stew with your children for lunch?" The woman affirmed her invitation. So, Moni-Mambu went to the woman's hut and ate the peanut stew together with her children. And when they finished the stew, Moni-Mambu roasted the children and ate them for lunch as well. Initially horrified at his outrageous act, the woman eventually agreed that Moni-Mambu was not to blame, because he did exactly what she invited him to do. One can see how this humorous tale may have served to teach children to select their words carefully or may have been a chiding commentary on the human tendency of carelessness.

A SUMMARY OF SOME ANANSI MYTHS[13]

One Anansi myth describes why the spider is thin and bald. He was not always thin but was big and round and loved to eat. However, the lazy spider did not want to work for his food. In his greed to get free food from more than one place, he had his sons pull ropes tied around his waist to inform him when the food was cooked. This allowed him to stay between two villages, ready to go in either direction. However, it so happened that the food was ready at the same time in both villages, and both sons pulled with equal strength from two directions, causing the ropes to squeeze tighter and tighter and his waist to grow thinner and thinner. He then had a big head, a big body, and a tiny waist in between.

Anansi's greedy appetite, along with his laziness, also contributed to his baldness. One day, he could not wait for lunch time to eat the beans his mother-in-law was preparing. He decided to place them secretly into his hat, but, just then, a crowd of people appeared. To cover his stealing, the spider put his hat on his head. The hot beans burned the hair right off his head.

Another Anansi story tells how the spider's greed caused him to eat so much of a melon that he was unable to get out of the hole through which he

---

12. Summarized from Belcher, *African Myths*, 83–84.
13. Summarized from Bowen, "Spiders," 40.

had entered. However, he soon discovered a way to overcome this obstacle. When Elephant came along, Anansi talked to him from inside the melon. Elephant soon had Hippo, Warthog, and Turtle all believing that they had found a magic melon, which could talk and was fit for their king. However, Anansi refused to speak when the melon was given to the king. Finally, the king said, "Oh, this stupid melon!" So, the melon spoke, "Stupid, am I? Why do you say that? I'm not the one who talks to melons!" At this, the king became so angry that he threw the melon against a tree, causing it to burst open, and Anansi was freed.

COMMENTARY

In Jamaica, Anansi's predominant character traits are those of cunning, greed, lewdness, promiscuity, slothfulness, and deceit. The Jamaican Anansi tales tell of how Anansi, the small spider, gets the better of powerful animals such as Tiger and Alligator or commands white humans like Massa and the King, using the only methods at his disposal, his intelligence and his wit and cunning. Anansi escapes the whip and steals the master's sheep or daughters.

Anansi tales told on the plantations reflected and inspired the trickster tactics that slaves adopted to outmaneuver their white masters. Anansi became a symbolic focus of resistance in the minds of the Africans. The stories reinforced the principles of deception and guile and inspired both psychological and practical methods of resistance and survival, allowing slaves to triumph in the face of a harsh environment.[14] "Anansi tactics" were often aimed at hitting Massa in his pocketbook—"where it hurt"—and included lying, stealing, cheating, working slowly, willfully misunderstanding instructions, breaking tools and machinery, and setting fire to the fields before harvest.[15] Trickster tales were a cathartic source of humor and an inspirer of trickster tactics that facilitated a form of resistance to the horrors of enslavement.[16] Further, these stories reinforced the slaves' African origins and created an occasion for them to come together communally through storytelling.

---

14. Marshall, "Anansi, Eshu, and Legba," 182.
15. Marshall, "Anansi, Eshu, and Legba," 183.
16. Marshall, "Anansi, Eshu, and Legba," 183.

QUESTIONS FOR REFLECTION: THE HUMAN DIMENSION

1. Are lessons received differently if they are voiced by animals or insects? Why or why not?
2. Define and identify tricksters in modern culture.
3. Do you sympathize with the victims in the Annancy myth? Why or why not?
4. If Anansi is a trickster, should he be thought of as a hero?

QUESTION FOR REFLECTION: CRITICAL ANALYSIS

As a speaker of life lessons, one title that can be given to the trickster is "teacher." Can you think of other titles he could be given that reflect his character and/or his role?

11

Myths of Filial Piety. Asian Ninja Filial Piety

HISTORICAL AND THEMATIC OVERVIEW

The Chinese character 孝 (*xiao*), is composed of two other characters: 老 (*lao*), which means elder, rests on top of 子 (*zi*), which means son.[1] The preferred meaning of this combination is that the elder generation is to be supported by the younger generation, illustrating the fundamental concept of filial piety. Many Asian cultures stress the importance of a child's respect for, obedience to, and provision for parents in their old age. This includes properly mourning them at an appropriate funeral and offering sacrifices to them after their death.

In ancient China, toward the end of the Warring States period (476–221 BCE), the term *gongyang*, which denotes the special feeding of elders, began to appear in literary sources.[2] The fundamental meaning of *gong* is "to provide" or "to supply," but it also has the extended meanings of "to offer respectfully" and "to present sacrifices."[3] The extended meaning of the word conveys that, in caring for one's elders, the caregiver was responding to a vertical hierarchy that existed within the home. This is often translated

---

1. Sha, *Care and Ageing*, 7.
2. Knapp, "Reverent Caring," 45.
3. Knapp, "Reverent Caring," 45.

as the idea that sons should utterly subordinate their interests to those of the extended family. For example, when trying to decide whether to support his mother or infant child, the filial exemplar Guo Ju said: "If we care for [*yang*] our son, I will be unable to engage in my occupation, which will hinder my effort to reverently care for [*gongyang*] our mother. We should kill the child and bury him."[4] Note that Guo merely "*yangs*" his child, but he "*gongyangs*" his parents. Furthermore, his decision makes it apparent that *gongyang* supersedes *yang* and is devotion to one's superiors. With the notion of a vertical hierarchy stressed in the term, the word *gongyang* can be understood to mean "reverent care."[5]

Myths of filial piety at times speak of dire supernatural consequences for those who do not provide reverent care for their parents. For example, after being sick for many years, Zhu Xu's mother suddenly desired to eat wild rice stew. Zhu tasted it first, liked it, and then gobbled it up. His mother angrily retorted, "If heaven is conscious, may you choke to death." When Zhu heard this, his heart became heavy and blood immediately began to run out of his body. By the next day, he was dead.[6]

The ancient Chinese work entitled *The Twenty-Four Exemplars of Filial Piety* contain myths of twenty-three filial sons and a filial daughter-in-law. It was compiled by Gui Jujing in the fourteenth century.[7] The stories were taken from different periods of Chinese history. While the stories reference a time and place, bringing a ring of truth to the narratives, they are too far-fetched to be true. A few examples of these myths are "For His Mother's Sake, He Would Bury His Child" and "He Slept on Ice to Procure Carp." These two myths are recounted below, following the summaries of the myths "Pari," "The Ancient Song of Doengving," and "With Deer's Milk, He Supplied His Parents."

MYTH SUMMARY: PARI

A Korean myth about a princess named Pari who was abandoned by her mother and father exemplifies extreme filial piety.[8] When a certain prince

---

4. Story taken from Knapp, "Reverent Caring," 46.
5. Knapp, "Reverent Caring," 44.
6. Knapp, "Reverent Caring," 55.
7. Chinnery, "China," 101.
8. Details of the myth come from Grayson, *Myths and Legends*, 352. The principal source for information about the legends and myths of the ancient period of Korean

became fifteen years of age, the king had him married and made him the heir to the throne. A fortune teller had predicted that, because the prince had married on an ill-fated day, there would be seven princesses born to him. Following the birth of his seventh daughter, Pari, the frustrated king ordered a chest to be made, put his seventh daughter in it, and threw the chest into the sea. The Buddha saw the chest, took the princess out, and instructed an old couple to raise her. The king and queen became seriously ill as a result of abandoning their daughter. The only way for them to be cured was to find the seventh princess and have her bring some magic medicinal water to them. The six other daughters had all refused to seek out the medicine. Princess Pari went to India and worked for nine years to secure the magic medicinal water. The king and queen, who had died, were revived by the magic water.

MYTH SUMMARY: THE ANCIENT SONG OF DOENGVING

Another myth concerning filial piety is "The Ancient Song of Doengving." It is one of the Chinese scriptures recited at funerals and during the annual New Year offerings to ancestors among the Zhuang people in the northwestern highlands of Guangxi.[9] The scripture presents a mythic narrative of the origin of funeral customs and a story that also illustrates filial piety. The boy, Doengving, was out herding buffalo one day, during which time he watched as a cow slowly and painfully was giving birth. He went back and told his mother, who assured him that human birth was much more difficult. Doengving was so moved by what he viewed and what his mother had told him that, when she died, he contravened established custom and put her body in a coffin. In doing so, he denied his kinsfolk and fellow villagers a certain burial custom. He proposed offering them the flesh of a buffalo instead of their ancient tradition of eating the bodies of the dead.[10]

---

history is the Samgukyusa (Memorabilia of the Three Kingdoms). This book was written in the thirteenth century (Grayson, *Myths and Legends,* 26).

9. Holm, "Ancient Song," 71.

10. This myth also presents an etiology of the origins of buffalo sacrifice (Holm, "Ancient Song," 73).

MYTH: FOR HIS MOTHER'S SAKE, HE WOULD BURY HIS CHILD[11]

In the days of the Han dynasty lived Kuo Chii, who was very poor. He had one child who was three years old. The family's poverty was such that his mother usually divided her portion of food with this little one. Kuo said to his wife: "We are so poor that our mother cannot be supported, for the child divides with her the portion of food that belongs to her. Why not bury this child? Another child may be born to us, but a mother, once gone, will never return." His wife did not venture to object to the proposal, and Kuo immediately dug a hole about three cubits deep, when suddenly he uncovered a pot of gold with the following inscription: "Heaven bestows this treasure upon Kuo Chii, the dutiful son; the magistrate may not seize it, nor shall the neighbors take it from him." Taking it up, they clasped their child with ecstasy in their arms and returned home, for now they had enough wealth to support their whole family.

MYTH: HE SLEPT ON ICE TO PROCURE CARP[12]

During the Chin dynasty lived Wang Hsiang, who lost his mother when he was young and whose stepmother Chu had no affection for him. His father also did not regard him with kindness. His mother was in the habit of eating fresh fish at her meals, but with winter coming, the ice bound up the rivers. Wang took off his clothes and went to sleep on the ice in order to seek the fish. His resolution was fixed, and although it was at the risk of his life, he was determined to go. The river was frozen, and the fish were hidden in their deep retreats. He was not dismayed at the coldness of the snow, nor terrified at the fierceness of the winds. Even the wicked spirits were deterred from injuring him and dared not molest him. Suddenly the ice opened and two carp leapt out, which he took up and carried to his mother. The villagers, hearing of the affair, were surprised and admired one whose filial duty was the cause of such an unusual event.

---

11. Chên, trans., *Book of Filial Duty*, 48–49.
12. Chên, trans., *Book of Filial Duty*, 55–56.

MYTH: WITH DEER'S MILK, HE SUPPLIED HIS PARENTS[13]

In the time of the Chou dynasty lived Yen, who possessed a very filial disposition. His father and mother were aged, and both were afflicted with sore eyes. They desired to have some deer's milk, which was believed to cure eye ailments. So, Yen concealed himself in the skin of a deer and went deep into the forests, among the herds of deer, to obtain some of their milk for his parents. He closely imitated the cry—yew, yew—of the fawns, watching for the tracks of the herds. While amongst the trees, some hunters saw him and were about to shoot at him with their arrows, when Yen disclosed to them his true character and related the history of his family and the reasons for his conduct. Yen was not deterred by the obstacles in the way of procuring the milk his parents desired.

COMMENTARY

The high level of filial care expected is seen in the belief that nurturing parents with food or physical care should be automatic, so it was not necessarily considered as virtuous behavior. Thus, to reflect a more virtuous behavior, a common means of reverent care was performed by offering delicacies to parents. It was believed that, by providing parents with delicacies, parents were honored, because such food was costly and difficult to obtain.[14] There was a financial and physical sacrifice involved. Reverent care for one's parents involved some act of self-deprivation, where children sacrificed their most basic needs, such as keeping themselves warm. Many myths illustrate this level of filial care and self-deprivation, which is expected in cultures that place a premium on elder care. Often the myths have a son searching for a food that is difficult, if not impossible, to obtain, usually because it is out of season. Often, when the food is acquired through the filial son's willingness to endure intense suffering, heaven will intervene on his behalf.

The highest level of self-deprivation was sacrificing one's wife and/or children for the sake of one's parents. Myths that illustrate this theme usually take the form of a moral dilemma in which a filial son must choose between two unpalatable options. Why must a filial son have to sacrifice so much to reverently care for his parents? Because he must repay the

---

13. Chên, trans., *Book of Filial Duty*, 41–42.
14. Knapp, "Reverent Caring," 46.

immense debt that he owes them for feeding and raising him when he was a child. When his parents become frail and helpless with age, he must carry out his end of the reciprocal bargain. Alan Cole has fittingly called this obligation a "milk-debt."[15] This level of filial piety was expected even if the parents did not love and care for the child as they should.

QUESTIONS FOR REFLECTION: THE HUMAN DIMENSION

1. Is it likely that anyone would literally behave in the manner described in these myths? If not, then what is the point of the stories? Why not write something more realistic?

2. Do these myths have any value today? If so, how? If not, why not?

3. Is filial piety a culturally specific ideal?

4. Confucius said, "Our body and hair and skin are all derived from our parents, and therefore we have no right to injure any of them in the least. This is the first duty of a child."[16] Do you agree with his statement? Why or why not?

5. Compared to the ancient world, modern society is highly mobile, often creating great geographical distance between adult children and their elderly parents. This is much different from societies where extended families often lived in the same home or at least in the same geographic area. Unlike ancient societies, modern society also has the benefit of social security, retirement savings, and senior citizen housing to care for the elderly. Nevertheless, David Gill believes that there is much to gain from extended families living, if not together, then in the same neighborhood, even if it involves some level of professional and personal sacrifice for adult children.[17] This arrangement allows for significant ongoing contact with one's parents. Do you agree or disagree with this viewpoint? Why or why not?

---

15. Knapp, "Reverent Caring," *Filial Piety*, 57.
16. Chên, trans., *Book of Filial Duty*, 16.
17. Gill, *Doing Right*, 178.

12

Sir Gawain and the Green Knight. British
Green and Gallant Knights

HISTORICAL AND THEMATIC OVERVIEW

DISPLAYED NEAR EACH OTHER in the public gallery of the British Library is a collection of England's greatest literary treasures. These artifacts consist of Jane Austen's writing table, Paul McCartney's scrawled lyrics to the song "Help," and as part of a collection of old manuscripts assembled by Sir Robert Cotton (1571–1631), the Arthurian romance[1] poem, *Sir Gawain and the Green Knight*.[2]

Sir Gawain is one of several significant poems assigned to the fourteenth century "Alliterative Revival."[3] This revival in England saw a

---

1. Medieval romances, as opposed to modern romantic love stories, narrated the deeds of a central, usually noble, person and his or her relationship to courtly society (Glaser, *Sir Gawain*, xv).

2. Glaser, *Sir Gawain*, xlix. While there is disagreement concerning the pronunciation of Gawain, it seems that when the author rhymes it with "to Frayne" (to pursue, l. 489) that he "was thinking Ga-WAYNE, with the accent on the second syllable" (Glaser, *Sir Gawain*, 18).

3. Benson, *Sir Gawain*, xii. It is called a "revival," because Old English poetry had employed a similar verse form, but it had disappeared from the written record over the centuries since the Norman Conquest (Cooper, ed., *Sir Gawain*, xxxiv).

burgeoning of poems that used alliteration as an essential formal device.[4] The following lines from *Sir Gawain* illustrate the alliterative style: "Where are your boasts of valor now, your bold victories, your pride, your prizes, your wrath and rousing words?"[5]

Sir Gawain was preserved in a small volume together with three poems of religious nature—*Pearl*, *Cleanness*, and *Patience*. All four poems are commonly attributed to the same anonymous writer. The precise date of the poems is hard to determine, but it is generally agreed that the manuscript was copied no later than 1400 and that the poems were composed sometime prior—perhaps as early as 1350.[6]

In addition to his proficiency in alliteration, the poet's skill is also exemplified in *Sir Gawain* by the clever use of mathematics and various symmetries and that are built into the narrative—parallels such as two castles and two courts, two beheading scenes, two confession scenes, a double identity for the Green Knight, and more. The three-part parallels are less frequent, but no less significant.[7] The poem is also rich in symbolism. A partial list of symbols includes the intruding knight's green color, the holly sprig he carries, the animals hunted, and the chapel.[8]

MYTH SUMMARY: SIR GAWAIN AND THE GREEN KNIGHT[9]

The poem, *Sir Gawain*, tells of how, during one New Year's Day feast at the court of King Arthur, an unknown monstrous green knight disrupts the festivities to challenge the reputation of the Round Table Knights. The knight was clothed entirely in green and rode his horse into the hall where the court was feasting. He carried no helmet, shield, or spear, but in one hand a sprig of fresh holly, and in the other an axe outlandish and huge, the

---

4. Benson, trans., *Sir Gawain*, xii.

5. Cooper, ed., *Sir Gawain*, 13 (Section 1, l. 311–312).

6. Cooper, ed., *Sir Gawain*, x.

7. Benson, trans., *Sir Gawain*, xxii. Some of those triplets are the three kisses, three hunts, and three blows of the axe.

8. Benson, trans., *Sir Gawain*, xxii–xxiii.

9. This summary is adapted from Morris (*Sir Gawayne*). The language has been updated and certain parts have been replaced with more scholarly translations. The significant changes will be noted. Sections and verses are from Cooper (*Sir Gawain*). Keith Harrison's translation in Cooper's edition is a good modern version for the reader who is interested in reading *Sir Gawain* in its entirety.

edge of which was as keen as a sharp razor. Thus arrayed, the Green Knight entered the hall without saluting anyone. Shockingly, the green man asked if anyone at the court would be so kind as to chop off his head—provided that the knight who accepted the challenge would, in a year and a day, allow the Green Knight to do the same to him. Everyone fell silent, but this caused the visitor to berate the court. In the face of an insult to the whole court, there was no recourse but for King Arthur himself to step up and take the challenge. Arthur's nephew, Sir Gawain, begged the king to let him undertake the encounter; and at the earnest entreaty of his nobles, Arthur consented "to give Gawain the game."[10]

The Green Knight adjusted himself on the ground, bent slightly his head, laid his long, lovely locks over his crown, and laid bare his neck for the blow. Gawain then gripped the axe, raised it high, letting it fall quickly upon the knight's neck, which severed the head from the body. The fair head fell from the neck to the ground, and many turned it aside with their feet as it rolled on the floor. The blood burst from the body, yet the knight never faltered nor fell; but boldly he started forth on stiff shanks and fiercely rushed forward, seized his head, and lifted it up quickly. Then he ran to his horse, stepped into his stirrups, and swung into the saddle. He held in his hands his head by the hair and sat as firmly in his saddle as if no mishap had harmed him. Before riding away, the head of the green man spoke, reiterating the terms of the pact, reminding Gawain to seek him in a year and a day at the Green Chapel. After the Green Knight left, the company went back to its festival, but Gawain was uneasy.

A year passed quickly. On All Hallows day, Arthur entertained the lords and ladies of his court in honor of his nephew, for whom all courteous knights and lovely ladies were in great grief. Sir Gawain, with great ceremony, was arrayed in his armor and was completely equipped for his adventure. He first heard mass, and afterwards took leave of Arthur, the knights of the Round Table, and the lords and ladies of the court, who kissed him and commended him to Christ. He bade them all good day.

In his travels, Gawain came upon the loveliest castle he had ever seen. Gawain urged on his steed Gringolet and found himself at the chief gate. He called aloud, and soon there appeared a porter who welcomed him. "Good sir," said Gawain, "would you go to the high lord of this house, and request a

---

10. Section 1, l. 336–365.

lodging for me?" "Yes, by Saint Peter!" replied the porter, "you are welcome to dwell here as long as you like."[11]

A table was soon raised, and Gawain, having washed, proceeded to feast. Many dishes were set before him—fish of all kinds, some baked in bread, others broiled on the embers, some boiled, and others seasoned with spices. The knight expressed himself well pleased and called it a most noble and princely feast.

After dinner, in reply to numerous questions, he told his host that he was Gawain, one of the Knights of the Round Table. When this was made known, great was the joy in the hall. Each one said softly to his companion, "Now we shall see a marvelous show of manners and learn from the intricate turns of his conversation. The prince of courtesy walks among us. "Surely God has showered his grace on us in granting us a guest such as Gawain."[12]

For sport, the host struck a deal with Gawain. The host would go out hunting with his men every day, and when he returned in the evening, he would exchange his winnings for anything Gawain had managed to acquire by staying behind at the castle. Gawain happily agreed to the arrangement and retired to bed.

Early before daybreak, the host and his men saddled their horses and tethered their bags. The first day, the lord hunted a herd of deer. On the morning of the first day, the lord's wife sneaked into Gawain's chambers and attempted to seduce him. Gawain put her off, but she did manage to give him a kiss. That evening, when the host gave Gawain the venison he had captured, Gawain kissed him, since he had won one kiss from the lady. The second day, the lord hunted a wild boar. The lady again entered Gawain's chambers, and this time she kissed Gawain twice. That evening, Gawain gave the host the two kisses in exchange for the boar's head.

The third day, the lord hunted a fox, and the lady kissed Gawain three times. She also asked him for a love token, such as a ring or a glove. Gawain refused to give her anything and refused to take anything from her, until the lady mentioned her girdle. The green silk girdle she wore around her waist was no ordinary piece of cloth, the lady claimed, but possessed the magical ability to protect the person who wore it from death. Intrigued, Gawain accepted the cloth, but, when it came time to exchange his winnings with the host, Gawain gave the three kisses but did not mention the lady's

---

11. Section 2, l. 812-813.

12. Cooper, ed., *Sir Gawain*, 34 (Section 2, l. 916-917, 921).

green girdle. The host gave Gawain the fox skin he won that day, and they all went to bed happy, but weighed down with the fact that Gawain must leave for the Green Chapel the following morning to find the Green Knight.

Having thanked his host and all the renowned assembly for the great kindness he had experienced at their hands, he stepped into stirrups and saddled the horse. Gawain then pursued his journey, rode through the valley and looked about. He saw no signs of a resting place, but only high and steep banks, and the very shadows of the high woods seemed wild and distorted. He could not find a chapel. After a while, he saw a round hill by the side of a stream; he went there, dismounted, and fastened his horse to the branch of a tree. He walked about the hill, debating with himself what it might be. It had a hole in one end and on each side and was everywhere overgrown with grass, but whether it was only an old cave or the crevice of an old crag, he could not tell.

Gawain said, "This place is a desert, a desolation. This sinister shrine is ugly with herbs overgrown. It is a fitting place for the man in green to deal his devotions after the devil's manner. Now I feel in my five senses it is the fiend (the devil) that has covenanted with me that he may destroy me. This is a chapel of misfortune! It is the most cursed church that ever I came in."[13] With his helmet on his head and spear in his hand, he roamed up to the rock, and then he heard from that high hill beyond the brook a wondrous wild noise. Lo! It clattered in the cliff as if one upon a grindstone were grinding a scythe. It whirred like the water at a mill and rushed and re-echoed, terrible to hear. "Though I may lose my life," said Gawain, "no noise shall cause me to fear." Then he cried aloud, "Who dwells in this place that keeps covenant with me?"[14] Without halting, Gawain walked up to the place and said, "Finish this business off now or never."[15]

Intent on fulfilling the terms of the contract, Gawain presented his neck to the Green Knight, who proceeded to fake two blows. On the third swing, the Green Knight nicked Gawain's neck, barely drawing blood. Angered, Gawain shouted that their contract had been met, but the Green Knight merely laughed, revealing his name as Lord Bertilak and then explaining that he was the lord of the castle where Gawain recently stayed. Because Gawain did not honestly exchange all his winnings on the third day, Bertilak drew blood on his third blow. Gawain was confounded, the blood

---

13. Section 4, l. 2189–2196.
14. The term "covenant" is from Cooper, ed., *Sir Gawain*, 79.
15. Section 4, l. 2210-16. The last line is adapted from Cooper, ed., *Sir Gawain*, 79.

rushed into his face, and he shrank within himself with shame. "Cursed," he cried, "be cowardice and covetousness both; in you are villainy and vice, that virtue destroy."[16] Then he took off the girdle and threw it to the knight in green. The Green Knight laughed and said: "You have confessed so clean, and acknowledged your faults, that I hold you as pure as if you had never sinned since you were born. I give you, sir, the gold-hemmed girdle as a token of your adventure at the Green Chapel. Come now to my castle, and we shall enjoy together the festivities of the New Year and make peace with my wife."[17]

When Gawain questioned Bertilak further, he explained that the old woman at the castle was really Morgan le Fay, Gawain's aunt, and King Arthur's half-sister. She sent the Green Knight on his original errand and used her magic powers to change Bertilak's appearance. Relieved to be alive but extremely guilty about his sinful failure to tell the whole truth, Gawain wore the girdle on his arm as a reminder of his own failure.

Gawain returned to Arthur's court and recounted his adventures. Groaning for grief and shame, he showed his fellow knights the cut in his neck, which he had received for his unfaithfulness. The king and his courtiers comforted the knight: they laughed loudly at his adventures and unanimously agreed that those lords and ladies that belonged to the Round Table, and each knight of the brotherhood, should ever after wear a bright green belt for Gawain's sake.

COMMENTARY

Stories like *Sir Gawain* were told to nobility as a way of training them in virtues such as loyalty, honor, courtesy, and bravery. Loyalty and honor are two virtues explored in this myth. Has Gawain demonstrated failure or success in living out these virtues? Scholars point to the structure of the story to support both Gawain's success and his failure in modeling these qualities.

On the one hand, it has been suggested that the structure of the myth is better viewed as a circularity, which stresses the return to a beginning point and underscores that the knight has returned as the same honorable and loyal knight that he was at the beginning of his journey.[18] Examples of a circular structure include the poem's setting, which begins in Arthur's

---

16. Section 4, l. 2375.
17. Section 4, l. 2391–2403.
18. Margeson, "Structure and Meaning," 16.

Court and ends there as well. The narrative also begins on New Year's and finishes at the beginning of the calendar year. When Gawain returns, having satisfied all the requirements of the challenge, the court contends that Gawain has retuned the same worthy knight that he was when he left. For the court, Gawain's quest has been circular, starting and finishing in perfection.[19]

Gawain though, cannot accept this view. He is keenly aware that he has forsaken his nature as a knight. Gawain was "so shaken with guilt, so grief-struck that he quaked within,"[20] upon the realization that his loyalty had failed by not revealing the girdle to green knight. He states, "And the noble and generous code of knightly men. I am proved false, faulty . . . ."[21] Gawain realizes that in his quest, he has changed from one state (perfection) to another (imperfection).[22] Unlike the court's circular view of his journey, Gawain believes it has been linear. Things have not come full circle. This view of the structure finds support in various ways. First, while there are two Christmas celebrations for the knight, he is humble and happy at the first, honored but troubled at the second.[23] Likewise, the two New Years are not identical. The first is joyous in the castle; the second is set in a freezing cold wilderness and marked by Gawain's pending death. The different circumstances demonstrate a linear view of time. Nothing is the same as previously.

QUESTIONS FOR REFLECTION: THE HUMAN DIMENSION

1. The Green Knight's two challenges test Gawain's loyalty on two fronts, the public and the private. The Green Knight plays the role of antagonist and challenger to Arthur's court to test whether it has the right to its reputation as the greatest court of chivalry in history. Lady Bertilak plays the role of temptress and challenger to Gawain's virtue to test his honor: Can he keep his promises to her husband? The first challenge is to determine if he can keep his word when his life and honor are publicly on the line. The second will ascertain if he will also keep his

---

19. Margeson, "Structure and Meaning," 17–18.
20. Section 4, l. 2370.
21. Cooper, ed., *Sir Gawain*, 84–85 (Section 4, l. 2381–2382).
22. Margeson, "Structure and Meaning," 18.
23. Margeson, "Structure and Meaning," 20.

word in trivial matters that are secret. In your opinion, are both public and private integrity equally as important? Why or why not?

2. The poem recounts King Arthur's emotional response upon hearing the Green Knight mock the cowardice of the Round Table Knights. It states, "With this he [the Green Knight] laughed so loud that Arthur blushed in shame as blood shot up to shine in his cheeks and face."[24] Antonina Harbus states that this manner of evoking a familiar and heartfelt emotion through reference to the bodily sensation, invites the reader to recall that bodily sensation, and thereby more easily empathize with the character.[25] Do you believe this is true? If you can obtain a full copy of the myth, identify a character in a particular part of the poem with whom you strongly empathize and describe why you have that strong connection.

3. What may be the morals of the story?

4. Danko Kamčevski states that *Sir Gawain* "provides a good example of the complexities of life, where it is hard to differentiate between 'good' and 'evil,' 'right' and 'wrong.'"[26] Can you find support in the narrative for this perspective?

5. Did Gawain behave with honor, as Bertilak and Arthur's court seem to believe, or did he bring shame to his reputation, as he himself seems to think?

QUESTIONS FOR REFLECTION: CRITICAL ANALYSIS

1. Scholars have struggled to identify the symbolic nature of the color green given to the knight. Some have suggested it is a courtly color; others associate it with springtime, innocence, gaiety, beauty, courtesy, and hope.[27] Green has also been considered a dangerous color, associated with the Devil, demons, witches, dragons, and poison.[28] What do you think it may symbolize? Support your answer from the poem.

---

24. Cooper, ed., *Sir Gawain*, 13 (Section 1, l. 316–318).
25. Harbus, "Emotion and Narrative," 600.
26. Kamčevski, "Orality and Humour," 271.
27. Gentile, "Shape-Shifter," 230–231.
28. Gentile, "Shape-Shifter," 230–231.

2. What are the three assessments (Gawain's, Bertilak's, and the court's) of the success or failure of Gawain's challenge? How do they compare to one another? In your opinion, which is the correct assessment? Why?

3. Sir Gawain is depicted as experiencing emotions of fear, anger, disgust, sadness, joy, shame, and guilt in a variety of situations. Identify an example of each of these emotions from the summary above.

4. A. C. Spearing refers to the moment when Gawain is caught by Bertilak for concealing the girdle gift as a "situation of public shame and private guilt." According to Spearing, for Gawain, his frustration was not because he has been unfaithful to his agreement with the lord of the castle, but that his unfaithfulness is now public and was uncovered by the lord himself. Do you agree with Spearing? Why or why not?

5. Do you think that the poet has structured the poem in a linear fashion in order to stress that Gawain's interpretation of his sin is the correct one? Explain why or why not.

13

The King, the Pigeon, and the Hawk. East Indian Animal Rights and Wrongs

HISTORICAL AND THEMATIC OVERVIEW

THE *MAHĀBHĀRATA* IS AN epic of the Hindu scriptures compiled in the third or second century BCE. It is ascribed to the sage Vyāsa.[1] In the original language of Sanskrit, the composition runs one hundred thousand stanzas in verse, making it the longest piece of literature in the world.[2] It is eight times longer than the *Iliad* and *Odyssey* combined.

Its contents are of varied interests, containing stories of heroes, villains, beautiful women, and kings. It also describes the duties of the ideal, righteous king, the importance of rituals for worship, and instructions on how to properly perform the rituals. There is a great deal of philosophical discussion in the epic, deliberating on life and proper conduct.

One of the stories in the *Mahābhārata* is the myth "The King, the Pigeon, and the Hawk," which tells of a king who gave his own flesh in order

---

1. The term "Vyāsa" could have been a generic title (Narayan, *Mahabharata*, vii–viii).
2. Narayan, *Mahabharata*, vii.

to redeem a pigeon chased by a hawk. It is one of the most widespread and celebrated stories in India.[3]

MYTH: THE KING, THE PIGEON, AND THE HAWK[4]

Once upon a time, a beautiful Pigeon, followed by a Hawk, dropped from the sky and sought protection from the King.[5] The single-minded King, seeing the Pigeon's terror, said to it: "Be comforted, good bird. Why are you afraid? You are so beautiful, your color is like a fresh-blown blue lotus, your eyes like the flower of an ashoka tree! Do not be afraid, for none need fear who seek protection here. For your protection, I will surrender all my kingdom, if need be, life itself. Be comforted, my Pigeon." But the Hawk took up the King's words. "This bird," he said, "is my appointed food. You should not protect my lawful prey, won by hard endeavor. O king, hunger is gnawing at my stomach. The Pigeon is my lawful prey, and he bears the mark of my talons on his body. You have the right to intervene when human beings fight; but what lawful power do you possess over the birds in the sky? Or, if you seek to earn religious merit by granting your protection to the Pigeon, have regard also to me, who am likely to die of hunger." Then said the King: "So be it. Let a bull or boar or deer be dressed for you for you cannot have the bird." But the Hawk replied: "I do not eat the flesh of bulls or boars or deer. Pigeons are my appointed food. But, O great King, if you have such affection for the Pigeon, give flesh from your own body equal to the Pigeon's weight." The King answered: "Great is your kindness in suggesting this to me. What you suggest shall be done." Saying this, the King began to cut away his own flesh and to weigh it in a scale against the Pigeon. Meanwhile the gold-decked queens and the ministers and servants raised a bitter wail of grief that rose from the palace like the sound of roaring clouds. The earth quaked because of that act of truth. But the King cut flesh from his arms and thighs, filling the scale in vain; for the bird weighed heavier and heavier against the flesh. Then, when the King was nothing but a skeleton, he desired to give his whole body, and stepped himself into the scale. Then there appeared the gods, headed by Indra, and the sound of heavenly music was heard; a shower of nectar fell on the King, whereby

---

3. In some versions, it is called a Dove instead of a Pigeon.
4. Noble and Coomaraswamy, *Myths of the Hindus*, 369–370.
5. Another version of the myth says the bird landed on the king's thigh (e.g., Sharma, *Hindu Narratives*, 50).

all his body was restored. Heavenly flowers fell from the sky, there came a splendid car, and when the King was seated, it bore him away to heaven. And it was said, "Whosoever protects another shall certainly attain the same good end. And he who tells this story shall be cleansed of every sin, and he also that hears it."

COMMENTARY

The King, the Pigeon, and the Hawk has come down to us in several versions, Hindu epic as well as Buddhist and Jain versions, and the story has even found its way into other tales.[6] In the Buddhist and Jain versions, the myths highlight the themes of protection and generosity offered by those who possess power and voice to those who are weak and voiceless.[7] In Hinduism, as early as the literature of the *Rig Veda*, human virtue was described as always giving out help and never asking for help. The gods rejoice when one's happiness is a result of another's voluntary sacrifice.[8]

Several studies have explored possible reasons for the presence of animals in the *Mahābhārata*.[9] Some of the conclusions reached for the animal's presence in stories have been, first, that animal myths reflect a primitive mind, which believed that all things of the world—trees, birds, animals, etc.—were equal with human beings. By projecting human qualities on animals, the otherness between humans and animals is reduced. Second, some scholars have concluded that the ancient Hindu collection uses talking animals to make the message easily accessible to children. Finally, it has been suggested that the animal myths enable the voiceless creatures' needs to be communicated.

Overall, the *Mahābhārata* recognizes the hierarchy of birth, whereby, according to the Indian philosophical theory of karma, animals are lower than humans.[10] But the tale cautions humans to treat the nonhuman beings as possessing as much agency and responsibility as their own, because the individual soul moves constantly up and down the karmic ladder.

---

6. Gaál, "King Śibi," 1.
7. Howard, "Lessons from 'The Hawk,'" 119.
8. Gudorf, *Comparative Religious Ethics*, 216.
9. Howard, "Lessons from 'The Hawk,'" 121.
10. Howard, "Lessons from 'The Hawk,'" 129.

QUESTIONS FOR REFLECTION: THE HUMAN DIMENSION

1. Is this a myth that teaches about care of animals, or does it function to encourage compassion and generosity of the powerful toward people who are weak and voiceless? Support your answer.

2. In his exploration of animal suffering, Henry S. Salt, who has been credited as being one of the earliest animal rights activists, reasoned that "the cruel man is cruel because he cannot put himself in the place of those who suffer, cannot feel with them and imagine the misfortunes from which he is himself exempt. The cure for cruelty is therefore to induce men to cultivate a sympathetic imagination."[11] How much do you agree or disagree with this statement? Explain your answer.

3. Is the Pigeon's life equal to the King's? Or is a balanced substitution impossible? Support your answer from the myth.

4. The myth creates a reality in which humans, animals, and gods co-exist, demonstrating a principle of radical interconnectedness among species, despite the Hindu belief in a karmic hierarchy among them. Animals, far from being mere sacrificial and utilitarian objects (that is, means, rather than ends), are sentient beings deserving just treatment and human empathy. Do you agree with this view? Why or why not?

QUESTIONS FOR REFLECTION: CRITICAL ANALYSIS

1. Why should the king differentiate between the lives of the bird and the beasts by offering the Hawk any food, as long as the food is not the Pigeon?

2. Why do the divinities choose to present themselves as mere animals to test the rectitude of the righteous king? Of the various suggestions noted in the commentary, with which do you agree? Why? If you do not agree with any, then suggest another reason. Support your answer.

---

11. As cited by Howard, "Lessons from 'The Hawk,'" 126.

14

The *Aeneid*. Roman
Rome Wasn't Built in a Day. Here's How Long It Really Took.

HISTORICAL AND THEMATIC OVERVIEW

IT IS NOT OFTEN that one culture unapologetically and boldly borrows another culture and incorporates every aspect as its own. This is, however, the case in first-century Rome, which borrowed heavily from Greek literature, religion, and ideals. The Greek gods, for example, were given different names but were otherwise the same gods with the same characteristics and family ties. Zeus became Jupiter, Hera became Juno, and Aphrodite became Venus.

This acculturation is evident in the great national epic poem of ancient Rome, the *Aeneid*. The author Virgil sought to record the story of the founding of Rome and drew heavily from Homeric literature in composing his epic poem. The opening of the *Aeneid*, for example, closely parallels the *Odyssey*. As in the *Odyssey*, the *Aeneid* starts with a storm blowing the hero's ship to a foreign land, the hero meeting a disguised goddess, the hero attending a banquet with a foreign ruler, a bard's song, and the narration of the hero's story.

Virgil, who grew up well-educated, although apparently not wealthy, began writing poetry around 42 BCE. He first produced books of poems such as the *Eclogues* and *Georgics*. Virgil had never written an epic but began composing the *Aeneid* in 31 BCE at the behest of Caesar Augustus. The civil war at Actium had ended, and Caesar Augustus (who at that time was known as Octavian) saw the need to restore patriotism and a return to ancestral religion, a kind of "back to God and country." He wanted to restore Roman customs and morals and create a sense of national pride. He believed that by revisiting the early days of Rome, the Roman people could be persuaded to return to the honorable Roman values of duty and responsibility. The *Aeneid* was to describe the founding of the Roman Empire and remind Rome of its divine destiny. Rome was at a golden age when the *Aeneid* was published, and this story rooted in mythology and history was considered central to its founding.

During the eleven years that it occupied his creative efforts, Virgil wrote out this epic, first in prose, and then began the arduous task of converting it into poetry, following the same pattern of dactylic hexameter as the *Iliad* and *Odyssey*. Each hexameter is a line of verse containing six metrical feet. This was a monumental task. Such a meter is more natural in Greek than in Latin, but Virgil wished to imitate the style and form of the Greek classics.

In writing the epic, Virgil used the works of Homer as a template and incorporated similar stories with different heroes. He tended to compare the heroes, always placing the Roman hero in a morally superior position to that of the Greek hero. Whereas Greek heroes tended to be in it for themselves, the heroes in the *Aeneid* tended to follow their destiny for the greater good, despite personal cost.

Virgil did not finish the *Aeneid*. He started to sail for Greece in 19 BCE, perhaps to better understand the Greek culture in which part of the *Aeneid* is set. On the ship, he caught a fever and had to return to Italy, where he died soon thereafter. He had planned on spending an additional three years on the epic. As he lay dying, Virgil asked his friend Varius to burn the manuscript. Varius refused, and Caesar Augustus ordered Virgil's friends Varius and Tucca to complete the poem.[1] While there are some obvious discrepancies that Virgil likely would have cleaned up, it remains a highly admired piece of literature and a testimony to the talent of Virgil. The *Aeneid* was immediately recognized in the Roman culture for its quality of writing and was used as a textbook for centuries. Other cultures have recognized its value as well. In fact, the *Aeneid* has been so influential that

---

1. Constantakis, ed., *Epics for Students*, 2.

it has affected the course of literary history and culture. The *Aeneid* and the Bible were likely the two most consistently read books in Western Europe for two thousand years.[2] It has been influential in specifically English literature, too, inspiring John Milton's *Paradise Lost* and Edmund Spenser's *The Faerie Queen*.[3] It remains one of the most studied works of literature in the world.

Early in the fifth and sixth centuries CE, the *Aeneid* began to be thought of as an allegorical precursor of Christianity. This view gained popularity especially in the Middle Ages, in reference to a section of Virgil's earlier poem, the *Eclogue*, which contained a prophesy of the birth of a child who would overcome sin and restore peace. This was believed to be a prophecy of the birth of Christ.[4] Also, the main character in the *Aeneid*, Aeneas, is similar to Christ, in that both had divine missions and neither deviated from his mission, despite the profound personal cost. Virgil's writings began to be viewed as God's preparation for other cultures to understand the concept of the Messiah, that when others heard the story of Jesus Christ, they might turn to him as Lord.

The backstory for the *Aeneid* is the Trojan War. The *Aeneid* gives the most complete account of the Trojan horse of any surviving manuscript. Virgil assumed that his readers would be familiar with the Trojan War as well as with a mythical story often called the Judgment of Paris, which involves a conflict between three goddesses:

Discordia, the goddess of strife, is not invited to a wedding celebration. She arrives at the feast anyway and throws an apple onto a table, as a prize for the "fairest" goddess. Three goddesses claim the apple, insisting that they are the fairest. Paris, a mortal and the prince of Troy, is appointed as the judge. Although each goddess offers Paris a bribe if he chooses her, his choice was Venus. Her bribe is to promise Paris the most beautiful woman in the world as his wife. Unfortunately, the most beautiful woman in the world is already married to Menelaus, the king of Sparta. Nevertheless, Paris kidnaps Helen (perhaps she goes willingly), and the Greeks go to war against Troy to reclaim her. The Trojan War lasts for ten years, and the hero of the *Aeneid*, Aeneas, fights for the Trojans.

The Trojan horse was a ploy used by the Greeks to overthrow the Trojans at the end of the war. After a ten-year siege, the Greeks infiltrate

---

2. Constantakis, ed., *Epics for Students*, 1.
3. "Virgil."
4. "Virgil."

the city of Troy, using the trick of the Trojan horse. The Greeks pretend to sail away, leaving word that they plan to return with reinforcements. They leave a large wooden horse outside the city gates as an offering to Athena, and unbeknownst to the Trojans, Greek soldiers are hiding inside. Trojan leaders debate what to do with the horse. In the most famous and often misquoted line from the *Aeneid*, the Trojan priest Laocoon warns his countrymen, "I fear Greeks, even those bearing gifts." Ultimately, the Trojans are duped into bringing the large wooden horse inside their city gates, and once inside, the Greek soldiers overthrow the Trojans.

The epic opens with words that would cause audiences to recall a Homeric epic, but, unlike the Homeric hero Odysseus, the hero Aeneas makes it clear that this is not something he wishes to recall. He claims he is bound by fate and does not wish to retell the past horrific events.

As the epic begins, Aeneas and his fleet are sailing to Italy. The goddess Juno asks Aeolus, god of the winds, to blow them off course. They land in Carthage, in North Africa. Early in the epic, it is established that Juno hates the Trojan people for several reasons, not the least of which is that she is angry over the judgment of Paris: "Juno, with her deep, unhealing heart-wound...."[5] Venus, the goddess mother of Aeneas, is concerned about her son and reminds Jupiter of his promise that Rome will rule land and sea.

MYTH SUMMARY: THE AENEID

Aeneas and his crew were seven years into their return journey home from the Trojan War when they were blown off course by Aeolus, god of winds, who had been instructed by Juno to do so. They landed in Carthage. Some of the fleet was lost, and Aeneas was nearly devastated by this. Yet he regrouped and encouraged his people. While in Carthage, he met Dido, queen of Carthage, who pitied him and invited him to dine. At a banquet, she asked him to recount the war. He told the story of the Trojan Horse and how the city had been destroyed and he was persuaded by his father to leave the city. He told of how he left with his wife, son, and father. His wife was lost as they fled, and when he returned to look for her, he was met by her ghost. Aeneas told how he learned more about the prophesy for Italy.

As Aeneas told his story, Dido became more and more sympathetic and infatuated. Venus intervened and sent Cupid in disguise. A dart from Cupid's arrow caused Dido to fall desperately in love with Aeneas. This

5. Virgil, *Aeneid*, 35.

caused Dido great internal struggle because she had taken a vow of fidelity to her dead husband. Yet, with Cupid's arrow, she had no choice but to fall hopelessly in love with Aeneas. They began to spend time together and she lost interest governing the city. During a wild storm, both Aeneas and Dido took refuge in the same cave, and sheltering overnight, they consummated their love affair.

> The Trojan lord and Dido found the same cave.
> Primeval Earth and Juno, giver of brides,
> Signaled, and in collusion lightning flashed
> At the union.
> On the mountaintops nymphs howled.
> From this day came catastrophe and death.
> No thought of public scandal or of hiding
> Her passion troubled Dido any longer.
> She called it marriage, to conceal her shame.[6]

Aeneas and Dido became lovers, despite Dido's internal struggle with the vow she had made to her deceased husband. To ease her conscience, she referred to her union with Aeneas as marriage, even though it was not a marriage. Their bliss was short-lived as Jupiter sent Mercury, the messenger god, to remind Aeneas of his duty. He realized he must follow the will of the gods, leave Dido, and continue his journey.

> What will this loitering in Libya bring you? . . .
> This apparition left Aeneas stunned.
> His hair stood up, and words stuck in his throat.
> He burned to run—however sweet this land was.
> The gods' august command had terrified him.
> But how? What would he dare say to the queen
> In her passion?
> What beginning could he make?
> His mind kept darting and his thoughts dividing
> Through the whole matter and each baffling question.
> After much wavering, this seemed the best plan:
> He called Mnestheus and brave Serestus
> And Sergestus: they must get the men together
> Quietly, rig the fleet, and hide the reason
> For the stirring.
> Meanwhile the good lady Dido

---

6. Virgil, *Aeneid*, 75.

Would not expect such strong love could be broken.[7]

Indeed, Dido did not think it even possible that Aeneas would leave her. But he was sworn to duty, and so he quietly rigged up the fleet. Dido could hardly imagine this was happening and begged Aeneas to stay. He refused, and Dido cursed as he left. She was devastated and killed herself with the sword Aeneas left behind.

After sailing away from Carthage, the Trojans landed in Sicily. This provided a brief time of relaxation, but disaster struck when Juno intervened again and influenced the Trojan women to burn the ships. Aeneas was distraught and considered giving up, until his father appeared as a ghost and implored him to continue. Some of Aeneas's fleet stayed, but the rest boarded the remaining boats. Soon they reached the promised land of Italy.

Aeneas decided he needed some guidance from the underworld and consulted a priestess of Apollo, who instructed him and sent him below. There he encountered the usual underworld characters: the three headed guard dog Cerberus; the river Styx and boatman Charon; Tartarus, the deepest underworld; and Elysium, the place for the blessed dead. He also encountered his dead father and Dido, who refused to speak with him.

> "She only glared in fury
> While he was pleading, while he called up tears.
> Her eyes stayed on the ground, her face averted,
> As changeless in expression, while he spoke,
> As granite or a jagged marble outcrop.
> At last she darted bitterly away
> To the dark forest, where her spouse Sychaeus
> Felt for her sorrow and returned her love."[8]

While in the underworld, Aeneas also encountered those who had died in the battle. He was filled with sorrow at the human cost of the war and journey.

Aeneas was allowed to leave the underworld and was welcomed by King Latinus, who viewed the Trojans' arrival as a fulfillment of the prophesy that foreigners will intermarry and form a great kingdom. Latinus offered his daughter Lavinia in marriage to Aeneas. Once again, the goddess Juno, whose hatred of the Trojans ran deep, intervened and created a

---

7. Virgil, *Aeneid*, 78.
8. Virgil, *Aeneid*, 131.

three-way dissent between King Latinus; Lavinia's mother Queen Amata, who opposed the marriage; and a local chieftain, who wanted Lavinia for himself. Juno orchestrated a fight between the men and this resulted in the killing of a pet deer. War broke out between the Italians and the Trojans. During a brief interlude, Aeneas visited Evander, the king of Pallanteum. Evander offered his son Pallas with a band of warriors to fight with Aeneas. Venus provided new armaments for her son, made by the god Vulcan.

Meanwhile, at the Trojan camp, Turnas attacked. When Pallas and Aeneas returned, Turnas chose Pallas for single combat. Pallas was killed. This enraged Aeneas, who savagely killed those around him until he was overcome with regret and anguish.

Aeneas officiated at Pallas's funeral. A messenger arrived to ask for a ceasefire to bury the dead. Aeneas wanted a truce, but Turnas was determined to destroy the Trojans. Camilla, who was an ally of Turnus, was killed, and this caused the Italians to retreat. Turnas and Aeneas decided to settle the war with a fight between the two. Aeneas promised to leave if he lost; and if he won, to unite the two groups without domination. Before that fight could begin, another fight broke out among the Trojans and Italians. Aeneas was wounded, but he was healed by divine intervention. Both he and Turnus raged in the battlefield, slaughtering many.

Turnus was protected by Juno. The Trojans surrounded the Italian capital, and in her despair, Queen Amata committed suicide. The duel between Turnus and Aeneas began but was suspended when the scene switched to a battle between Juno and Jupiter.

Jupiter forbad Juno from intervening further. She agreed, but she requested three things: that the descendants be called Latins, that they speak Latin, and that they wear the native costume, a toga.

The final scene returned to the fight between Turnus and Aeneas. Aeneas wounded his opponent, and Turnas begged for mercy. Aeneas considered sparing him, but upon noticing that Turnus was wearing Pallas's vest, he killed him in a fit of vengeance.

COMMENTARY

A key theme in this story is the concept of duty. Augustus wanted to motivate the Roman people to remember and live out their duty to the country, gods, and their family and friends. Virgil's intent was to portray the joy of fulfilling one's duty, even though there might be sorrow created by a conflict of private and public duty. The character Aeneas struggles with this conflict, as evidenced in the love story between Dido and Aeneas. Dido struggles with her vow never to marry again after her husband died. Yet she is unable to resist Aeneas, in part because of the intervention of Cupid. Aeneas also appears to struggle over leaving Dido, although he subjugates his emotion to duty when he is reminded of his mission. In his portrayal of these conflicting emotions, Virgil conveys that duty supersedes one's personal struggles. If one follows one's duty, then personal struggles, no matter how terrible, can become bearable.

Morality is another important theme in the *Aeneid*. The Romans looked upon the Greeks as cultural models, yet they viewed Greeks as untrustworthy, sneaky, decadent, and soft.[9] Virgil tended to portray his characters as morally superior to their Homeric counterparts. For example, in the *Odyssey*, Odysseus displays great cleverness in returning home, yet he is self-centered and individualistic. Aeneas, on the other hand, loses almost everything—his wife, his home, his country—in order to fulfill the ordination of the gods that he be founder of a new country and people. Aeneas, when asked to recount his journey, says, "Must I renew a grief beyond description, telling how the Greek destroyed the power of Troy, that tear-stained kingdom—since I saw the worst, and played a leading role?"[10] Aeneas exhibits other indications of moral superiority, such as rescuing a character whom Odysseus left behind in the *Odyssey*. Also, the Cyclops blinded by Odysseus makes an appearance but is treated in a more compassionate light. One of the most emotive examples of a higher morality is when Aeneas gives up his relationship with Dido in order to complete his duty, whereas Odysseus rarely gave up anything out of a sense of duty,; rather, his motivation was a sense of longing for his home.

Violence and war are part of the story as an intentional commentary. As previously noted, the *Aeneid*'s backstory is the Trojan war, where the city of Troy was destroyed and many lives were lost. In the second half of the epic (Books 7–12), countless people are killed. Some of these appear in the underworld, and Aeneas grieves them. In the last and final scenes, Aeneas loses control and slaughters Turnus and others. Virgil makes the point that even the most heroic man can be in a situation where he loses control. Virgil intends to question the purpose of war, from the Trojan War lasting ten years over a woman to the war to claim Rome: When is war justified?

9. Vandiver, *Odyssey*, 5.
10. Virgil, *Aeneid*, 24.

The *Aeneid*. Rome

Another important theme is the role of fate. In the *Aeneid*, fate is a principle which supersedes even the power of the gods. Aeneas must fulfill his destiny to found Rome. Fate determines how history will evolve and is the driving force behind the building of the Roman Empire. Dido is a victim of fate—she has little control over her love of Aeneas—and yet fate denies her his presence. Aeneas gives up his own desire to fate.

But fate is not all that drives the story. Virgil also intended to increase reverence for the gods. In the *Aeneid*, characters who ask for the help of the gods are given help, whereas those who ignore or disparage the gods are punished. Respect for the gods means making sacrifices and prayers. When Aeneas calls upon Apollo for help, he is victorious, whereas Mezentius dies after saying he does not care for any of the gods.

QUESTIONS FOR REFLECTION: THE HUMAN DIMENSION

1. When is it imperative to attend to one's duty over personal self-interest? Can you think of a time when you chose duty over your own future and a time when you chose your own interests over duty? How did you feel in each case?
2. Dido broke her vow to her dead husband. When might a vow be broken? When *should* a vow be broken? What are the consequences to one's sense of honor in each case?
3. Sorrow and regret play an important role in this epic. How do sorrow and regret influence decisions and outlooks of people today? Provide examples.
4. There are several perspectives on war in the *Aeneid*. Name a few and describe which perspective is closest to yours.
5. What is your opinion on fate?

QUESTIONS FOR REFLECTION: CRITICAL ANALYSIS

1. What does the *Aeneid* imply about submitting to divine will?
2. Do you think the *Aeneid* may have influenced the ancient Romans toward piety and patriotism? Why or why not?

3. Does the *Aeneid* portray war as justified? Does it convey a position on war? Defend your answer.

4. Poetry was an important, highly prized, and respected form of literature in ancient Rome and Greece. Today, that is not so much the case. Why do you think poetry was greatly respected in Greek and Roman culture, and why is it no longer considered essential?

15

Antigone. Greek
C'mon, King Creon. May I Please Bury My Brother?

HISTORICAL AND THEMATIC OVERVIEW

SOPHOCLES (496 TO 406 BCE) was one of the great dramatic poets of Ancient Greece and wrote throughout his life, even producing two masterpieces at age ninety. There is a story, perhaps apocryphal, that, in his old age, one of his sons wanted Sophocles's money and tried to declare him incompetent. Sophocles recited from memory one of his current compositions from *Oedipus at Colonus*, and the case was dismissed.[1]

Dramas by Sophocles and other playwrights were performed at the Theater of Dionysus in Athens, often during the festival of Dionysus. Attending drama was considered a civic duty. Crowds of fifteen thousand people were regularly present at such a performance, and even criminals could attend.[2] The drama productions were competitions between contemporary playwrights who each produced four plays: three tragedies and a satire. The audience cheered or jeered based on their preference, and judges who had been selected from across the tribes of Athens cast votes into an urn.[3] Of the approximately one hundred and twenty plays he wrote, Sophocles won

1. Bender, Review of *Masterpieces*, 63.
2. Moss and Wilson, "Antigone," 20.
3. Moss and Wilson, "Antigone," 20.

either first or second place in every competition.[4] Unfortunately, only seven of his plays survive today. *Antigone*, the third in a series of tragedies, was first performed in Athens in 442 BCE and was a huge success.

The story of Oedipus, the tragic king of Thebes, was a favorite subject of many playwrights in the time of Sophocles. *Antigone* draws from this tale but can be viewed as a kind of sequel to another play, Aeschylus's *Seven Against Thebes*. The backstory centers on the children of the ill-fated King Oedipus, who unwittingly killed his father and married his mother (see the chapter on *Oedipus the King*). The children of King Oedipus included daughters Antigone and Ismene and sons Polynices (alternatively Polyneices) and Eteocles. Initially, Polynices and Eteocles were to share the throne upon their father's death, trading off each year. However, Eteocles refused to relinquish it when it was Polynices's turn to rule. The two sons had insulted their father and as a result were cursed, resulting in the prophesy that they would kill one another. Polynices, who had married outside of Thebes, returned with an army of foreign princes to fight his brother. During this war, Eteocles killed his brother and himself suffered a mortal wound. The dead Polynices was deemed a traitor because of his ongoing war against his brother.

MYTH SUMMARY: ANTIGONE[5]

The play begins with Antigone revealing to her sister Ismene that their uncle, the new King Creon, had declared that Polynices should not be buried.

> Ismene, dear sister,
> You would think that we had already suffered enough
> For the curse on Oedipus:
> I cannot imagine any grief
> That you and I have not gone through. And now—
> Have they told you of the new decree of our King Creon?[6]

Antigone relayed the news that anyone who attempted to bury Polynices would be stoned. Antigone did not accept this. She believed she was following a higher directive, and she planned to bury her brother. She told her sister, "Ismene, I am going to bury him. Will you come?" Ismene was

---

4. "Sophocles," 343.
5. Myth summary from Sophocles, *Antigone*.
6. Sophocles, *Antigone*, 189–190

fearful and advised against it, "But think of the danger! Think what Creon will do!" She gave her reasons, "We are only women, we cannot fight with men.... I must yield to those in authority."

Antigone countered, "You have made your choice, you can be what you want to be. But I will bury him, and if I must die, I say that crime is holy."

Antigone symbolically buried Polynices outside of Thebes in a secret ritual, sprinkling some dust on her brother's corpse. Even this symbolic burial would allow her brother's spirit to enter the underworld.

Creon was informed that someone had defied his order. The guard reported, "The body, just mounded over with light dust: you see? Not buried really, but as if they'd covered it just enough for the ghost's peace." The guards arrested Antigone, and Creon learned from the sentry that Antigone had been the one to bury Polynices. Creon was furious that she would not obey him. She passionately defended herself by insisting she was doing the right thing based on a higher law than that of Creon, that is, the law of the gods.

> It was not God's proclamation. That final Justice
> That rules the world below makes no such laws.
> Your edict, King, was strong,
> But all your strength is weakness itself against
> The immortal unrecorded laws of God.
> They are not merely now: they were, and shall be,
> Operative for ever, beyond man utterly.[7]

Creon was unresponsive to her plea and condemned Antigone to be locked in a cave with barely enough food to survive. Antigone's fiancé, who was Creon's own son Haemon, tried passionately to reason with his father, arguing on her behalf. Creon, however, was firm in his conviction that she must be punished.

The blind prophet Tiresias stepped in to advise Creon that Polynices be buried: "Give in to the dead man, then: do not fight with a corpse— What glory is it to kill a man who is dead?" Creon reluctantly agreed, but it was too late. A messenger arrived with the news that Antigone had hanged herself, and Haemon, upon discovering her, had killed himself as well. As a result, Creon's wife killed herself. When the messenger delivered this news, Creon lamented, "All true, all true, and more than I can bear! O my wife, my son!" The play ends with Creon bowed in grief, and the Chorus warning

---

7. Sophocles, *Antigone*, 208.

that pride is punished. "There is no happiness where there is no wisdom; no wisdom but in submission to the gods. Big words are always punished, and proud men in old age learn to be wise."

COMMENTARY

Sophocles's view was that there are times when natural law overrules the laws dictated by rulers. He takes the side of Antigone and writes the play in such a way that even the gods affirm her position. Antigone believes in her right to bury her brother, based on both her duty as a surviving member of the family as well as the natural or unwritten law.

Nevertheless, there are no winners in this drama. While Antigone could be said to win from the grave, she still is dead. Creon has defended his rights as a lawgiver, yet lost his son and his wife. The message may be that staunch adherence to one's principles without considering another's point of view may bring misfortune.

It is significant that Sophocles used a woman protagonist. In a society where females were not considered citizens, and where women had no voice in politics, Antigone makes a strong statement by opposing a male ruler. Creon says that she must be defeated because she is a woman. Later, when he begins to realize his mistake in not allowing Polynices to be buried, he changes his defense, saying that admitting defeat to a woman would be a violation of divine law. This misogynistic mentality, combined with his pride, is his undoing.

Antigone's sister Ismene is the foil to Antigone's boldness. Obedient, timid, and submissive, Ismene submits to male authority, in contrast to the moody, bold, and declarative Antigone. Antigone, however, is the one who makes the most impact and stands up for what the gods deem is the right thing to do. Note, however, that Antigone was a little too bold, and paid the ultimate price for going beyond gender boundaries.

In modern times, Antigone's sense of familial duty and Creon's sense of order might appear admirable, but, in ancient Greece, moderation was the key to successful living. Both Antigone and Creon violated this key measure of moderation.

Antigone's uncle Creon made the death and banishment decrees, even though these went against cultural norms. The play raises the question of what powers should be obeyed. Should Creon's decree stand when it denies a basic human dignity? Does Creon abuse his power? Sophocles may be implying that there is a place for civil disobedience when authority is misused.

Sophocles contrasts the blindness of the sighted Creon with the perception of the blind prophet Tiresias. Creon remains blinded by his pride and obstinacy, until the end, when he curses his own blind pride. Tiresias, though sightless, could always see the truth.

QUESTIONS FOR REFLECTION: THE HUMAN DIMENSION

1. What is your view on divine or natural law versus human law? Should an individual who believes in a higher authority stand against an earthly authority? Why or why not?
2. Antigone remained devoted to her family throughout the play. Do one's family ties become more important than following the law? For example, if you knew a relative was participating in organized crime, would you let law enforcement know?
3. Think of an example of a law or laws that have been unjust and have denied basic human dignity. Who spoke against these laws? What was the result?
4. How might the Greek concept of the value of moderation benefit our current political landscape?
5. Which of the sisters are you most like? Why?
6. Provide a modern example where a deviation from gender expectations caused conflict.

QUESTIONS FOR REFLECTION: CRITICAL ANALYSIS

1. Identify the uses of irony in the play. In your opinion, what is the effect of irony?
2. Tragic plays in ancient Greece were seen as a way to allow catharsis to occur, a kind of purging of negative emotion in the audience so that they could make better decisions without being hampered by negative thoughts. In what way or ways might Sophocles's play have been cathartic?

16

The *Odyssey*. Greek
Cyclops and Sirens and Sun Gods, Oh My!

HISTORICAL AND THEMATIC OVERVIEW

IT WOULD BE HARD to overstate the importance of the *Odyssey*, the epic poem of ancient Greece. The *Odyssey* has been an extraordinarily influential piece of literature in ancient Greece and throughout world history. Along with the *Iliad*, the *Odyssey* has functioned almost as a sacred text or a kind of textbook used by the ancients to teach values and moral codes. The *Odyssey* was also used as a precedent to shape the political systems in ancient Greece and, by extension, shapes our governmental system of democracy, which modeled that of the Greeks.[1] It offers us an insight into what it meant in the ancient world to be civilized, hospitable, moral, and dedicated. The *Odyssey* has influenced centuries of writers, artists, and philosophers, including Virgil in his composition of the *Aeneid*, Michelangelo, John Milton, Thomas Jefferson, and Ralph Waldo Emerson.[2]

In this epic, Homer examines the concepts of family and homecoming. The *Odyssey* is a poem about the returning war hero and king of Ithaca, Odysseus. It tells of his struggles as he returns home from the Trojan War, a journey that takes ten years. He is aided by the goddess Athena, but

1. "Odyssey," 4:783.
2. "Odyssey," 4:783.

hindered by Poseidon, and along the way loses his ship and crew. He arrives home, but his homecoming is endangered by usurpers of his family and throne.

Who wrote the *Odyssey*? Was it Homer, a blind poet, as the ancient Greeks believed? Scholarship suggests a variety of scenarios. Some scholars think it the work of a single genius; others imagine a conglomeration of stories compiled into an epic by one or more bards and scribes. What few details that can be gleaned come from the poems or from scant archeological evidence. There are no other clues as to authorship.

While authorship is debated, dating is even more so. There are few contemporary clues in the form of art or literary style that would help date the *Odyssey*, and therefore there is significant disagreement as to its exact date of composition. The best estimate is within a hundred-year window, with the general consensus that the *Odyssey* was composed at some point between the eighth and late seventh centuries BCE. What is not debated, however, is that the *Odyssey* provides a viewpoint which is markedly different from the focus of the *Iliad*, an earlier work attributed to Homer. Whereas the *Iliad* illuminates the glory of battle, the *Odyssey* explores the theme of homecoming as developed in the adventures of one man, Odysseus.

The backstory of the *Odyssey* is the Trojan War. While no historical accounts of the Trojan War exist, the war is referenced in several Greek literary works and has been pieced together from sometimes contradictory accounts. While stories of the war have undoubtedly been embellished, it does appear from archaeological evidence that Troy was destroyed shortly after 1200 BCE, perhaps by the Trojan War.[3] There is much distortion and exaggeration in historical narratives of the day, so we cannot know for sure if the heroes named were contemporaries or separated by decades or even centuries. Homer's embellished version includes involvement of the Greek gods. The *Odyssey* is an epic poem in dactylic hexameter. Originally one work, the poem was later divided into twenty-four books for easier reference.

3. "Troy," 110.

MYTH SUMMARY: THE ODYSSEY[4]

Odysseus was returning home. It was high time he did so; he had been gone at war for ten years. Odysseus's family and country were in dire need of their husband, father, and king.

The *Odyssey* begins by describing the sad state of affairs in his own household. Penelope, his wife, was in the midst of tremendous internal struggle. Odysseus's extended absence meant that Penelope had no way of knowing if he was alive or dead. There were a number of suitors—one hundred eight, to be exact—who were courting Penelope, each with the hope that he would marry her and perhaps take over the kingdom. It was her cultural obligation if her husband were alive to remain utterly devoted and faithful to him, and it was her cultural obligation if her husband were dead to remarry.

Penelope and her son Telemachus were in limbo as they tried to determine the proper course of action. Penelope had held the suitors at bay for several years. When Telemachus was younger, Penelope had used the excuse that she needed to tend to her son. As he grew older, she held off the suitors for three years with the excuse that she was fulfilling her final duty as a daughter-in-law by weaving a burial shroud for her father-in-law. She would weave during the day and secretly undo the weaving at night. The suitors discovered her trick, and Penelope could delay no longer. She had to decide. Twenty-year-old Telemachus was also torn. Should he guard the kingdom for his father's return or claim the kingdom as his own? With no father to guide him, Telemachus was immature and had not yet asserted himself as would have been expected of a male of that age in that culture.

To further complicate the issue, the suitors who were vying for Penelope's hand threatened both Odysseus and Telemachus. Homer's original audience would have known that, in the *Iliad*, King Agamemnon returned home from war, only to be murdered by his wife's lover; and the same fate may well have awaited Odysseus. The suitors were also threatening Telemachus's life.

Not only was Odysseus's household in disarray, but the kingdom of Ithaca was also in disorder, having suffered for ten years—twenty, by the time Odysseus returned—without a king.

The issue that caught the attention of the gods, specifically Zeus, was that the suitors crassly ignored the rules of hospitality (*xenia*) that were so

---

4. Myth summary from Homer, *Odyssey*.

important in Greek culture. Zeus was the god designated to ensure that proper hospitality rules were followed. Zeus became aware that the suitors spent their days in Penelope's presence, devouring Odysseus's food and wine and threatening his marriage, a gross violation of *xenia*. While Zeus is utterly indifferent to Odysseus's plight, he is not indifferent to the violation of hospitality.

The first four books of the *Odyssey* make it abundantly clear that it is extremely urgent that Odysseus return home to address the threats to his kingdom, marriage, and son. Telemachus is in danger, and Penelope must choose a suitor. It is all the more urgent that Odysseus return home *now*.

We encounter Odysseus for the first time in Book Five in what seems to be a confusing chronology. While complex, the presentation of the storyline indicates a degree of literary sophistication far more impressive than a straightforward chronology would be. Our first encounter with Odysseus takes place on the nymph Calypso's island towards the end of Odysseus's journey. Odysseus had been held captive on Calypso's island for seven years, where she offered him immortality if he would consent to be her husband. Odysseus, however, longed to return to his role as husband, father, and king. His longing for home was so intense, he longed to "see even just the smoke that rises from his own homeland."

When we first encounter Odysseus, he was finally about to set sail again, thanks to an intervention from the goddess Athena. Throughout the epic, Athena made appearances and often helped Odysseus in significant ways. In this case, Athena saw that Odysseus had been held captive and she asked Zeus to command Calypso to release him. Calypso reluctantly agreed and aided Odysseus in building a raft. He set sail; but Poseidon, who hated Odysseus for reasons that will become evident later, sent a violent storm which wrecked the raft. Odysseus barely made it to the island of Scheria, where exhausted, bruised, and battered, he fell asleep in a forest bed of leaves.

Athena inspired Nausicaä, the princess of the Phaeacians (residents of the island of Scheria), to go wash her clothes by the seashore, near where Odysseus was sleeping. He awakened and uttered a line he repeats elsewhere on his journeys: "What is this country I have come to now? Are the people wild and violent, or good, hospitable, and god-fearing?"

Uncertain of the kind of response he will receive while naked and battered, Odysseus had to ask Nausicaä for help. He delicately covered himself with a branch and approached carefully to reassure her that she was in no danger of rape. He references the virgin goddess Artemis as a way both of indicating his social standing and reassuring her that he means no harm. The princess Nausicaä offered him clothing and food and instructed him to come to the palace after she returned home.

Odysseus entered the palace and was extended proper hospitality by Queen Arete and King Alcinous. They arranged for festivities in his honor, and there Odysseus recounted his adventures (Books Nine to Twelve), including the attrition of his men throughout the voyage and eventually the loss of the entire fleet of twelve ships.

Odysseus opened his story by recounting that, upon returning from war, his men decided to partake in a bit more looting. He told of entering the land of the lotus-eaters, where crew members ate the lotus and lost both pain and ambition. He had to drag them off the island, and they resumed the journey to what is the most widely known story from the *Odyssey*, the encounter with the Cyclops.

Odysseus and his men arrived on the island of the Cyclopes (plural of Cyclops) and hoped to be treated with hospitality. However, instead of being welcomed, they were held captive by one of the Cyclopes named Polyphemus. Polyphemus ate some of the men, and the rest he trapped in his cave. But Odysseus was clever and came up with a plan. The men plied Polyphemus with a potent wine, and when he was sufficiently relaxed, they stabbed him in his single eye to blind him. Odysseus had told Polyphemus his name was "No one" or "No man," so, when the other Cyclopes heard Polyphemus screaming in pain, they asked, "Why are you screaming through the holy night and keeping us awake? Is someone stealing your herds or trying to kill you by some trick or force?" Polyphemus replied, "No man is killing me by tricks, not force." They responded, "If no one hurts you, you are all alone, Great Zeus has made you sick, no help for that. Pray to your father, mighty Lord Poseidon."

Odysseus proposed a daring escape by instructing his men to cling to the undersides of the sheep belonging to the now-blinded Polyphemus when Polyphemus released the sheep to graze. The ruse worked, and the men escaped to their ship. Here Odysseus made an error of pride. Odysseus could not resist telling Polyphemus his name. "If someone asks you who did this, the name is Odysseus!" This was a mistake of ego that followed Odysseus for the rest of his journey.

Polyphemus called upon his father Poseidon to avenge his blindness. Poseidon cursed Odysseus, saying, "Grant that Odysseus, the city-sacker, will never go back home. Or, if it is fated that he will see his family, then let him get there late and with no honor, in pain, lacking ships, and having caused the death of all his men, and let him find more trouble in his own house." The latter is indeed what happens.

Following the encounter with Polyphemus, the crew arrived on the island of Aeolia, the home of the guardian of the winds, Aeolus. Aeolus showed Odysseus appropriate hospitality and sent him with a bag containing the winds. The crew set sail and were within sight of Ithaca when the crew became suspicious that there might be a treasure in the bag. In their greed, they opened it, and the winds flew out of the bag and drove the ship back to Aeolia. This time, Aeolus reasoned that Odysseus must be hated by the gods and refused to have any more to do with him. So the crew sailed on and encountered the island of Aeaea, where the goddess Circe lived. Half the crew went to explore the land, and Circe turned the men into swine. One crew member, Eurylochus, escaped and returned to Odysseus. Hermes intervened and gave Odysseus instructions on how to avoid Circe's curse. Odysseus became her lover for a year, until finally his crew convinced him he must return home.

But Odysseus was not quite ready. He said he must first seek out the prophet Tiresias in the land of the dead. The crew sailed to the edge of the world and made the appropriate sacrifice, blood poured into a pit, designed to awaken the spirits of the dead. Odysseus encountered Tiresias, who offered instructions and predictions with regard to Odysseus's return home.

They traveled to the island of the Thrinacie, where the cattle of the Sun god were kept. Odysseus repeatedly warned his men not to eat the cattle because they were the property of the Sun god and immortal. The men listened until the winds refused to blow, and they were marooned there for month. Facing starvation, the crew slaughtered and ate the cattle while Odysseus was asleep. But, because the cattle were immortal, the hides were moving about even after they had been eaten. The men set sail but were all drowned by a storm Zeus sent, all except for Odysseus, who was shipwrecked on Calypso's island. She nursed him back to health, became his lover, and kept him captive for seven years. By day, he wept for home; by night, he slept with Calypso. He finally was released and made his way to the Phaeacians, where we first heard of him in Book Five.

After hearing of his adventures, the Phaeacians gave him food, clothing, and a vessel, and returned Odysseus to Ithaca. From Books Thirteen to Twenty-Four, the narrative is straightforward chronology. The second half of the *Odyssey* describes Odysseus's homecoming, and while it does not contain the fast-moving adventures, nevertheless it is filled with suspense.

During his adventures, Odysseus had often longed for his homeland and had longed to see even the smoke arising from the fires of Ithaca. Ironically, on his voyage home, he arrived in the mist while sound asleep and so missed his long-anticipated arrival. Once he awakened, Odysseus did not know where he was. He once again asked the question: "Where am I now? Are those who live here violent and cruel? Or are they kind to strangers, folk who fear the gods?"

Odysseus encountered Athena disguised as a young man, and she informed him that he was back in Ithaca. Odysseus was aware that he could not just show up at the palace unannounced. He recalled King Agamemnon, murdered by his wife's lover upon his homecoming. So, to avoid detection and danger, Odysseus disguised himself as a beggar, aided by the goddess Athena, and made his way to the palace. In a poignant scene, Odysseus was recognized by his elderly dog, who died immediately thereafter. The feeble dog was covered with ticks and fleas, lying atop a dung heap, symbolic of the neglect of Odysseus's kingdom.

Odysseus encountered and tested his servants to see who was loyal. He met with his son Telemachus, and after a tearful but short reunion, the two launched a plot to kill the suitors. He was there just in time. The suitors had been pressuring Penelope to choose her new husband, and she could no longer hold out. She decided on a test: Whoever could string Odysseus's bow and shoot an arrow through twelve axes would be her choice. Each suitor tried in turn, and all failed. When at last the beggar, who was Odysseus in disguise, asked to try, he was met with derision. Yet Penelope insisted he be given a chance to do so. He strung the bow easily, and Telemachus, knowing the killing was about to begin, insisted his mother retire upstairs for the evening. The few faithful servants whom Odysseus could trust were apprised of the situation, and they locked the room so the suitors could not escape. Against all odds, with the help of the goddess Athena, Odysseus and Telemachus killed every single suitor. Odysseus then had to convince his wife Penelope that he was who he said he was. Penelope put forth a test whereby she ordered her marriage bed to be moved outside the bedroom. Both she and Odysseus knew this would be impossible because one of the bedposts was a living olive tree; his response to the order was the final test, confirming Odysseus's identity.

COMMENTARY

Central to the plot of the *Odyssey* is the theme of homecoming. By way of comparison, in the *Iliad*, the central theme was glory in battle and how one might be remembered, a concept referred to as *kleos*. A young man's early death in battle may yield glory and praise which outlasts him, but Odysseus discovers that glory is not as desirable as the happiness of hearth and home. Achilles, whom Odysseus encountered in the underworld, says as much: "I would prefer to be a workman, hired by a poor man on a peasant farm, than rule as king of all the dead."[5]

Odysseus is concerned about his *kleos*, but at the end of his travels he seems to conclude that it is best to be content with a life that brings happiness instead of glory. There is, however, an element of ambiguity at the end of the epic. Instead of a "happily ever after" ending, Homer seems to indicate that happy home life is fragile, easily threatened and displaced. Similar to the theme invoked by Thomas Wolfe's posthumously published book *You Can't Go Home Again*, the *Odyssey* seems to indicate that home is not the permanent fixture we often think it to be.

Another important concept in the *Odyssey* is *xenia*, loosely translated as "guest-host relationship." The concept of *xenia* is considerably more complex than those three words, however. The Greek word *xenoi* is a reciprocal relationship, meaning all at once guest, host, stranger, friend, and foreigner.[6] *Xenia* is the base root for the English word "xenophobia," meaning fear of foreigners, as well as the less common usage, "xenophilia," the love of strangers.

Xenia is a relationship based on mutual obligation, and it was considered an affront to Zeus himself if the principles of *xenia* were violated. In a typical interaction in ancient Greece, a stranger arrives in a town and finds an individual of similar social standing. The host welcomes the guest and invites him in, no questions asked. The host feeds the guest and offers a bath and night's lodging, and only after these obligations have been met is it permissible to ask the guest about himself. Upon the guest's departure, transportation is arranged for the guest, and gifts are given to the guest. The understanding was that, at some point, this kindness would be repaid. It likely would not be to the same host, but the reciprocal nature of *xenia* implies that this bond would continue between families in future generations,

---

5. Homer, *Odyssey*, 295.
6. Vandiver, *Odyssey*, 8.

that eventually the host's family would someday be a guest and balance would be achieved.

The *Odyssey* contains a number of episodes in which this concept is explored. We see Telemachus visiting Nestor, where Telemachus is treated well by Nestor and *xenia* practiced appropriately. Telemachus is fed, given a guest gift, and provided with transportation to visit Menelaos. Likewise, when visiting Menelaos, Telemachus is fed, given gifts, and bathed by the women of the palace (Greek men were customarily bathed by women). Another example of appropriate *xenia* occurred when Odysseus washed up on the shore of the Phaeacians' island. Nausicaä provided him with clothing, and offered her maidens to bathe and feed him. At the palace, he is offered appropriate *xenia,* and the King Alcinous orders his subjects, "Come, let's give him the parting gifts a guest deserves. Let us each contribute a fresh cloak and shirt and a bar of precious gold."[7]

On the other hand, there are numerous examples where *xenia* is ignored or snubbed. The most blatant examples are seen in the behaviors of the suitors and Polyphemus the Cyclops. The suitors continue to ignore the reciprocal nature of *xenia*, continually eating Penelope's food (which rightfully belongs to Odysseus) and threatening his marriage. The Cyclops demonstrates violation of *xenia* in the worst possible way. Odysseus hopes and rightly expects to receive appropriate hospitality. But not only does the Cyclops refuse to provide the suppliants with food, he eats them. His "guest gift" is the promise to eat Odysseus last.

Coming of age is also an important theme, particularly as it relates to Odysseus's son Telemachus. Initially, Telemachus is an immature and uncertain adolescent, afraid to confront the suitors' exploitive behavior. By the end of the epic, he has matured into a decisive and formidable young man who fights alongside his father. In Book One, Telemachus demonstrates a defeatist, passive hopelessness, saying, ". . . there was once a time when this house here was doing well, our future bright, when he was still at home. But now the gods have changed their plans and cursed us. . . ."[8] In subsequent books, however, Telemachus takes small steps toward growth. He calls an assembly of leaders from Ithaca to discuss the suitors' inappropriate behavior. Nothing comes of this, however. Not until he travels to visit Nestor and Menelaus does he realize and begin to incorporate into his worldview appropriate behavior and leadership. As Telemachus and his father fight the

7. Knipfer, "Development of Xenia."
8. Homer, *Odyssey,* 112.

suitors, Telemachus mistakenly leaves the door to the weapons storeroom wide open. Melanthios climbs through some vents to get armor for the suitors. Odysseus blames the maid, but Telemachus admits that it was his fault, this admission being another indication of his maturity.

A fourth theme which is prominent in the study is the concept of cleverness, the Greek word *metis*. Odysseus's *metis* is displayed in several examples throughout the narrative. Odysseus displays his *metis* by telling Polyphemus his name is "No one." It should be noted, however, that in a moment of pride (hubris) as they sail away, Odysseus cannot resist shouting Polyphemus his real name. This of course led to Poseidon's curse, which follows Odysseus throughout the epic.

Another example of Odysseus's cunning takes place on Calypso's island, where he demonstrates great tact and diplomacy in order not to offend the goddess. Calypso offers Odysseus immortality if he will stay with her. "What does Penelope have that I don't have?" is the gist of her request. Odysseus cannot risk offending the goddess, so he very tactfully steers the conversation away from Calypso and focuses on his longing for homecoming. He makes homecoming central to his refusal, the one desire that not even a goddess can fulfill.

When Odysseus is with the Phaeacians on the island of Scheria, we see his tact and cunning again. A naked man approaching a group of young girls would obviously be frightening, and yet Odysseus uses tact and self-depreciation, while at the same time indicating his good breeding with appropriate references, responses, and observations. The princess responds in accordance with her breeding and tact. Later, when Odysseus is under the care of the Phaeacians and enjoying their hospitality, yet still under disguise, he longs to know what people are saying about his exploits at the Trojan War. Had his skill and cunning been recognized and appreciated? He asks the local bard to sing of the story of the Trojan Horse in order to hear how he is perceived.

When Odysseus finally returns home, he uses the disguise of a beggar to ascertain who among his servants and family has remained loyal. He does not even know if Penelope is still his wife. He does know that it is likely there are those who would kill him, so the disguise of a beggar is a clever way to be invisible.

Penelope is also clever and cunning. Her ruse of weaving during the day and unwinding at night to keep the suitors at bay lasted for three years, until she was betrayed by a palace maid. Upon Odysseus's return, Penelope is circumspect instead of emotional as she seeks to ascertain if the beggar is indeed her husband. She displays many of the same characteristics of Odysseus.

This theme of cleverness is commonly found across myths of every culture, including today's movies, where the protagonists often use exceedingly clever language and tactics to achieve their goals.

QUESTIONS FOR REFLECTION: THE HUMAN DIMENSION

1. How does Telemachus's maturation process reflect your own coming of age? Have you observed in yourself a significant behavior that indicated to you your own maturation?

2. What do you think Homer is trying to say about home and family versus warfare and glory? Would your preference be to have a long, uneventful life, or a short life with a significant legacy?

3. How does Homer contrast the gods and goddess's cavalier attitude about time with the human understanding of mortality? Does the knowledge of your mortality motivate you to accomplish in life? How so?

4. For the Greeks, *xenia* was an extremely important social practice. What social practices are most important to our society? How do you think our society might change if *xenia* were as important a concept to us as it was to the Greeks?

QUESTIONS FOR REFLECTION: CRITICAL ANALYSIS

1. Why do you think Homer chose a complicated chronology in the epic?

2. Odysseus bragged about his identity when he escaped from the Cyclops. What was the tragic result, and did he learn from that?

3. Consider how Telemachus matures in the epic. Compare and contrast Telemachus's actions in Books 1–4 with his actions at the end of the epic against the suitors.

4. Consider the double standard for men and women in the Greek culture as it relates to sexual fidelity. Why do you think males were not expected to be faithful, but women were?
5. Trace Penelope's interactions with the beggar. At what point do you think she recognized Odysseus? At what point was she certain that it was her husband? What ironies do you detect in her comments to him?

17

The Boy who Was Kind to Animals.
Tibetan

The Vegetarian Boy Who Sits
on a Pink Shell Throne

HISTORICAL AND THEMATIC OVERVIEW

TIBETAN MYTHOLOGY STEMS FROM both Buddhism and an ancient spiritual practice known as Bön. Bön defies categorization, but is often described as animistic and shamanistic, with a folk belief in psychic powers of divination.[1] Bön myths are typically related to origins and involve rituals which recall these origins. In the retelling, the rituals are made effective. For example, in a marriage ceremony, the story of the first marriage may be told and reenacted by the priest and empowers the modern marriage.[2]

The Bön and Buddhist influence are seen in Tibetan origin stories. Some Tibetans believe their ancestry to be derived from a Buddhist goddess who initiated a magical monkey into a monastery. The monkey eventually married a mountain ogre, and their children lost their long tails and began speaking. Reality is not quite so colorful. While there is no way to know definitively, as corroborating historical data has been lost, some of

1. Yuan, Kunga, and Li, *Tibetan Folktales*, 12.
2. Leeming, "Tibetan Mythology."

The Boy who Was Kind to Animals. Tibetan

the Tibetan folktales indicate that the Tibetans are descendants of a defeated Indian army who fled to the region. Genetic research indicates Mongolian background with genetic similarities to those of North Asia.[3] The ancestors of Tibetans were hunter-gatherers who lived in the forests of the Tibetan Plateau between six thousand to seven thousand years ago, eventually turning to farming.[4] The Tibetan mountains influence the Tibetans' food production, because Tibet covers about one-eighth of the Chinese mainland, sharing Mount Everest with Nepal. Growing crops is difficult in such a mountainous region.

Tibetan literature developed out of oral tradition and reflects religious motifs of ghosts, demons, and supernatural heroes. The overarching theme one sees in Tibetan mythology is the reward of good deeds and the punishment of evil. Tibetan Buddhism emphasizes compassion and an appreciation for life in all forms, from amoebas to human beings.

As is the case for many myths, there are multiple versions of this Tibetan myth.

MYTH SUMMARY: THE BOY WHO WAS KIND TO ANIMALS[5]

Tashi was the only son born to parents with three daughters, and each of his older sisters had married rich husbands. Tashi's parents lamented that their only son would not be able to provide for them in their old age. This was because Tashi refused to hunt or eat meat, insisting, "All of life is sacred. I cannot kill another living being."

Still, his father insisted that Tashi hunt with him. His father recognized that taking a life is opposed to Buddhist beliefs, yet he felt he needed to provide food for his wife and son. One day, the father went hunting and caught a small rabbit but nothing more. During the expedition, Tashi sat on a rock, eating fruit and cheese and praying to Chenrezik, the patron saint of Tibet, Lord of Compassion.

The two continued on, and the father saw a large hare. The hare froze, and the father took aim with his sling. Just before he was ready to send the stone, Tashi cried, "No father, no, do not kill him!" The hare escaped, and Tashi's father was furious. He lunged at Tashi with a large rock, yelling, "I

---

3. Yuan, *Tibetan Folktales*, 5.
4. Yuan, *Tibetan Folktales*, xi.
5. Myth summary from Hyde-Chambers and Hyde-Chambers, *Tibetan Folk Tales*.

will hurt you!" Tashi squeezed inside a nearby small cave just as his father threw the rock. The rock struck his leg, and Tashi bled profusely. The cave opening was too small for Tashi's father to come after him, so Tashi inched his way back and fell unconscious.

He was eventually awakened by footsteps, and he called pitifully for help. The travelers stopped, and men peered in. They were three monks on a pilgrimage. One small, robed body appeared and helped Tashi out of the cave onto a soft bank of grass. There, the monks tended to his leg. They invited him to tell his story, and Tashi told of how his father was driven to despair over food and even tried to kill his only son. The monks invited Tashi to join their pilgrimage and dressed him in a mendicant monk's robes.

The monks traveled to Tashi's oldest sister's house to ask for donations. She did not recognize Tashi and asked if they had seen her brother. The same thing happened at the next sister's house. The youngest sister, however, recognized Tashi and begged him to stay. As a gesture of good will, the three sisters came together for a feast, and the monks were given gifts. Despite this show of family support from his sisters, Tashi decided he would not stay but instead go out into the world. As a parting gift of good will, his sisters gave a speaking magic horse.

Tashi left with the horse, who soon thereafter asked Tashi to kill him, saying, "Put my skin on the plain and scatter my hair all around so that the wind will carry it to the far corners of the plain." But, of course, the kind Tashi refused. That night, the horse purposely ran over a cliff and died. When Tashi awoke in the morning, he saw the horse's crushed body. With great sadness, he did as the horse had asked of him. He gathered the skin and spread it on the plain and threw the horsehair into the wind, so it would be scattered. The skin became a huge mansion, and the hair became herds of sheep and yaks. The horse then appeared and said to Tashi, "You have shown compassion toward other living things; this is your reward." He galloped away, leaving gold patches on the ground where his hooves touched.

Tashi returned to his parents' home dressed in his monastic robes. He climbed onto the roof and threw down a pancake for each of his parents. He knocked on the door, and his overjoyed mother hugged him and begged him not to leave again. His father asked for Tashi's forgiveness. Tashi invited his parents to come to his mansion on the plain. There he put his mother on a golden throne, his father on a silver throne, and Tashi himself sat on the more pure throne of a pink shell.

COMMENTARY

The Tibetan climate makes it difficult to grow food. Meat is more readily available. Yet Buddhism teaches that we must not harm living creatures; therefore, there is an innate conflict in eating meat. Tibetans realized the incongruity of their diet and their religion and sought to be compassionate with regard to taking animal life. This myth uplifts the ideal of compassion in several ways. Tashi is unwilling to kill an animal, even for food. The monks show great compassion in helping a wounded traveler. Tashi's sisters show compassion by providing alms for the monks, and finally, Tashi himself shows great compassion as he remembers his parents and invites them to live with him, despite his father's attack.

Tashi demonstrates strength and inner resolve in his refusal to kill, despite pressure from his parents and culture. He does the most honorable thing in every situation: always protecting animal life, refusing to retaliate against his father, and bestowing gifts on his parents.

QUESTIONS FOR REFLECTION: THE HUMAN DIMENSION

1. How might one reconcile dissonance between religious beliefs and life practices?
2. What do you find valuable about the Buddhist belief in compassion for all creatures?
3. What parallels are there with honor today?

QUESTIONS FOR REFLECTION: CRITICAL ANALYSIS

1. How might religion influence this myth?
2. What may be the significance of the horse's sacrifice?
3. Discuss the use of irony in the myth.

18

The Old Woman Who Was Kind to Insects. Inuit

What's This about Marrying a Blowfly?

HISTORICAL AND THEMATIC OVERVIEW

SURVIVAL IN THE ARCTIC requires innovation and resourcefulness. The Inuit, the indigenous population of Canada, Alaska, and Greenland, have lived in the Arctic region for roughly four thousand years. Up until approximately 1948 through 1970, the Inuit people lived a nomadic life. During that twenty-two year stretch, they began to settle around Hudson Bay trading posts.[1] The Inuit people were astonishingly resourceful and efficient in using available resources. Blocks of snow became building materials, animal parts served as both fuel and food, animal skins were used for clothing and even frozen sled runners, seal intestines made lightweight clothing, and bones were used for tools and weapons.

In such a harsh environment, starvation was a constant threat. Both women and men worked tirelessly to find and prepare food. With very little plant-based food available, the Inuit relied heavily on animals such as caribou, whales, walruses, and seals, in addition to fish and other sea creatures. Their existence depended on the constant killing of these animals,

---

1. Finckenstein, ed., *Celebrating*, 39.

The Old Woman Who Was Kind to Insects. Inuit

and they were ever aware that they needed to stay within the limits of their food supply.[2] This meant limiting their population, even practicing female infanticide in order to conserve resources for the necessity of raising young males who functioned as hunters. Suicide and even assisted suicide was practiced among the elders, who believed that they were a drain on the family's meager resources. Even so, family relationships were highly valued and children seen as a great blessing.

The Inuit believed that hunting is both sacred and dangerous and had great respect for nature and the animals they consumed. They believed that all living things had a soul, that people became spirits after death, and that animals' spirits went to new generations of their species.[3] They did not worship a single deity; rather, they had an understanding of and cooperation with the forces of nature.

Not surprisingly, cooperation and kindness were highly valued in the culture. Many of these societal themes are evident in the short Inuit myth "The Woman Who Was Kind to Insects."

MYTH SUMMARY: THE WOMAN WHO WAS KIND TO INSECTS[4]

One winter, an old woman was left behind in the tribe's summer campground. She was too old to move on and was no longer an asset to the leather-making business of her tribe. She had few teeth left to chew the leather, and she could barely walk.

The family left her in the camp with just a few insects for food. She decided she could not eat the insects, thinking that perhaps some of these poor creatures were young insects with their whole lives before them. She set the insects free from the cage.

Later, a fox appeared and began to linger around her hut. One day, it came right into her hut, leapt up, and bit her. The woman thought she might die, but the fox did not bite deeply, rather just nipped at her skin all over her body, almost as if her skin were a set of clothing. The fox nipped until all her skin fell away. New skin was under that skin, and it was the skin of an attractive young woman. The insects returned and began to buzz around

---

2. Madsen, "Theological Reticence," 119.
3. Wolfson, *Inuit Mythology*, 9.
4. Myth summary from Millman, ed., *Kayak Full of Ghosts*.

her, thanking her for their freedom. They had sent their friend the fox to rid the woman of her old skin and bring her new life.

When the tribe returned to the campground the next summer, they expected to find the woman's body. But she had vanished, having gone to live with the insects and perhaps even to marry a blowfly who had been particularly kind to her.

COMMENTARY

The story turns on the ambiguity of the value of human life. In a climate where survival is on a razor's edge, when do the needs of the many outweigh the needs of the one? The woman was left to die because she could no longer contribute. However, her compassion greatly exceeded the compassion of her tribe. Her decision not to eat the insects meant death for her, yet she chose it in order to save something as insignificant as juvenile insects.

The story critiques the idea that the worth of a life is dependent upon one's contribution. At the same time, it lifts up the idea that self-sacrifice is appropriate, when driven by compassion. As a reward for her compassion, the woman was reborn.

The old woman is both compassionate and giving, qualities that were not recognized by her tribe, yet were noticed by both the insects and the fox. The reborn woman leaves the tribe to live with the insects and perhaps even to marry a kind blowfly. This detail is significant, possibly signifying a snub to the callous tribe; the old woman chooses insects over rejoining her tribe. This might be an element of injected humor, providing the opportunity for the woman to "win out" over the short-sighted tribe.

No doubt, when hearing this story, tribe members would consider their honored and beloved elders with whom they had grown up and consider how it would feel if they left them to die. This myth is intended to address the ambiguities of the value of life, while taking into account the reality of hardship.

QUESTIONS FOR REFLECTION: THE HUMAN DIMENSION

1. Do you think that there is a time when the needs of a group outweigh the value of a life? Explain your answer.

2. Is the worth of a life dependent on what one contributes? How does our society view that question, and how do you view it? Be honest in your self-appraisal.

3. Can you imagine a scenario in which you would have to choose between leaving a loved one to die and the survival of a larger group? How might this myth be instructive?

4. The indigenous peoples of the Great Plains used every part of the bison. The Inuit also were extremely careful to use every bit of the animals they harvested. What might we learn from such conservation of resources?

QUESTIONS FOR REFLECTION: CRITICAL ANALYSIS

1. What might this teach the Inuit people about kindness toward all creatures?

2. What might this teach about self-sacrifice?

3. What do you think is the intent of including the marriage to the blowfly at the end of the story?

19

The Tale of the Orphan and the Old Woman. African

I Prefer to Vomit Gold and Jewels Rather than Toads and Vipers, Thank You.

HISTORICAL AND THEMATIC OVERVIEW

SLIGHTLY SMALLER THAN THE state of Colorado, the African country Gabon was named by Portuguese navigators after a hooded cloak called a gabão.[1] The explorers noticed a similarity between the Gabon estuary and the Portuguese style of cloak. Gabon is located on the west coast of Africa and straddles the equator. It is home to at least forty distinct ethnic groups, including the original inhabitants, the Pygmies. The largest ethnic group, the Fang, arrived from the north in the eighteenth century and currently comprises about thirty percent of the population.[2]

French colonialism had a profound influence on the culture, pervading its language, institutions, and social structures.[3] French was adopted as the national language, and although challenges to their traditional practices have threatened the culture, the Fang have maintained some identity and

1. "Gabon," 313.
2. "Gabon," 313.
3. Boussougou and Menacre, *Impact of French*, 12.

have adapted. One such adaptation is a syncretic religion containing elements of Catholicism as well as native religions, known as Bwiti Fang.[4]

This Fang story teaches many important tribal values. The main character in this story is a motherless girl. The story refers to the girl as an orphan, which in our Western culture is someone who has lost both parents. However, for the Fang, an orphan is one who has lost his or her mother. This in part is due to the practice of polygamy, as in the case of an extended family with many wives, it is the child's birth mother who would ensure affection and comfort for her child, even if the father is still alive.[5]

MYTH SUMMARY: THE TALE OF THE ORPHAN AND THE OLD WOMAN[6]

A woman died shortly after giving birth to a daughter. There was no one to nurse the infant, so her husband looked for a wife. He found and married a woman whose ugliness contrasted sharply with the beautiful orphan girl. After a time, the stepmother gave birth to a daughter who looked exactly like her mother.

The stepmother always mistreated the orphan girl and sent her on many errands at all hours of the day and night. The orphan's most frequent assignment was to walk through the forest to fetch many buckets of water from the lake.

One day, the orphan girl was sad, and she arrived at the edge of the lake crying. She was drawing water when she was approached by a very old, wrinkly woman who smelled and looked filthy and repugnant. The old woman begged her, "My child, give me some water to drink." So the kind-hearted orphan girl did. As soon as the old ugly woman drank, she turned into a strikingly beautiful young woman, saying, "My child, because you gave me water to drink when I was thirsty, and you saw me dirty and repulsive and nevertheless approached me to give me water, you will find in your life all the happiness in the world. One day when you open your mouth, gold and ivory and precious objects will come out." And then suddenly she disappeared.

The stepmother, who had been waiting in the village for the orphan girl to return, came barreling down the forest path, carrying a large stick.

---

4. Mvé Ondo, *Wisdom and Initiation*, ix.
5. Mvé Ondo, *Wisdom and Initiation*, 132.
6. Myth summary from Mvé Ondo, *Wisdom and Initiation*, 128–130.

When she met the orphan girl, she angrily yelled, "What have you been doing? You've been gone too long!" The child did not respond, and the stepmother smacked her with the stick. The girl opened her mouth to cry out, and from her mouth flowed gold, ivory, and precious stones of every kind.

The stepmother ran back to their home and told her daughter, "Run quickly to the river, and bring us the same happiness!" The stepsister ran to the river and found the distasteful old woman in the same place her stepsister had. The old, wrinkly, and repulsive-smelling woman also asked the stepsister for a drink of water. "What's this? Who are you? Get out of here!" the stepsister angrily ordered. She continued to shout insults at the old woman. The old woman turned into a beautiful princess and said to the child, "Since you wouldn't give me water when I asked for it, and instead you insulted me beyond all limits, you will encounter unhappiness. There will come a moment when you open your mouth, and out will come frogs, toads, vipers, and snakes."

The disappointed girl walked back home, where her mother waited impatiently with her large stick. She struck the girl on her back, saying, "Speak and hurry up!" The girl opened her mouth to cry, and out poured toads, vipers, and frogs. The mother fled, chasing the girl from the village. There is a proverb that says, "Generosity enriches the donor, just as avarice deprives the miser." Is it not this way?

COMMENTARY

This tale is reminiscent of Cinderella, where a young girl is hated for her innocence and beauty but endures mistreatment patiently and without complaint. In this story, as in Cinderella, the young girl is rewarded, and the perpetrators get their due.

The story displays a symmetry of action with two quests, the positive quest of the orphan and the negative quest of the stepsister.[7] The orphan child starts with unhappiness, has an encounter with an old woman, then a trial, and ends with happiness. The negative quest is reversed: initial happiness, encounter with an old woman, trial, unhappy end. The trial for both girls includes the practice of politeness, obedience, respect for elders, and helpfulness despite injustice.[8]

---

7. Mvé Ondo, *Wisdom and Initiation*, 129.
8. Mvé Ondo, *Wisdom and Initiation*, 130.

The Tale of the Orphan and the Old Woman. African

The orphan girl is said to be beautiful in contrast to both her abusive stepmother and lazy stepsister. But her beauty is more than skin-deep. The gold which poured from her mouth is reflective of the gold in her heart. The stepsister has few, if any, chores; she has had a bad example in her mother, and she responds to the old woman harshly. The stepsister fails her test of character. Both girls had the same opportunity to show kindness, and the end result was in part due to their choices.

The orphan girl was sent to draw water from the lake deep in the forest. The choice of errands is significant. As in many myths, water is symbolic. It can represent life-giving forces, and in this case, the old woman recovers her beauty when she drinks it. For the Fang, water is the place where souls are created and purified.[9] The forest also has significance in Bwiti Fang religion. It is seen as an ambiguous meeting place which may contain evil but is also a place where one can discover true knowledge.[10]

The story teaches the value of obedience, patience, good manners, and kindness. It also teaches the results of mistreating an orphan. Humility and respect are essential to the moral code.[11]

QUESTIONS FOR REFLECTION: HUMAN DIMENSION

1. Both sisters went through a trial of character. The orphan girl showed compassion and kindness, while her stepsister did not. When have you experienced a trial to test your compassion? How did you fare?
2. The stepsister's fate is to be chased away by her own mother. Is this fair? How might you write this to make this a more satisfying ending?

QUESTIONS FOR REFLECTION: CRITICAL ANALYSIS

1. The idea of character on trial is common to many myths. How might a hero's trial be effective in teaching moral codes?
2. Why do you think the father is absent, except for the very beginning?
3. Unpack the proverb that ends the myth: "Generosity enriches the donor, just as avarice deprives the miser."

---

9. Mvé Ondo, *Wisdom and Initiation*, 136.
10. Mvé Ondo, *Wisdom and Initiation*, 135.
11. Mvé Ondo, *Wisdom and Initiation*, 144.

20

Sedna. Inuit
What Kind of a Dad Would Chop Off His Daughter's Fingers?

HISTORICAL AND THEMATIC OVERVIEW

BAFFIN ISLAND IS A huge island east of Greenland and north of Hudson Bay. The Inuit people who lived on the island hunted seals, whales, and walruses in the winter and caribou in the summer.[1] Hunters followed the migrating herds, moving from one place to another with the seasons and living in skin tents. In the fall, salmon began to spawn, and the Inuit built stone enclosures to trap them. Food was frequently cached for the hard winter.

In the Arctic region, where edible vegetation is scarce, food cannot be grown, so the Inuit rely on hunting and fishing for food, clothing, and the raw materials for tools. The Inuit routinely kill animals, and it is fitting that a hunting deity would be an important part of their tradition. The myths which surround the deity Sedna explain the origin of sea creatures, as well as of the turmoil of the Arctic region. Sedna is often considered the most important deity because she provides life-sustaining food from the surrounding seas.

1. Wolfson, *Inuit Mythology*, 68.

The animals are considered both to have originated from and to be controlled by Sedna. Sedna was said to be the liaison between the Inuit people and her children (the animals that the Inuit need to survive) through religious rituals.[2] If animals were scarce, it was thought that Sedna had sent the animals away because of broken hunting, birth, or death taboos. Order and successful hunting could be restored with the intervention of a shaman.[3] While in an ecstatic trance, the shaman had to enter the goddess's home beneath the sea to convince her to release her children so the Inuit could survive.[4]

The Inuit on Baffin Island held feasts in which Sedna was ritually killed by thrusting a harpoon through a coiled thong on the floor, which represented a seal's breathing hole.[5] The intent was to ritually cleanse the broken taboos of the previous year to ensure good hunting in the following year.

The dark winter marked the end of celebrations and festivals and began the time for storytelling. The story of Sedna was told with many variations.

MYTH SUMMARY: SEDNA[6]

An Inuit man lived with his only daughter Sedna on an isolated coast. His wife had died, and the two led a solitary life. Many suitors came to court Sedna, but she was too proud to accept any of their proposals.

On another distant shore, a seabird looked with distaste on the female seabirds and desired a human wife. He flew from house to house, looking for the perfect mate, and much to his delight, he found Sedna. He was determined to make Sedna his wife through courtship and fashioned a sealskin parka to adorn his human form. When spring came, he came to Sedna's dwelling and began to woo her, saying, "Come with me, my dear, to the land of my people, the land of the birds. There you will live in a beautiful skin tent, you will sleep on the softest bearskin mat. My people will bring you whatever you wish. Their feathers will clothe you, your lamp will always be lit, and your pot will be full of meat." Sedna was impressed, and

---

2. Rosenberg, *World Mythology*, 638.
3. "Sedna," 5:916.
4. Rosenberg, *World Mythology*, 638.
5. Kleivan, "Sedna," 12:8221.
6. Myth summary from Driscoll, "Sedna," 35, and Rosenberg, *World Mythology*, 638–41.

unlike her response to the previous suitors, she became interested in the bird-man. She could not resist the comfortable lifestyle that he proposed, and she longed for the luxuries he promised. She ran to her tent to collect her belongings and informed her father she had found her suitor. Her father was not so sure and tried to dissuade her. But Sedna would not listen to her father's counsel against marrying a bird-man. She climbed into the bird-man's kayak and made the long journey with the bird-man.

When they arrived in the distant land of the bird-man, she discovered it had all been a ruse. Instead of a beautiful tent, she was given a small, smelly tent made of fish skin that let in every blast of bitterly cold wind. She slept on a hard walrus hide. She had only a small portion of raw fish to eat.

By day, she sang, "O Father, if you knew how wretched I am, you would come to me, and we would hurry away in your boat over the waters. I am miserable. Please come for me to return me to our home."

After a long year, the father came to visit Sedna. She was very happy to see him and told him of her misery. When he heard of her life among the seabirds, he was furious. In a fit of vengeance, he killed the bird-man and he and Sedna paddled off toward their home.

The other seabirds flew by and discovered the body of Sedna's birdman husband. They immediately pledged to avenge his death, and so, flying over the sea, they spotted the kayak, where Sedna and her father were rapidly paddling toward their home. They flew down upon the kayak, causing a terrible windstorm. Sedna's father became frightened at the attack of the sea birds. He knew he would die unless he took action. "This is no fault of mine!" he exclaimed. "If she had just accepted a husband from her own people, this would never never happened. I will rid myself of Sedna, and perhaps the seabirds will call off the storm!" So he threw Sedna overboard. She immediately swam to the side of the kayak and hung on for dear life. In fear and desperation, her father cut her fingers at the nail. As these fingertips fell into the water, her nails became whalebone, and her flesh became the whales. Sedna grabbed on with her finger stubs, but her father cut her fingers off from the first joint to the middle joint. These became seals. Still Sedna clung to the side of the kayak. Her father once again cut off the last bit of finger and her thumbs. Her finger stubs became bearded ground seals, and her thumbs became walruses. The seabirds believed that Sedna would die, so they flew away, and gradually the winds and waves grew calm. Sedna's father helped her climb into the kayak, but Sedna was enraged with her father. That night, she invited the sled dogs into the tent to eat her father's hands and feet. He awakened in pain, cursed her, himself, and the dogs, and the earth opened up and swallowed them all. They fell down, down, down into the land of Adlivun, where Sedna rules from the bottom of the ocean.

Sedna creates animals and commands them to give themselves to those people in the tribe who are good and to hide from those who are evil. Sedna has no fingers left to comb her hair. When she becomes angry, her hair becomes tangled, and she withholds animals from the Inuit hunters. The Inuit shaman must comb her tangled hair and plead with her to forgive her people who broke taboo. If the shaman is successful in easing the tangled hair, the village hunters will be successful.

COMMENTARY

Cooperation and mutual respect are essential in Inuit culture, as survival may depend upon consideration for others. Both Sedna and her father exhibit disrespect. Sedna does not respect her father when he discourages her from marrying the bird-man. Her father is both cowardly and self-centered when he completely disregards his daughter's life in trying to save himself from the seabirds. Both suffer severe consequences. Sedna lives in impoverished misery, and her father loses his hands and feet, then both are dropped into the Adlivun underworld. The myth illustrates the consequences of putting one's own concerns first.

The myth introduces the concept of taboo. Taboo means "prohibited," and it has parallels in both primitive and highly developed societies. Every culture has actions and words that are forbidden for religious and social reasons, and violation of these can lead to negative consequences. In this case, the Inuit believed they must observe certain practices and rituals in order to avoid offending Sedna. Breaking taboo meant failing to observe the appropriate rituals and thereby risking her anger, which could lead to famine.

Sedna is seen as benevolent and malevolent, reacting to human behavior with reward and punishment. Having participated in and experienced the worst of human (and bird) behavior, Sedna reacts with the same duplicitous conduct.

QUESTIONS FOR REFLECTION: THE HUMAN DIMENSION

1. What is behind the human tendency to assign cause and effect, even if there may be none?
2. What taboos are in our society? What are the results of broken taboos?
3. How do you feel about Sedna as a deity? Explain your answer.

QUESTIONS FOR REFLECTION: CRITICAL ANALYSIS

1. How might the prescribed societal norms of the Inuit help them survive? What environmental conditions might dictate needs for such societal norms?
2. What may be the advantages of a society with strict taboos? Are there disadvantages?
3. How effective do you think this myth would have been in teaching young Inuit children? Explain your answer.

21

Genesis. Ancient Hebrew
The Start of Something New

HISTORICAL AND THEMATIC OVERVIEW

BIBLICAL TRADITION ASSIGNS MOSES as the author of the book of Genesis.[1] The Bible describes how Moses was chosen by God to lead the Israelite people out of slavery in Egypt to Canaan in the thirteenth century BCE (Exod 3:7–12).[2] While neither Genesis nor the rest of the Bible specifically attributes authorship to Moses, logic and tradition are enough to attach a significant guiding role to him—a role which includes both authorial and editorial functions.[3] Genesis chapters 1 and 2 are of special interest, because they recount an ancient Israelite creation narrative.

It may be troubling for some to label the creation account in Genesis as myth. This is true for those who consider it a misrepresentation of the Bible to situate it alongside stories of Greek mythology, where the gods act in undignified and perverse ways. However, it is helpful to remember that

---

1. Traditionally, Moses is regarded as the author of the first five books of the Hebrew Bible, which includes Genesis.

2. An early dating of Moses's leading the Israelite people out of Egypt places it in the fifteenth century BCE.

3. For a more complete discussion of authorship, see Whybray, *Introduction to the Pentateuch*, 12–28.

WORLD MYTHOLOGY

a function of some mythology in ancient cultures was to explain how the world came into existence and how it functions. Many of the biblical writings, including the creation account in Genesis, functioned in the same manner as mythology. They gave the Israelites, the original audience of the book of Genesis, "a literary mechanism for preserving and transmitting their worldview and values."[4]

MYTH: GENESIS 1:1–2:4[5]

> In the beginning when God created the heavens and the earth, the earth was a formless void[6] and darkness covered the face of the deep, while a wind[7] from God swept over the face of the waters. Then God said, "Let there be light"; and there was light. And God saw that the light was good; and God separated the light from the darkness.[8] God called the light Day, and the darkness he called Night. And there was evening and there was morning, the first day. And God said, "Let there be a dome in the midst of the waters, and let it separate the waters from the waters." So God made the dome and separated the waters that were under the dome from the waters that were above the dome. And it was so. God called the dome Sky. And there was evening and there was morning, the second day. And God said, "Let the waters under the sky be gathered together into one place, and let the dry land appear." And it was so. God called the dry land Earth, and the waters that were gathered together he called Seas. And God saw that it was good. Then God said, "Let the earth put forth vegetation: plants yielding seed, and fruit trees of every kind on earth that bear fruit with the seed in it." And it was so. The earth brought forth vegetation: plants yielding seed of every kind, and trees of every kind bearing fruit with the seed in it. And God saw that it was good. And there was evening

4. Walton, *Genesis*, 27.

5. NRSV.

6. The earth's condition as a formless void describes it as inhabitable and unproductive (Mathews, *Genesis*, 115). By describing the condition of the earth as "a formless void," a foil is provided, by which God directs his creation agenda.

7. The term "wind" has been traditionally rendered as "Spirit," referring to the divine Spirit, but "wind" is also a likely possibility, fitting the context, since the earth is described with natural phenomena, such as seawater (Mathews, *Genesis*, 136).

8. The term translated as "good" indicates not only that creation was exceptional in quality, but also was likely intended to communicate that it was fitting or appropriate for the purpose for which it was created.

and there was morning, the third day. And God said, "Let there be lights in the dome of the sky to separate the day from the night; and let them be for signs and for seasons and for days and years, and let them be lights in the dome of the sky to give light upon the earth." And it was so. God made the two great lights—the greater light to rule the day and the lesser light to rule the night—and the stars. God set them in the dome of the sky to give light upon the earth, to rule over the day and over the night, and to separate the light from the darkness. And God saw that it was good. And there was evening and there was morning, the fourth day. And God said, "Let the waters bring forth swarms of living creatures, and let birds fly above the earth across the dome of the sky." So God created the great sea monsters and every living creature that moves, of every kind, with which the waters swarm, and every winged bird of every kind. And God saw that it was good. God blessed them, saying, "Be fruitful and multiply and fill the waters in the seas, and let birds multiply on the earth." And there was evening and there was morning, the fifth day. And God said, "Let the earth bring forth living creatures of every kind: cattle and creeping things and wild animals of the earth of every kind." And it was so. God made the wild animals of the earth of every kind, and the cattle of every kind, and everything that creeps upon the ground of every kind. And God saw that it was good. Then God said, "Let us make humankind in our image, according to our likeness; and let them have dominion over the fish of the sea, and over the birds of the air, and over the cattle, and over all the wild animals of the earth, and over every creeping thing that creeps upon the earth."[9]

So God created humankind in his image,
in the image of God he created them;[10]
male and female he created them.

God blessed them, and God said to them, "Be fruitful and multiply,[11] and fill the earth and subdue it; and have dominion over the fish of the sea and over the birds of the air and over every living thing that moves upon the earth." God said, "See, I have

9. This task of preserving order is passed on to humanity, one of the ways in which the human being, male and female, fulfils the high destiny of being created in the image of God.

10. In the ancient world, kings would set up statues, icons, or images in the various territories over which they ruled. The images would mark the king's territory and remind the subjects who was in charge, who sat on the throne.

11. God is offering the first couple a blessing, rather than issuing them a command to have children. In the ancient world, the ability to reproduce was viewed as a gift from God.

given you every plant yielding seed that is upon the face of all the earth, and every tree with seed in its fruit; you shall have them for food. And to every beast of the earth, and to every bird of the air, and to everything that creeps on the earth, everything that has the breath of life, I have given every green plant for food." And it was so. God saw everything that he had made, and indeed, it was very good. And there was evening and there was morning, the sixth day. Thus the heavens and the earth were finished, and all their multitude. And on the seventh day God finished the work that he had done, and he rested on the seventh day from all the work that he had done. So God blessed the seventh day and hallowed it, because on it God rested from all the work that he had done in creation. These are the generations of the heavens and the earth when they were created.

COMMENTARY

The creation account in Genesis 1:1–2:4 is only one of many biblical creation accounts (e.g., Gen 2:5–25; Ps 8, 33, 74, 90,102; Jer 27, 32; Ezek 28). The account in Genesis 1:1–2:4 presents creation in an orderly, balanced, and symmetrical fashion. The narrative describes creation as moving from a situation of chaos to one of order. The narrative is structured around the idea of forming and filling, with two sets of three acts corresponding to one another. In the first set of three, God creates a space or environment; in the second set of three, he creates the corresponding actors to fill that space.[12]

Day 1: Forming the light (Gen 1:1–5); Day 4: Filling with Sun and Moon (Gen 1:14–19).

Day 2: Forming the sky and seas (Gen 1:6–8) Day 5: Filling with fowl and fish (Gen 1:20–23)

Day 3: Forming the dry land (Gen 1:9–13) Day 6: Filling with earth creatures (Gen 1:24–31).

Repetition plays an important role in this narrative. "And God said" occurs ten times at 1:3, 6, 9, 11, 14, 20, 24, 26, 28, and 29. The repeated divine mandate (e.g., "Let there be . . .") is followed each time by an executed response (". . . there was . . ."). The repeated phrase, "And God said, let there be . . .," gives the impression of "a magisterial and in-charge deity whose

12. Anderson, "Creation."

word is all powerful."[13] By bringing the world into existence by utterance, the imagery is of a powerful sovereign (a king) who utters a decree from the throne, and in the very spoken word, it is accomplished, done, finished, and obeyed. Noteworthy is that, in this creation account, God is not depicted as a craftsman but as a king. His worker is his word. Thus, he needs no assistants or servants. God is the sole operative cause.[14] In contrast to the creation of the cosmos and of the plant and animal kingdoms, the creation of humanity in Genesis 1:26–28 comes about, exceptionally, not through a word-act but as the result of deliberation: "Let us make humankind."

QUESTIONS FOR REFLECTION: THE HUMAN DIMENSION

1. What questions about the earth's origin are not answered for you in this creation account?

2. According to this account, what is the purpose for which humanity was created? Does this purpose seem satisfactory or fulfilling for you personally? Why or why not?

3. John Oswalt maintains that one ruling idea in the worldview of myth is the idea that all things that exist are part of each other. There are no fundamental differences between the three realms: humanity, nature, and the divine.[15] Do you agree with this view? Why or why not? Does that view apply to the Genesis creation myth?

QUESTIONS FOR REFLECTION: CRITICAL ANALYSIS

1. If Israelite values are expressed in this account, what does the story highlight as significant, and how does it emphasize this value?

2. How is God characterized in this narrative? List at least three attributes with support from the text.

13. Niditch, *Oral World*, 13.

14. McKenzie, *Myths and Realities*, 96. It is true that deities in other myths exhibit the power of the spoken word. For example, Marduk, a god in Mesopotamian mythology, demonstrates his verbal power by annihilating and restoring a garment by the command of his mouth. However, this is more like the work of a sorcerer performing stage magic (McKenzie, *Myths and Realities*, 100).

15. Oswalt, *Bible among the Myths*, 48.

3. At the end of the account, it says God rested. Does this convey exhaustion on the part of God? Support your answer from the text.

4. What is the pinnacle of creation: the creation of humanity, the blessing of the seventh day? Support your answer from the text.

22

Popol Vuh. Mayan
Word Power

HISTORICAL AND THEMATIC OVERVIEW

THE QUICHÉ-MAYANS WERE INDIGENOUS people from Mesoamerica.[1] They likely were descendants of migrants from Siberia who came across the Bering Strait during the last ice age and settled North America.[2] These hunter-gatherers reached Mexico and Central America about ten thousand years ago. As the climate warmed around 7000 BCE, these peoples began domesticating and cultivating plants and practicing agriculture. Some of the Mayan's striking cultural traits include their two calendars of 260 and 365 days, hieroglyphic writing, screenfold books, and masonry courts for playing a game that used a ball and rings.[3] The Mayans also had a collection of mythological tales, including a story of the creation of the world.

According to the Quiché-Mayan account of creation, the first four humans whom the gods successfully created (they had failed in earlier attempts) had the ability to see everything in the future. The gods had not intended to create persons capable of being their equal, so they eliminated

---

1. The name given to that part of Central America (primarily Mexico) that was civilized before the Spanish conquest in the early sixteenth century.
2. Taube, *Aztec and Maya Myths*, 8.
3. Taube, *Aztec and Maya Myths*, 7.

their powers of foresight. However, the lords who ruled the kingdom of Quiché had in their possession an instrument for seeing into the future. The instrument, which they had acquired on a pilgrimage, was not a crystal ball, but a book called the Council Book or *Popol Vuh*.[4] The lords consulted their book whenever they sat in council. Not only did the *Popol Vuh* foretell when there would be war, famine, strife, and death, it also detailed events before the creation of the world down through the Mayan kings in 1550.[5] The Council Book also provided useful information for the survival of the people, such as instructions on when to plant and harvest based on astronomical signs.

In the form that is known to us today, the *Popol Vuh* is thought to have been written between 1554 and 1558 (based on references to contemporary historical events) by Quiché speakers most likely from the Mayan nobility, who were trained to read and write the Latin alphabet.[6] It was likely composed in reaction to the Spanish oppression, with the aim to preserve Mayan native beliefs and stories important to their cultural identity.[7] The content of the original manuscript is known to us today thanks to the copies made in the beginning of the eighteenth century by Francisco Ximénez, a Dominican friar serving as the parish priest. He discovered the text and was permitted to copy and translate the book from the original Quiché language.[8]

In translation, the *Popol Vuh* is divided into four or five sections. The first part covers creation. The following two sections recount the adventures of a pair of trickster twins who rid the world of demons and monsters. In the final sections, the history of the Quiché people is recounted.

MYTH SUMMARY: THE POPOL VUH CREATION ACCOUNT[9]

In the beginning, only the gods existed in the middle of the dark waters. The gods assembled, discussed, and decided to create the world by command. "And the earth arose because of them, it was simply their word that

---

4. Tedlock, *Popol Vuh*, 21.
5. Sproul, *Primal Myths*, 287.
6. González, "*Popol Vuh* for Children," 217.
7. Anton, "Power of the Word," 8.
8. Tedlock, *Popol Vuh*, 27.
9. Myth summary from Sproul, *Primal Myths*, 287–96.

brought it forth. For the forming of the earth, they said, 'Earth.'"[10] The gods also made all the animals and birds to live on the earth. But these creatures were flawed because they could not speak or praise their creators. The gods said, "'Speak now: speak, pray to us, keep our days,' they were told. But it didn't turn out that they spoke like people: they just squawked, they just chattered, they just howled."[11] So the gods set out to make people. The first attempt failed because the clay they were using melted in the water. The second attempt to make people was with carved wooden creatures, but they were too dry and brittle. They had no blood and no memory and lacked anything in their hearts or minds. This race of people was destroyed by their talking cooking pots, tortilla griddles, and other kitchen utensils. The gods tried a third time to create humanity. This time they used plants (mostly varieties of corn and beans, the main diet of the Mayan) and made four people. These people were gifted with great vision and understanding. These abilities frightened the gods. The creatures turned out to be too perfect for the gods' liking, causing them to limit the humans' profound understanding of the world. The humans were grateful to their creators for being given mouths, faces, and ability to speak and listen. Next the gods formed four women. From these first people descended all the ancestors of the Quiché and other Central American tribes.

COMMENTARY

From the opening of the creation account, the power of the gods and their words seems to be limitless, yet when confronted with failed attempts at making creatures that would give thanks to the gods, the power of the divine beings and their words is called into question. It seems that the spoken word is indeed an important motif, not only in the creative act but as a purpose as well. The intention of the gods was to bring rationally speaking beings to life, who would honor their creators.[12] The importance of the spoken word manifests itself in this narrative in various aspects, such as creating, planning, glorifying, and uniting. In later parts of the *Popol Vuh*, the spoken word is used to deceive and punish.

In the *Popol Vuh*, the gods also interact with the stuff of creation to make things happen. Nature does not yield to their will. The work of

10. Tedlock, *Popol Vuh*, 65.
11. Tedlock, *Popol Vuh*, 67.
12. Anton, "Power of the Word," 10.

trial-and-error is demonstrated as the way to improve on initial concepts. The gods learn as they go.

QUESTIONS FOR REFLECTION: THE HUMAN DIMENSION

1. How much value might you place on having a resource to be able to see into the future?
2. How have you experienced words functioning to bring about change for good?
3. Are you comfortable with gods who appear to not be perfect? Explain your answer.

QUESTIONS FOR REFLECTION: CRITICAL ANALYSIS

1. The Mayan gods tried numerous times to create humanity a certain way. What might this tell you about the Mayan worldview?
2. A culture's story about the origins of the world is most often informed by that culture's view of what is meaningful, valuable, and acceptable, and of what is evil, disposable, and taboo. What does the Mayan creation story suggest might be true for each of these?
3. What reasons can you suggest that might account for the importance of speech and the power of the spoken word in the creation account?
4. Compare and contrast this creation account with other creation accounts in this book.

23

Völuspá Part 1, Creation. Norse
From Chaos to Calm

HISTORICAL AND THEMATIC OVERVIEW

On April 21, 1971, a Danish frigate came steaming into the harbor of Reykjavik, the capital of Iceland.[1] Waiting for the ship were fifteen-thousand Icelanders. The rest of the nation, not present at the harbor, were witnessing the event on television or listening to it unfold on the radio, for shops and schools had been closed for this historic occasion. Once docked, three packages were then carried off the ship. These packages had been locked in a cabin on the ship all the way from Denmark. Twice a day, the cabin was unlocked by the captain to verify that the room was at the optimal humidity and temperature for preservation of the contents. Among the packages was one of the most valuable treasures of Icelandic literature, the Codex Regius (the King's Volume), which had been taken from the Icelandic colony two hundred fifty years earlier. The Codex was discovered in 1643 on an Icelandic farm, when it came into the possession of Brynjólfur Sveinsson, then Bishop of Skálholt. In 1662, the Bishop sent it as a gift to King Frederick III of Denmark, thus the name the King's Volume. It was then preserved in the Royal Library in Copenhagen until it was eventually returned to

---

1. The historical overview relies primarily on Magnusson, "Introduction," 1.

Iceland, where it is now housed in the Árni Magnússon Institute for Icelandic Studies.

The Codex Regius, written down in the thirteenth century, contains the collection of thirty-one poems known as the *Poetic Edda*.[2] These are anonymous poems from the Viking Age about the gods and heroes of Norse mythology.[3] Because the poems in the *Edda* build on a long oral tradition, it is impossible to give an exact date for the composition of a poem or to determine a specific origin. However, the Vikings, who told and enjoyed the myths collected in the *Edda*, refers collectively to the Danes, Norwegians, and Swedes—Norsemen active during the period of 780 to 1070 CE.[4]

Before the poems were written down, they were passed on by poets who were skilled at selecting meters and constructing images. As previously noted, the poems in the *Poetic Edda* build on a long oral tradition. Viking people were mainly illiterate, so storytelling was an oral, communal activity. Family members shared tales around the fireside, itinerant storytellers brought the latest news and gossip, professional bards recited grandiose narratives at feasts. Like political speeches today that are adapted for different audiences, some of the ancient traditions likely changed in oral transmission.

Völuspá is the most noteworthy and most often discussed of the Eddic mythological poems. It opens with a creation myth and then proceeds to describe the events that led up to the climactic battle at Ragnarok (RAG-na-rock; the fate or doom of the gods), the battle itself, and its aftermath. The most coherent and variant account of Norse creation also occurs in the *Prose Edda*.[5] There is also a vague and somewhat different partial account of the beginning of the world in the poem *Vafthruthnismal*.

MYTH SUMMARY: VÖLUSPÁ[6]

Völuspá recounts the events of the past and future, which are told in the first person by a seeress. For now, we will focus on the events of that portion

---

2. Lindow, *Norse Mythology*, 12.
3. Lindow, *Norse Mythology*, 12.
4. Crossley-Holland, *Norse Myths*, xiv.
5. The *Prose Edda* was written by the Icelander mythographer Snorri Sturluson (1129–1241). *Völuspá* is also found in a variant version in *Hauksbók*, a large, early fourteenth-century compendium of prose and verse (Larrington, trans., *Poetic Edda*, 274).
6. Benjamin Thorpe translated the *Poetic Eddas* from the original Old Norse text into

of the myth describing origins. The poem begins with the seeress calling for the attention of an audience. The invocation communicates a sense of religious solemnity as her voice breaks through the noise of the banquet hall at the court of the chieftain.[7] She requests both the greater and lesser offspring of Heimdall to listen:[8]

> Listen all sacred children,
> great and small, offspring of Heimdall [HAYM-dahl],
> Corpse-Father wished for me to recount
> men's ancient stories,
> those that I remember.[9]

The Norse god Odin had consulted a seeress to find out what had transpired in the past. She recounted a time when nothing existed:

> There was in times of old, when Ymir[10] [EE-mere] lived,
> no sand, no sea, no cool waves,
> no earth existed, no heaven above,
> a chaotic chasm, and grass nowhere.[11]

The active agents in creation were referred to as the sons of Bur, who were Odin, Vili, and Ve.[12] The three gods raised the shores from the primeval sea and laid the foundations for Midgard, a space to be inhabited by human beings. The heavens and earth came into existence, but in chaos:

> The sun from the south, the moon's companion,
> cast her right hand over the horizon.[13]
> The sun knew not where she had a dwelling,
> the moon knew not what power he possessed,

English. The quotations are based on his work *The Elder Eddas*. The language has been updated. In parts, alterations also have been made, when necessary, from more recent scholarly translations. These changes are referenced.

7. Lönnroth, "Founding of Miðgarðr," 12. The setting for the poem appears to be like the banquet hall of the Icelandic chieftains. Iceland functioned as a commonwealth, in which judicial power was in the hands of a group of chieftains, and there was no king or other central authority (Lindow, *Norse Mythology*, 6).

8. Heimdall is the watchman of the gods who sits at the edge of Asgard, the gods' domain. He was called "the father of the races of men."

9. Stanza 1.

10. Ymir is a primordial being or giant.

11. Stanza 3.

12. Larrington, trans., *Poetic Edda*, 283.

13. The phrase "over the horizon" is from Lönnroth, "Founding of Miðgarðr," 17.

the stars knew not where they had a station.[14]

The gods levied order on this chaos and then constructed religious edifices and fabricated tools:

> Then went the powers all to their judgment-seats,
> the holy gods, and they held council:
> and to night and to the moon they gave names;
> morning they named, and mid-day,
> afternoon and evening, so they could calculate the years.
>
> The Æsir[15] met on Idavoll Plain;[16]
> they constructed altars and temples high;
> they established furnaces, and forged precious things,
> formed tongs, and fabricated tools.[17]

After creation, the gods enjoyed a time of leisure, playing games. The board game described may have been a game of chance[18] and was considered a special pleasure among the Icelandic chieftain class. In *Völuspá*, the game was a symbol for the highest and purest joy.[19] The myth then describes the creation of the dwarfs and of humanity:

> Breath they possessed not, spirit they had not,
> nor blood or complexion.
> Breath gave Odin, spirit gave Haenir,
> blood and complexion gave Lodur.[20]

Following the creation account, the seeress then narrates the arrival of a female practitioner of magic amongst the Æsir tribe of gods.[21] Because of her arrival, the Æsir find themselves at war with another tribe of gods, the Vanir. The Æsir family consisted mainly of the gods of war and sky. They included Odin, his wife Frigg, Thor, and Baldr (Bal-DURR). The Vanir consisted of the gods of fertility and sensual pleasure as well as of wealth and commerce. They included the gods and goddesses Njörd (NI-yord), Freyr

---

14. Stanza 5.
15. Æsir (ā-sir, sing., *áss*) are a tribe of gods.
16. The phrase "Idavoll Plain" is from Larrington, trans., *Poetic Edda*, 4.
17. Stanzas 6–7.
18. Boyer, "On the Composition," 120.
19. Lönnroth, "Founding of Miðgarðr," in Acker and Larrington, *The Poetic Edda*, 18.
20. Stanza 18. This stanza relies on Larrington, trans., *Poetic Edda*, 6.
21. Lindow, *Norse Mythology*, 23.

Völuspá Part 1, Creation. Norse

(FRĀ-r), and Freyja (FRĀ-a). When a truce is eventually reached between the two warring factions, the gods must repair the war-damaged walls of Asgard (ASS-guard; enclosure of the Æsir), home of the gods. A builder offers to rebuild the ramparts in a very short time in exchange for the sun, moon, and Freyja. The gods agree, thinking the task impossible, but the builder was on schedule to complete the project by the agreed upon deadline. So, the gods attempt to thwart the builder's progress.[22] Consequently, the builder becomes enraged, revealing his identity as a member of the race of giants, ancient enemies of the Æsir. Thor is summoned, and on the grounds that the builder was not who he purported to be, Thor annihilates the giant with his hammer Mjölnir (MYOL-nir):[23]

> There alone was Thor with anger swollen.
> He seldom sits, when of the like he hears.
> Oaths were not kept, nor words, nor pledges,
> binding compacts reciprocally made between them, broken.[24]

At stanza twenty-eight, no longer is the seeress discussing the past. The creation account is complete. Odin then questions the seeress about what is to transpire in the future.

COMMENTARY

Völuspá likely created a mystical environment when it was performed before spectators. It is written in the first person, which serves to "summon up" the seeress from another world in front of a live audience.[25] The seeress

---

22. Loki (LOW-key) is blamed for persuading the gods to accept the original agreement. While Loki does not appear in this portion of the poem, other sources reveal that he finds a way of disrupting the builder's schedule by turning himself into a mare, who entices the builder's helpful stallion away from the building project, causing the promised construction timetable to be broken.

23. Thor is the god of thunder and lightning. He rules the sky, the wind, rainstorms, and sunshine. Those credentials made him the natural god of farmers, responsible for ensuring the fertility of the soil and the health of crops. Most Icelandic men were farmers or herders. Some did metalworking, construction work, or shipbuilding, either as a sideline or main occupation. Others were merchants who travelled widely overseas, artisans who decorated their handiwork with exquisite patterns, professional courtiers, soldiers, or legal experts. It was not unusual for men to join raiding expeditions, either for a single season or on a regular basis (Kerven, *Viking Myths*, 16).

24. The last two lines are adapted from Woolf, "*Spaewife's Prophecy*," 28.

25. Gunnell, "Eddic Performances," 104.

seems to speak directly to the spectators in the performance space. Further, those present at the time of the performance would be watching and interpreting the poet's gestures, movements, and facial expressions, which would have enlivened the numinous experience even more.[26]

Odin is the god of wisdom, yet he seeks out knowledge from the seeress. In the second stanza, the seeress begins to unveil the hidden wonders. Creation demands an explanation, and mythology provides this by addressing certain questions: What was the beginning? How did things start? The creation myth opens in chaos, and it is eventually brought to a state of order.

Eddic poetry at times employs kennings—a poetic phrase used in conjunction with or in place of the common name. For example, a kenning for the sun is "the sky-candle." A kenning for arrows is "war-needles." In the first stanza of *Völuspá*, the god Odin is called a "Corpse-Father" or, more literally, father of the slain. Odin is called "Corpse-Father" because he reigns over those who die in battle and are taken up to Valhalla, the resting place of dead heroes.[27] These riddle-like phrases add color to the story and invite listeners to participate by unpacking their meaning.

QUESTIONS FOR REFLECTION: THE HUMAN DIMENSION

1. What evidence in *Völuspá* can you find to support that the principle force in the evolution of the universe is fate? How would you define fate based on this account? Do you agree with the poem's fatalistic outlook on life? Why or why not?

2. Answer the following according to *Völuspá*: What is a human being? What is the purpose of existence? What is the meaning of life? What is the nature of the world, and what is humanity's relationship to the world? Where did the universe come from? Is there an ultimate being? Do the answers to these questions seem satisfactory or fulfilling for you personally? Why or why not?

---

26. Gunnell, "Eddic Performances," 95.

27. Throughout the poem, Odin is given different names, alluding to his varying characteristics and functions. One of the most popular and important attestations for Odin is "All-Father." He acts as a father to all the gods, and because he and his brothers created the first humans, he is a father to all. Odin is considered the chief Norse god and the god of warriors and wisdom. Odin is also the god of poets.

Völuspá Part 1, Creation. Norse

3. What evidence can you find that wisdom is a topic of the poem? What is wisdom, or how is it defined, according to *Völuspá*? Is this a type of wisdom you find valuable? Why or why not?

4. What do you find appealing or unappealing about the poem?

QUESTIONS FOR REFLECTION: CRITICAL ANALYSIS

1. Little space is devoted to the creation of humanity. What might this suggest about the purpose of the poem?

2. Part of the purpose of kennings is to explore new ways of describing and understanding the world around us. If you can obtain a copy of *Völuspá*, select three kennings from the creation myth and explain how they function to describe something differently. What effect does the new way of naming the object (the kenning) have on the context in which it is used?

3. If you can obtain a full copy of *Völuspá*, read through the creation narrative. Based on the different types of creation myths described in the chapter "How to Read a Myth," decide if this account exemplifies "creation out of nothing" or "creation out of chaos." Support your answer with quotations from the myth.

4. Why might the poet repeat the phrase "knew not" in stanza five?

24

Creation of the Titans and Gods. Greek

Let's Not Eat Our Offspring, Dad.

HISTORICAL AND THEMATIC OVERVIEW

The Creation of the *Titans and Gods* is part of Hesiod's *Theogony*, a thousand-line poem written in the eighth century BCE. Not much is known for certain about Hesiod, but he did provide some autobiographical data. His father was a trader who was "fleeing wretched poverty" and became a farmer near Ascra in Boeotia.[1] Hesiod worked the land for his father, and it was there that he said the Muses appeared to him while he was tending sheep. They commanded him to write poetry, so he did.

We know more about Hesiod than we do about Homer, the contemporary of Hesiod who wrote the *Iliad* and the *Odyssey*. Hesiod's writings provide more biographical information. Hesiod wrote about his brother Perses, with whom he had a bitter legal dispute over inheritance. In the eight-hundred-line poem *Words and Days*, Hesiod describes how Perses had taken the larger share of the family inheritance and had wasted it. The poem also contains advice on how to ethically conduct one's affairs. Hesiod, who was a thoughtful man, valued honesty and hard work and condemned

---

1. "Hesiod," 7:631.

laziness and dishonesty. In some of his writings, Hesiod mixes observations on farming with proverbs on how to live.

Hesiod also mentions his personal encounter with the Muses, who appeared to him as he was tending sheep. They provided him with the gift of song, and he was able to compose lyrical poetry. His two major surviving works are *Theogony* and *Works and Days*.

The *Theogony* was Hesiod's attempt to compile into some semblance of order a number of primitive myths about the origin of the gods, providing readers with a more systematic and progressive story. He intended to incorporate the myths into a rational explanation of how Zeus became the "father of men and gods."[2] The section *Creation of the Titans and Gods* is a complex, multi-generational story of divine beings, whereby each generation overthrows the previous generation. It likely represents a snapshot portrait of the myths at the time, as they continued to develop and as the gods were endowed with different characteristics.

MYTH SUMMARY: CREATION OF THE TITANS AND GODS[3]

In the beginning there was just Chaos, but from Chaos emerged three divine beings: Gaea, or Mother Earth; Tartarus, ruler of the deepest and darkest underworld; and Eros, a beautiful god of love. Gaea was able to produce Uranus without a partner, but, once she had produced him, she made him her equal and her mate. Gaea also produced Mountains and Pontus, the Sea.

Gaea and Uranus produced the twelve Titans; three Cyclopes; and three Hecatoncheires, beings with fifty heads and a hundred arms. Uranus proved to be a difficult father, and the three Hecatoncheires hated him. Uranus pushed them all back into Gaea's womb, causing her great pain. She began to plot against Uranus and attempted to enlist her other children's help. Only Cronus, the youngest Titan, dared to avenge his mother.

Cronus did so by emasculating his father with his mother's sickle, saying, "Your reign is over, Father! Now I shall reign in your place. You may challenge me, but my power is clearly greater than yours." Uranus, being immortal, could not die, but he was in great pain, both physical pain and the pain of knowing his power was gone. The blood dripping from his

2. "Hesiod," 7:632.
3. Myth summary from Rosenberg, *World Mythology*, 85–7.

wounds created the Furies, who punished children who killed their parents; the ash-tree nymphs; and a race of fearsome giants. Cronus threw Uranus's genitals into the sea; there they foamed, and arising from the foam came Aphrodite, goddess of sexual desire. Uranus threatened vengeance on Cronus and his Titan brothers.

Cronus became the ruler of the sky like his father before him, but he forgot his promise to his mother that he would release his brothers in Tartarus. Gaea was disappointed in him, and she informed him that one of his sons would overpower him some day. To this prophesy, Cronus replied, "I shall fool the Fates. If do not have any children, then I will be able to rule forever!"

Cronus married his sister Rhea, and in time she produced a daughter she named Hestia. When she proudly presented the infant to her husband, he remembered the prophesy and swallowed the baby whole, uttering, "Now I have cheated the Fates of their prophesy and my child of his throne!" This pattern was repeated with each infant: Demeter, Hera, Hades, Poseidon. Finally, Rhea got wise, and when she presented her sixth child, Zeus, she substituted a rock wrapped in a blanket. Cronus swallowed the stone unknowingly.

Zeus was hidden away throughout his youth and grew up. When he reached maturity, he consulted with a Titaness named Metis (one of the descendants of the original twelve Titans) on how to overthrow his father. Rhea prepared a delicious drink, and Cronus wanted more. A young stranger walked in and gave him another cup which he drank down immediately, not realizing that this was a potion designed to make him vomit up his children. This young stranger was his grown son Zeus. Rhea said, "Your destiny is upon you, Cronus! The Fates prophesied that your son would overpower you, just as you overpowered your own father. That son, Zeus, now stands before you." Sure enough, the children of Rhea and Cronus were vomited up and in this way, Zeus, who was the youngest, was also considered the oldest. It had been Zeus who was able to grow up, living outside of his father's stomach. Together, Rhea and Zeus bound Cronus in Tartarus, the underworld.

The fight for ultimate power was not yet over. The other Titans engaged in fierce, ongoing battles until Zeus and Tartarus released the Cyclopes and the Hecatoncheires. The Titans were defeated, and Zeus condemned them to Tartarus; there they were guarded forever by the hundred-headed giants.

Creation of the Titans and Gods. Greek

Atlas, one of the Titans, was strong and massive, and he was to forced stand forever at the edge of the world and hold up the world.

Gaea was upset that her children the Titans had been defeated. She gave birth to one last being, Typhoenus, a hundred-headed dragon that needed no rest. Most of the gods fled in fear of this unique creature, but Zeus stayed to fight. Zeus was captured briefly but released by Hermes and killed the dragon by hurling lightning bolts.

The three male gods drew lots for their kingdoms. Zeus drew the sky, Poseidon drew the sea, and Hades drew the underworld. Zeus married his sister Hera, who gave birth to Athena, Apollo, Artemis, Hermes, Persephone, Ares, and Hephaestus.

COMMENTARY

Central to the story are the themes of power and dominance. Each of the characters aims for control and dominance over the others. Cronus castrates his father, imprisons his brothers, and swallows his children. His son Zeus overthrows Cronus and fights others to retain power. The fight for supremacy is central, and it is force that determines who will rule.

This myth also addresses how order develops out of chaos. The story literally begins in chaos. By the end, there is an established leader, although chaos has not been easily or completely tamed. Hesiod was combining a number of early stories as a rationale for why Zeus is the chief god. In the end, it is force that brings order out of chaos.

QUESTIONS FOR REFLECTION: HUMAN DIMENSION

1. What might be the effect of a worldview where power and supremacy are shaped by fighting and force? How does this compare to your worldview?
2. Did each of the defeated gods get what they deserved? Defend your answer.

QUESTIONS FOR REFLECTION: CRITICAL ANALYSIS

1. How does the Greek concept of chaos compare to disorder in other mythologies?

2. How does this compare to the Genesis account of creation? Why do you think the Genesis account is so much more well-known than the *Creation of Titans and Gods*?

25

The Emergence. Native American
From Bugs to People in Five Worlds

HISTORICAL AND THEMATIC OVERVIEW

THE NAVAJO, WHO CALL themselves the Diné, meaning "The People," are the largest Native American group in North America. They descended from a group of Athabascan-speaking clans originally from Alaska and western Canada.[1] Primarily a herding and farming tribe, the Navajo lived in mud hogans in the western United States before being forced into slavery by the Apache and later relocated by the U.S. government.

The Diné have an emergence-style creation story. As with many myths, there are several versions of this creation account, but all involve the movement through underworlds in a progressively more civilized and sophisticated environment. The creatures overcome issues like hunger and overcrowding as they progress up and onward through these underworlds while evolving, and they emerge as people in the final world, sometimes the fourth or, in this version, the fifth world.

Navajo culture typically emphasizes a "fourness" to its worldview. In this myth, the number four is sacred, reflective of the four cardinal directions, four seasons, four sacred mountains, four sacred colors (black, white, yellow and blue), and four sacred plants (corn, squash, beans, and

---

1. Lynch, "Navajo," 75.

tobacco).[2] Also, four humans are created by the gods (the First Man and Woman, First Girl and Boy).

This myth is notable in its portrayal of a close, intimate relationship among all species in nature, from insects to human beings. Each has a purpose, and each has gifts which are used for the greater good.

MYTH SUMMARY: THE EMERGENCE[3]

In the first world, there was just blackness in a land ringed by burning resin. This world was inhabited by wingless insects, including locusts, ants, dragonflies, beetles, and flies. These creatures lived in holes in the ground until one day they gathered and said, "This place is too small, too dark, and too unpleasant! We must find a new world that will be larger and lighter."

The insects made wings and tied them to their bodies. Locust found a crack in the roof where a blue light shone through. The insects flew through the hole and found themselves in the Second World.

This was the Blue World, inhabited by a variety of birds, including the white crane, the blue heron, the yellow loon, and the black loon. It was a much larger world and full of light. The insects separated themselves from the birds so that each group could have enough food.

As the insects grew in numbers, food became scarce. The insects invaded the birds' territory to find food, and as they swarmed into the territory, four great birds called for their kind to battle the invaders. The birds were victorious. Locust gathered the surviving insects and urged them to find a better world. They all flew quickly to the roof of the Blue World, where Blue Wind led them to the Third World.

This was the Yellow World. It was full of grass, bushes, springs, rivers, and mountains, and had ample food. Living creatures there spoke the same language and had the teeth, claws, feet, and wings of insects. Human beings were present and wore their insect wings as part of their outer coat which could be removed. The people lived in caves and ate only the raw food they could gather.

In the autumn, four gods, including White Body, Blue Body, Yellow Body, and Black Body, appeared before the people. Black Body god told the people that the gods wanted to create people who had the same appearance as they, saying, "Many of you have bodies like the gods, but you have the

2. Rosenberg, *World Mythology*, 615.
3. Myth summary from Rosenberg, *World Mythology*, 616–20.

teeth, claws, and feet of insects and animals. Be clean and ready when we return to you in twelve days."[4]

In twelve days, Black Body god and Blue Body god returned and brought two sacred buckskins. White Body god returned with two perfect ears of corn. They covered the ears of corn with buckskins and placed an eagle feather under each ear of corn. The White and Yellow Wind blew on the corn, giving them life, and each ear of corn became a human, the First Man and the First Woman.

The First Man and First Woman lived peacefully until the population increased and food again became scarce. The strong were able to find food, but those who were stronger and more clever stole it. The First People met together and decided to leave the Yellow World to escape hunger. People from each of four regions tried to choose a leader, but they could not reach an agreement. Each of their representatives returned with gifts, and the people decided that they needed a council, not an individual, to rule. They still needed to find food, so they flew to the roof of the Yellow World. They could not find a crack, but they heard voices from each of the four directions. They divided into four groups. The Navajo flew east and were directed by the First Woman in the Fourth World.

This was a Black and White world inhabited by other humans and Native American tribes. The First Man and First Woman taught their people how to live. Coyote, the lazy trickster, came and angered the Water Monster. He sent a flood, and the people were forced to leave behind their crop and escape to the high mountain. The people planted and prayed over a bamboo until it grew into one tree. Spider helped the people make a ladder, and they climbed the bamboo tree, where they were safe and dry inside. The people showed the First Woman all they had brought with them from the Fourth World. Turkey brought all kinds of seeds, and the people honored his wisdom. Locust made another hole in the sky and won the island in the Fifth World for the people of the Fourth World. Everyone used the treasure they had taken with them to make a better Fifth World.

In the Fifth World, people were still threatened by the flood. They discovered Coyote had stolen Water Monster's babies and hidden them in his coat. First Man and First Woman took the coat with the babies in the pocket and sent them out into the lake in a boat. The boat came near a large blue bubble which suddenly burst open, and the boat and babies disappeared. The Water Monster never troubled the people again. The Navajo

---

4. Rosenberg, *World Mythology*, 617.

made a home out of the Fifth World, growing in number and honoring certain laws, becoming a great civilization.

COMMENTARY

Interwoven in the myth are all types of creatures, from insects to human beings. The Navajo worldview is somewhat animistic; geographic regions, plants, and animals are often considered living and gendered beings with feelings and powers that should be respected.[5] Everything is animate and is connected with everything else in the world. Furthermore, treating the world kindly will result in reciprocal behavior, since the cosmos is reciprocal and can be personally helpful to humans.[6] Creatures at each level, therefore, are respected as an essential part of the universe. Furthermore, there is a level of comfort with the paradox of the unity and differentiation of all creatures.

In each world, there is a process of physical evolution. In the First World, the insects banded together to enter a better world. By the time they reach the Third World, the creatures have evolved, and while there are differences, they work together. They establish a council instead of a single leader, respecting the differences and gifts of each group. The gods appear and direct their movement to further encourage evolution. In the Fourth World, the people and animals bring individual gifts for the greater good, and in the Fifth World they honor laws and become a civilization. Nevertheless, there is still acknowledgement of imperfection. The Navajo tend to view life realistically, recognizing the good and evil in everyone. Theirs is an acknowledgement of both/and, not either/or. Yet, the focus is working together with all of nature for the greater good of the Diné, The People.

QUESTIONS FOR REFLECTION: THE HUMAN DIMENSION

1. Do you think that diversity in nature is valued in our own culture? Do you think that diversity among humans is valued? Explain your answers.

---

5. Vecsey, "Navajo Morals," 85.
6. Vecsey, "Navajo Morals," 86.

2. The motivating factor for moving is often the search for food. What else motivates humans to evolve and change?
3. How might the growth of the people in this myth be reflective of individual human maturation?

QUESTIONS FOR REFLECTION: CRITICAL ANALYSIS

1. What might be the advantages of viewing society as becoming more complex and civilized versus viewing society as descending into depravity?
2. What obstacles are overcome by the creatures in each world? What might they represent?
3. How is peaceful transition to growth portrayed in this myth as compared to the creation of the Titans and gods?
4. Why do you think the number four was a sacred number for the Navajo, and how might that idea have developed? Reflect also on the four sacred colors.

26

Creation of the Universe and Ife. African

A Cat Just Isn't Enough Company for a God. Gods Need People.

HISTORICAL AND THEMATIC OVERVIEW

The twelve to fifteen million people of the Yoruba tribe in western Africa are a long-lived group of people living in the same area since at least the fifth century BCE.[1] Today, most Yoruba make their homes in Nigeria and the Republic of Benin. They have a complex cosmogony, with a chief god named Olodumare who designated the council of some four hundred gods, called Orisa, to create the world. Olodumare is considered one supreme yet remote god.

Central to the creation story in the Yoruba tribe is a divine being called Obatala. He is one of several deities who are thought by the Yoruba to have been living people. He is also part of the Orisa, the council of gods assigned to bring order out of chaos. Obatala is the god who was tasked with creating solid ground and human beings.

African mythology is fluid and non-linear, so these myths tend to be reinterpreted and accounts vary between generations and individuals.

1. Pemberton, "Yoruba Religion," 9909.

MYTH SUMMARY: THE CREATION OF THE UNIVERSE AND UFE[2]

In the beginning there was only water and sky, each ruled by a god or council of gods. A god named Obatala decided to create dry land. He asked permission from Olokun, goddess of the sea, and advice from one of the council of gods.

"You will need a long gold chain, a snail's shell filled with sand, a white hen, a black cat, and a palm nut," said Orunmila, a god of prophesy.

Obatala asked the other gods in the Osira for their gold, and they willingly provided him with gold necklaces, bracelets, and other items. When Obatala brought the items to the goldsmith to create the chain, the goldsmith informed him that there was still not enough gold to create a chain long enough to reach the sea. Obatala instructed him to use what he had. Obatala obtained the snail shell, hen, cat, and palm nut that Orunmila had instructed him to gather and put them in a knapsack. He hung the chain in the sky and climbed down, down, down to the bottom of the chain. Just as the goldsmith had forewarned, the chain was not long enough to reach the sea, and Obatala knew it was too far for him to jump. From far above, Orunmila instructed him to pour out the sand from his snail shell. Obatala did so, and it formed land. Then Obatala released the hen, who pecked and scratched, scattering the sand, which turned into land, forming the hills, valleys, and mountains. Obatala let go of the chain and dropped down, now able to reach land. He walked around enjoying this new creation. Although there was no life yet, it was a grand start.

After enjoying the creation for a little longer, Obatala planted his palm nut. It immediately grew into a forest. Obatala named the land Ife and settled there, living with his cat for company. After some time, he became both bored and lonely and decided to make some clay figures. He was overcome with intense thirst while making these figures, so he drank some fermented palm juice deeply. He did not realize how drunk he was and continued to model the clay figures. Soon he asked Olorun, god of the sky, to breathe life into these figures. The next day he noticed the figures were misshapen and he vowed never to drink again. He vowed, "I will devote myself to protecting all the people who have suffered from my drunkenness." He became the protector of all who are born with any deformity.

---

2. Myth summary from Rosenberg, *World Mythology*, 512.

The next day, Obatala made new, perfect beings from clay, and when Olorun breathed life into these perfect forms, they began to build houses and cities. The Yoruba people grew and prospered. Eventually Obatala tired of city living, so he returned to his great home in the sky. The Orisa was pleased with his work and did not tire of hearing about life among humans, except for one. Olokun, ruler of the sea, felt slighted that she was not consulted, and she sent a great flood which wiped out almost all of creation. Orunmila climbed down the golden chain and caused the waters to recede. The goddess Olokun sent a message challenging Olorun, ruler of the sky, to a weaving contest. He cleverly used a chameleon to match her every shade of cloth. She told the chameleon to convey the message that he is the superior god, and peace was restored between the sky and the sea.

COMMENTARY

African mythology frequently has animals as co-creators of humanity, underscoring the significance of the connection between humans and nature and elevating the status of animals. In this version, we see a snail shell, a white hen, and a black cat as coworkers in the creation account. Obatala uses a hen to help him create and he lives comfortably with his cat for some time before longing for more company.

In many African creation stories, the creator is portrayed as a potter who creates humans from clay and breathes life into them. His motivation for creating humans is both loneliness and boredom, implying that the gods enjoy the company of humans. This makes for a likeable pantheon of deities. Furthermore, the gods have human characteristics of compassion, creativity, and a willingness to expand beyond themselves, as seen in Obatala's interest in creating people.

The mythology of the Yoruba is elaborate, reflecting the complexity of the natural world and an appreciation for the interconnectedness of humanity, the world, and the gods. This story contains a large council of four hundred gods, called the Orisa. While Obatala is central to the story, when he has finished his part, another god Ogun is said to have taken over and completed the final details.[3] Ogun still presides over the finer details of creation, such as tribal markings.[4]

---

3. Zuesse, "African Religions," 1:95.
4. Zuesse, "African Religions," 1:95.

QUESTIONS FOR REFLECTION: THE HUMAN DIMENSION

1. How are human deformities viewed in various cultures? Do you see the Yoruba view of humans born with deformities as compassionate? Why or why not?
2. In your mind, what positive qualities do the gods exhibit? What negative qualities?
3. Were you surprised to read of a flood in this myth? Take into consideration the size of the continent of Africa. Explain your answer.

QUESTIONS FOR REFLECTION: CRITICAL ANALYSIS

1. What do think is the purpose of the large council of gods, the Orisa?
2. Might there be any advantages to having a remote supreme god and other gods who are more accessible to humans?
3. What might be the purpose of having a "god of finishing touches" (Ogun)?
4. Many cultures contain a flood story. How does this one compare?

27

Creation. Egyptian
From Nun to Nut

HISTORICAL AND THEMATIC OVERVIEW

THE ANCIENT EGYPTIANS WERE isolated geographically. This meant that, unlike most cultures, there was little influence from foreign deities, and the pantheon of gods and goddesses developed independently of synergistic influences.[1] There are four major creation stories in Egypt. In all of them, one god created all the rest, with some of the deities having different roles which evolved and overlapped. In general, the gods and goddesses were most often immortal and usually benevolent, although human disrespect or negligence would anger these deities. When angered, they would bring about misfortune. Goddesses were sometimes more powerful than gods and could be devastating when angered.

In Egyptian culture, the king was considered divine and was the link between humans and the gods. Through his activities of temple maintenance and support of religion, the king assisted in maintaining harmony in the culture.

The major deities included the sun god Ra (Re); the combined god Amun-Ra, the creator; another sun god, Aten; Anubis, God of the dead; Osiris, lord of the underworld and of rebirth; Isis, his sister, wife, and

---

1. "Egyptian Mythology," 2:333.

Creation. Egyptian

mother goddess; Set, the god of violent and chaotic forces; and Nut, the sky goddess.

Ancient Egypt had four different cult centers, Heliopolis, Memphis, Elephantine, and Hermopolis, each with a different creation myth.[2] The myths are named after the region where they developed. At one time, Egyptologists believed these to be separate creation accounts from various localities. However, the Egyptologist Erik Hornung has suggested the more likely scenario that these are complementary and mutually reinforcing stories.[3]

This version of the Egyptian myth of creation is known as the Heliopolis version, dating back from 5000 to 2500 BCE, found on a scrap of papyrus in the 1860s.[4] This version introduces the god Neb-er-tcher, translated "lord of the universe,"[5] who not only creates the world from the nothingness of Nun, but also creates the other gods. Neb-er-tcher changes his name to Khepri as he begins to create.

To create the world, Khepri simply utters a word, such as "land," and it is created from the primordial elements of Nun. To create the gods, he supernaturally reproduces, and his children mate to produce more. Humans are formed from his tears, making them a uniquely fashioned species.

MYTH SUMMARY: CREATION[6]

There was nothing except dark waters, the essence of the goddess Nun. Within the Nun there were all the components of the universe, but these substances were all disconnected and free floating. A form of energy known as Neb-er-tcher decided to create the world and transformed himself into the god Khepri (alternatively, Khepera). He created first a mound of mud, then land, sky, sun, and moon, each with only a word. On any given day, Khepri took one of three forms. His morning form was a scarab beetle, his daytime form was a man with a head of a falcon named Ra, and his evening form was an elderly man name Atum.

Khepri created gods who rule over the elements. Shu and Tefnut, gods of air and liquid, were born from Khepri through self-fertilization,

2. Netzley, "Creation Myths," 94.
3. "Cosmogony," 1:188.
4. Auerbach, "Egyptian Creation Myth," 99.
5. Auerbach, "Egyptian Creation Myth," 99.
6. Myth summary from Auerbach, "Egyptian Creation Myth," 99.

graphically described as having "union with [his] closed hand," masturbation. The resulting children Shu and Tefnut were the first gendered deities. Shu and Tefnut coupled to produce two more gods: Geb the earth god and Nut the sky goddess. Geb and Nut immediately procreated and gave birth to Osiris, Set, Nephthys, Horus, and Isis. Soon their father Geb separated them, and Nut was pushed to the sky to create the heavens. Later Shu and Tefnut returned to the Nun, and Khepri sent his eye (the sun) after them. He created a second eye, which was the moon. When Shu and Tefnut came back, Khepri wept tears that turned into human beings. His first eye was angry about being replaced, so he consoled it by making it the more powerful of the two.

COMMENTARY

According to the descriptions found in the pyramids, Nun is huge black sea without form or border, yet contains all the building blocks of the universe.[7] From nothingness, a powerful god willed creation into existence. This concept of something from nothing may have influenced the Hebrews, as it reflects the Hebrew understanding of creation as well, light from darkness, sky and sea and land, plants, animals, and finally humans. A notable difference from the Hebrew Scripture, however, is that in most Egyptian myths, the creators were self-created and not gendered until their subsequent offspring. The gods tend to grow more diverse with each generation. In this and other Egyptian stories, one god is responsible for initiating the creation process.

The black and formless nature of Nun is symbolic of the Nile River. The Nile flooded almost every year and in the flood's wake deposited a thick, black carpet of fertile soil.

Humans are said to be created as a result of Khepri's tears. There is a pun here, as "tears" in Egyptian are *remy*, and "people" in Egyptian are *remetj*.[8] Hornung suggested that the connection was deeper, that humans were created when the creator god's vision was blurred.[9]

The scarab beetle became an important symbol related to this myth. Also known as a dung beetle, the scarab rolls a ball of dung to its burrow, where it consumes it. It lays eggs in the dung, and as they hatch, they

7. Auerbach, "The Egyptian Creation Myth," 99.
8. Bleiberg, et. al., "Cosmogony," 189.
9. Bleiberg, et. al., "Cosmogony," 189.

seem to come from nothing. To further extend the metaphor, the Egyptians seemed to believe that the growth process from egg to beetle mimics the daily rebirth of the sun; thus Khepri was portrayed as a scarab beetle rolling the sun across the sky.[10] Scarab beetles became an important symbol in ancient Egypt, and the discovery of mummified scarabs indicates they eventually became sacred.[11]

QUESTIONS FOR REFLECTION: THE HUMAN DIMENSION

1. What might the Egyptians find appealing about humans being created from a god's tears?
2. The concept of the scarab beetle coming from nothing became an important symbol in Egypt. How might this serve as a symbol of hope for the Egyptians? What gives you hope?
3. We generally are repulsed by the concept of siblings mating. Why do you think this and other creation stories use sibling couples who become parents?

QUESTIONS FOR REFLECTION: CRITICAL ANALYSIS

1. How does the concept of the Nun compare to pre-existence in other culture?
2. What natural phenomena do you see reflected in this creation story? Why may it be important to have gods "assigned" to various natural occurrences?'
3. Khepri takes on three forms during the day. Theorize as to the significance of each form.

---

10. "Scarab," 976.
11. "Scarab," 976.

28

Pangu. Chinese
His Decaying Body Became the Earth.
And I Thought I Had Big Bones.

HISTORICAL AND THEMATIC OVERVIEW

DOES THE LAND OF China even have a creation myth? Historically, the claim has been that there is no evidence of one and, in fact, very little evidence of mythology of any kind. Recorded Chinese mythology is fragmented and frequently disguised to make it difficult to ascertain its meaning. Instead of specific stories featuring gods, leaders, and demigods, in Chinese mythology, we tend to find fragments of mythological characters with little to no storyline.

However, more recent scholarship has shown this to be a mischaracterization of Chinese culture. This is because Chinese mythology tends to focus more on structure than on narrative. For these and other reasons, scholars in the 1920s to 1940s began to move away from earlier claims and acknowledge that Chinese mythology played a unique and important role in developing China.[1]

Chinese myth appears to be different from typical ancient literature in that it does not sustain a consistent storyline, but instead could be considered

---

1. Girardot, *Encyclopedia of Religion*, 1622.

Pangu. Chinese

as employing a strategy that "constantly juggles, rearranges and transforms assorted mythological signs" to emphasize order and disorder and states of being.[2] This complicates the study of Chinese mythology, but the basic mythological themes can be extrapolated with reasonable confidence based on evidence from the Western and Eastern Zhou dynasties (1046–221 BCE).[3]

By the first century CE, several similar creation narratives had developed, all positing that life begins with a cosmic egg. The two oldest written versions were authored by Xu Zheng (220–65 CE).[4]

MYTH SUMMARY: PANGU[5]

In the beginning was an egg containing yin and yang as an opaque swirling mass. From inside this egg was Pangu born. He slept here for eighteen thousand years until he woke and realized he was in chaos. He began to writhe to be free and split the shell, lifting the light part of the egg upward with the heavy part sinking. Thus, yin and yang separated, yin forming the earth and yang forming the heavens. Pangu stood and grew each day for another eighteen thousand years, growing hairy and developing horns on his head. After these eighteen thousand years of growing, Pangu was so exhausted from his struggle that he died. His decaying body turned into the earth. His last breath became the clouds, his spine turned into mountains, his eyes became the sun and moon, his flesh turned to soil. As his arteries became canyons, his blood became rivers. His hair floated up to become the stars, and his teeth and bones formed precious metals and gems. The worms on his body, or the insects in his fur clothes, became the common people of the world. His limbs held up the sky.

COMMENTARY

Pangu is one example of a myth where the world develops from a cosmic egg or shell. The types of symbolic structures for myths include creation from nothing, creation from chaos, creation from world parents, creation

---

2. Girardot, *Encyclopedia of Religion*, 1623.
3. Girardot, *Encyclopedia of Religion*, 1623.
4. Lutz, *World Mythology*, 174.
5. Myth summary from multiple sources.

through the process of emergence, and creation through an earth diver.[6] The cosmic egg symbol represents fertility, potentiality, and complementary dualism, as represented by the egg yolk and white. From this duality—in this case, yin and yang—life emerges. This gives a visual image of creation and how yin and yang are related but separate.

It is likely that the Indian epic *Rig Veda* influenced this myth, as there are distinct similarities to the character Purusha, who created the world from his body.[7] The *Rig Veda* was composed from 1700 to 1100 BCE and likely traveled throughout China and Europe from the Middle East. This version underscores the Taoist principles of complementary forces ordering the world.

The Taoist principles of yin and yang are said to be interdependent. Much of Chinese culture is based on this concept of the natural flow of the universe, with both yin and yang dependent upon and in need of each other. Life should be lived in balance; yin/yang are opposites in balance, such as female/male, dark/light, and passive/aggressive. One's goal should be to live in harmony and flexibility to what life brings.

QUESTIONS FOR REFLECTION: THE HUMAN DIMENSION

1. Explain how balance in life could be helpful.
2. From Pangu's struggle and sacrifice come the elements of creation. Provide examples of some people in history whose struggle led to a greater good.
3. Explore the principles of Taoism. What principles of Taoism do you find helpful? What might be problematic?

QUESTIONS FOR REFLECTION: CRITICAL ANALYSIS

1. As noted, the *Rig Veda* probably influenced this myth. Where else have you seen similarities between stories of different cultures?
2. Pangu is looked upon with fondness and affection in Chinese culture. How might the imagery used in the myth contribute to that feeling? Explain your answer.

---

6. Long, "Cosmogony," 3:1986.
7. Lutz, *World Mythology*, 175.

29

Creation. Mongolian
Why Do Cats and Dogs Have Fur and We Don't?

HISTORICAL AND THEMATIC OVERVIEW

MONGOLIA IS AN ASIAN country about the size and latitude of western and central Europe, located between China and Russia. The Mongolian steppes were home to nomadic tribes for centuries. The two most famous leaders were Genghis Kahn (1162–1227), who unified the Mongol tribes, and his grandson Kublai Khan (1215–1294), who made Buddhism the state religion.[1]

A number of Mongolian creation stories reflect this Buddhist heritage. Typically, the stories contain a description of a dark and chaotic world before creation, but from there the accounts differ considerably. One account influenced by Buddhism describes creation through a lama (a spiritual leader or guru) named Udan. There are parallel creation stories in other Eastern cultures which probably indicate some acculturational influences. This story reflects the influence of Lamaism (a type of Buddhism with elements of the indigenous Bön religion), which spread to the Mongol regions following the spread of Buddhism.[2] Buddhists believe Buddha created the

---

1. Bareja-Starzynska, "Mongolia," 464.
2. Nassen-Bayer and Stuart, "Mongol Creation Stories," 324.

world, so the account of Udan is notable in that it contradicts some Buddhist beliefs.

There are three short creation myths below. The first is a short straightforward creation story, and the second is an attempt to explain natural phenomena, in this case, why dogs have fur and humans do not. The third explains the origin of the basic elements of the world.

MYTH SUMMARY: UDAN[3]

There was a lama named Udan who created the world and all that was in it. When he was five hundred years old, earth and creation had not yet appeared. When Udan reached the age of one thousand, he divided the heavens and the earth into nine entities, including a nine-story heaven and a nine-story earth, along with nine rivers. Finally, he made humans out of clay. The humans married, and from these two humans, all humanity is descended.

MYTH SUMMARY: WHY DOGS HAVE FUR[4]

In ancient days, a god named Burqan Tenger descended to earth and made a man and woman out of clay. When he first formed them, they were only clay figures covered with hair and contained no life or breath. Burqan Tenger intended to make them sentient life forms with holy water, but to get this holy water he needed to return to heaven. He told his dog and cat to protect the clay people from the devil. Just as the god left, the devil entered. The dog and cat successfully fended off the devil and protected the clay figures while Burquan was away. But the clever devil gave a piece of red raw meat to the dog and a bowl of silky, frothy milk to the cat. In that moment of distracted eating, they turned away and did not notice that the devil was wickedly urinating on the people. The devil quickly ran away. When the Burquan returned, he was enraged at this discovery and scolded the animals. He forced the cat to lick all the hair from the bodies of the clay figures that the devil had defiled. The cat licked everywhere except the groin, which had not been defiled by the urine, and the head and armpits, which were too difficult for the cat to reach. The hair from the humans

---

3. Myth summary from Nassen-Bayer and Stuart, "Mongol Creation Stories," 324–25.
4. Myth summary from Nassen-Bayer and Stuart, "Mongol Creation Stories," 327–28.

Creation. Mongolian

went to the dog, and this is why humans are no longer covered in hair. The tongue of the cat and the hair of the dog are considered dirty for this reason. The humans became animated due to the holy water, but they were mortal instead of immortal because of the devil's urine.

MYTH SUMMARY: THE ORIGIN OF THE EARTH AND ITS ELEMENTS[5]

In the old days, there was only an ocean. Buddha Shakyamuni was flying over the ocean looking for a way to create the earth. He observed a frog with a golden body swimming from north to south. He decreed that the earth should be created on this frog's back. Using his bow and arrow, he shot into the frog's east side. Fire erupted from the frog's mouth, and water sprang from the frog's rump. Buddha threw golden sand on the frog, and this became the earth. The arrow in the frog's eastern side became a forest, and an arrowhead on the western side of the frog became metal areas. The north end of the frog became fire, and the south end became water. Therefore, the earth consists of these five elements: fire, wood, metal, water, and sand. If the frog moves its legs or head, there is an earthquake.

COMMENTARY

The first story is notable in its use of the number nine. The number is considered to be auspicious or favorable, in some geographic regions. The second story explains why humans do not have fur like other animals and also why they are not immortal. The third story describes the five basic elements of the world and how they evolved. While these are all simple stories, some scholars speculate that they were originally longer and more complex, but were later pared down under the influence of Buddhism.

QUESTIONS FOR REFLECTION: THE HUMAN DIMENSION

1. Which of these three creation myths do you find most appealing and why? List two reasons.

---

5. Myth summary from Nassen-Bayer and Stuart, "Mongol Creation Stories," 328.

2. The issue of mortality is raised in the second myth. In your opinion, is this a satisfying story? Why or why not?

QUESTIONS FOR REFLECTION: CRITICAL ANALYSIS

1. Speculate about why the number nine is considered auspicious in this myth and in Mongolian teachings and fairy tales.

2. The second story explains the cultural taboo surrounding the cat's mouth and dog's fur. Speculate about how taboos arise and why they vary from culture to culture. Why might some cultures eat horses and dogs but consider eating pigs loathsome?

3. Why is number thirteen considered unlucky in our culture, but not in others? How and why might taboos endure in a culture?

4. Notice the similarities to the basic elements to the Western culture's elements of earth, air, fire, and water. Compare and contrast.

30

Rangi and Papa. Polynesian
Tawhiri-Matea Is Mad because His Parents Separated.

HISTORICAL AND THEMATIC OVERVIEW

POLYNESIA CONSISTS OF A culturally and geographically diverse group of islands in a vast region of the southern Pacific Ocean. These islands likely were built from volcanic residue and eventually became populated with flora and fauna prior to human habitation. It appears that humans first sailed to these uninhabited islands from Southeast Asia about two thousand years ago.

There is a surprising similarity in the creation stories of the Polynesian islands, despite their geographic disparity.[1] Not surprisingly, most of these stories involve water and the separation of water from sky. While there are numerous variations of this creation story, the basic theme is the same: plant, animal, and human life are created when Father Rangi and Mother Papa are separated. Light is introduced, and plants are allowed to grow.

Tangaroa is an important god to the Polynesians, appearing under several similar names. While many of the gods and goddesses in Polynesian literature are interrelated in families, Tangaroa exists as an independent

---

1. Kaeppler, "Polynesian Religions," 11:7312.

deity. Tangaroa is a creator god and sometimes seen as the supreme being. In some stories, Tangaroa sends a bird over the water and throws a rock to form an island.[2] The bird lands and creates the first people.

MYTH SUMMARY: RANGI AND PAPA[3]

In the beginning, there was nothing except a giant shell, the top of which was the sky (Rangi, the male,) and the bottom of which was the earth (Papa, the female). Rangi pressed down on Papa so tightly that nothing could live in that pressure. There was one god in existence, Tangaroa, the god of the sea, who dwelt between Rangi and Papa. He had no room, but he closely knelt, so as not to separate Rangi and Papa.

Rangi and Papa loved one another and produced six sons, the gods. The sons could only crawl in the small and pressure-filled area between Rangi and Papa. They were sorely tired of living in darkness and pressure, so they consulted with one another about what to do. One of the sons, the warrior god Tu-mata-uenga, urged his brothers to kill their parents so they could have light and space. But Tane-mahuta disagreed and suggested that they separate their parents to create room. Most of the brothers agreed with Tane-mahuta, and the sons in turn tried to separate the parents, each using various means in accordance with his unique skill. The only one who disagreed with the plan to separate his parents was Tawhiri-matea, the god of wind and storms. He was angered by the idea and he left his brothers, as he believed separating their parents might kill them. Even though the rest of the brother gods attempted to separate Rangi from Papa, earth and sky remain fused.

Tane-mahuta tried again, this time by lying in the middle of Papa and pushing up with his legs. It worked, and Rangi and Papa separated with deep groans, their blood becoming the red clay. Immediately, light entered, and soon plants began to grow. Tawhiri-matea remained angry at his brothers for splitting apart their parents, and stayed between Rangi and Papa, occasionally sending storms to remind the others of his anger.

The gods were pleased with the lush plants and abundant wildlife and decided to create people. They formed them from red clay, and Tane-mahuta breathed life into them.

---

2. "Creation Stories," 2:262.
3. Myth summary from Kaeppler, "Polynesian Religions," 11:7313–14.

Rangi and Papa. Polynesian

Now that so much life had been created, there was need for even more room. Tane-mahuta pushed his parents further apart. Rangi and Papa were pleased by the creation but missed each other's company. Papa sighs for Rangi, creating morning mist, and Rangi cries tears on Papa's bosom, creating dewdrops.

COMMENTARY

One of the major emphases in Polynesian mythology is the unity of sky and sea. In almost all versions of the story, Rangi and Papa love one another deeply and attempt to resist separation. Nevertheless, they are pleased with the life that emerges from their separation. Storms are caused by Tawhirimatea as an angry response over the separation of his parents. Yet, the world was created out of love. It was seen as a gift of love that came at a cost. It is not surprising, therefore, that Polynesian mythology places an emphasis on nature and on the ocean in particular. Occasionally, storms arise to remind people of the conflict and cost of separation.

The concept of creation from almost nothing is central to all Polynesian myths. In this myth, life begins in a shell. Creation is an act of the gods, and humans are formed from clay by the gods and breathed into existence, creating a connection between gods and humans. At the time of creation, all humans are infused with a power known as mana. Mana can be found in people, animals, objects, plants; it can be good or evil, and the amount of mana varies. This myth also serves the etymological purpose of explaining mist and dew.

A central theme is the concept of grief and separation. Rangi and Papa are forced apart, yet it is through their separation that other life begins, including plants, animals, and later, people. Rangi and Papa grieve their separation but celebrate the resulting creation. In life, grief and separation may lead to growth, as it does with Rangi and Papa. A casualty of separation and grief are storms, which come unexpectedly and often pass over quickly. This is true in both a metaphorical and literal sense.

QUESTIONS FOR REFLECTION: THE HUMAN DIMENSION

1. What is appealing about creator gods who love one another and create through their love? How does this compare to other cultures' views of creation?
2. How have you seen grief lead to growth? To metaphorical storms?
3. Explain the implied concept of Mother Earth and Father Sky. What other cultures are you aware of that have these designations?

QUESTIONS FOR REFLECTION: CRITICAL ANALYSIS

1. Based on what you know about Polynesian creation myths, how do you think that the Polynesians might explain aberrations in nature?
2. How does the Polynesian belief that the world was created by two parents compare to creation stories in other cultures?
3. Are these gods friendly or unfriendly? Support your reasoning.

31

Revelation. Middle Eastern
Then I Saw a Great White Throne.

HISTORICAL AND THEMATIC OVERVIEW

THE LAST BOOK IN the Christian Bible is entitled *Revelation*. The title of the book in the oldest existing manuscripts is simply *Apocalypse of John*. The term "apocalypse" in Greek means to expose in full view what was formerly hidden, veiled, or secret. Most of the book of Revelation (1:10-20; ch. 4-22) alleges to be a series of visions disclosing unseen realities and future events to a man named John.

The apocalyptic style of writing found in Revelation was used in both Jewish and Christian circles. It often has an angel or otherworldly being revealing heavenly mysteries to a human recipient. The mysteries are delivered in the form of visions placed in a narrative framework.[1] Revelation is not only apocalyptic in form, but is also prophetic. It is prophetic both by forthtelling (e.g., Rev 1:8) and foretelling ("Now write . . . what is to take place after this" [Rev 1:19]). Prophetic style is distinguished from apocalyptic by its more positive tone (repentance will forestall judgment) and its spoken nature (Rev 1:8; 22:12-13, 16, 20). Apocalyptic style tends to be

---

1. Collins, "Introduction," 9.

more negative in tone (not much hope in the present, yet future vindication and judgment are certain) and it is more visionary in form.[2]

The author of Revelation identifies himself as John, a servant of God and spiritual brother to the members of the seven churches to whom the author is writing (Rev 1:1, 4, 9; 22:8). John wrote and sent correspondence to the seven churches in Asia Minor.[3] John is further designated as a prophet (Rev 22:6, 9) who was confined to the island of Patmos in the eastern Aegean Sea, "because of the word of God and the testimony of Jesus" (Rev 1:9). Likely, his presence on Patmos was not for the purpose of proclaiming the word of God, but rather he had been exiled there as punishment by the state for preaching. Revelation may have been composed between 68 and 69 CE, during the religious upheaval following the reign of the emperor Nero, or around 95 CE during the reign of the emperor Domitian.

Evidence in Revelation indicates there was some local persecution of Christians, but not widespread state persecution (Rev 2:13). Christians in Asia Minor were also experiencing harassment from their Jewish neighbors (Rev 3:9). In addition, the letters to the seven churches reveal that the congregations were faced with strife within their communities. These problems were in the form of false prophets, whose teaching threatened to weaken community boundaries (Balaam, Rev 2:14; the Nicolaitans, Rev 2:6, 15; and Jezebel, Rev 2:20). Given these issues, there was a tendency toward complacency among Christians and a lack of desire and motivation to remain faithful.

The vision that follows describes the last judgment, the course of events that determines the eternal fate of all humanity. The scene is reminiscent of a courtroom. The giving up of the dead by the sea, Death, and Hades enables the righteous and wicked to stand before the throne of God, awaiting their sentence.

MYTH: THE GREAT WHITE THRONE JUDGMENT (REVELATION 20:11–15)

> Then I saw a great white throne and the one who sat on it; the earth and the heaven fled from his presence, and no place was found for them. And I saw the dead, great and small, standing

---

2. Osborne, "Recent Trends," 477.
3. Asia Minor is present-day western Turkey.

before the throne, and books were opened. Also another book was opened, the book of life. And the dead were judged according to their works, as recorded in the books. And the sea gave up the dead that were in it, Death and Hades gave up the dead that were in them, and all were judged according to what they had done.[4] Then Death and Hades were thrown into the lake of fire.[5] This is the second death,[6] the lake of fire; and anyone whose name was not found written in the book of life was thrown into the lake of fire.

COMMENTARY

There is a lot of symbolism in the book of Revelation. Bizarre imagery and comparisons using vivid symbolism would capture the attention of the listener and hold it; and because imagery demands and receives a greater amount of processing time than non-pictoral language, it is more memorable. By creating a picture in his audience's imagination, an author could exhibit an impressive truth, rather than just speak about it. Thus, interpretation of the book requires some knowledge of the meaning of the symbolism that was understood by the original audience for whom the book was written. The following explanations pertain to the symbolism in the above passage.

1. The great and small represent people of various levels of society.
2. The books, literally scrolls, are the heavenly records of human deeds. It was believed that these scrolls were to be opened at the final judgment so that people could be rewarded or punished (Dan 7:10). Record books of all humankind's deeds are probably metaphorical for God's unfailing memory.[7]
3. The scroll of life is the list of people who receive the gift of life with God (Rev 3:5; 13:8; 17:8; 20:15; 21:27). This text does not reveal how one's name is written in this book. However, Revelation 13:8 further

---

4. John seems to picture those who have died on earth being kept in Hades, the realm under the earth, until the last judgment.
5. This statement can best be taken to mean that the role of Death and Hades is ended. In the new creation, death will be no more (Rev 21:4).
6. The second death deprives a person of life in the age to come.
7. Beale, *Revelation*, 1033.

describes the book as "the book of life belonging to the Lamb slain from the foundation of the world," meaning that the basis for one's name being inscribed in the book was the sacrificial atonement of the Lamb, who is also described as the Lion of the tribe of Judah, the Root of David (Rev 5:8). These designations are epithets for Jesus. The conscious rejection of God's call to repentance for a person's evil deeds is a major theme in the book of Revelation (Rev 9:20–21; 16:9, 11; 20:7–8); expressing that personal choice determines whether or not one's name appears in the book of life. Recording people's deeds meant they would be held accountable at some point in time for those deeds (Isa 65:6; Mal 3:16).

QUESTIONS FOR REFLECTION: THE HUMAN DIMENSION

1. Does the Christian myth of the afterlife offer you a satisfying fate for the just and unjust? Why or why not?
2. What questions does this myth leave unanswered for you?

QUESTIONS FOR REFLECTION: CRITICAL ANALYSIS

1. What might the courtroom setting of this text reveal about the nature of the judgment?
2. Given the struggles facing the church as described in the historical overview, what might have been the effect of this text on the original audience?
3. What might the flight of a personified heaven and earth communicate?

32

Völuspá Part 2, Ragnarok. Norse Mistletoe Mayhem

HISTORICAL AND THEMATIC OVERVIEW

WHILE THE FIRST PART of *Völuspá* looks back at the past, the second half looks ahead to the future. The poem describes moral decay, death, and cosmic disruption. The sun will darken, the earth will sink, and stars will fall from the sky:

> The sun darkens, earth sinks in the ocean,
> from heaven fall the bright stars,
> fire's breath assails the all-nourishing tree,
> towering fire plays against heaven itself.[1]

This sounds much like the events described in the book of Revelation from the Bible. Given that this version of the poem is found in the Codex Regius, which may have been composed around the time that Norway was converting to Christianity (1000 CE), it suggests the likelihood of some Christian influence on its composition.[2]

---

1. Stanza 54. All quotations are based primarily on Benjamin Thorpe's translation, *The Elder Eddas*. The language has been updated. The stanza numbering comes from Larrington, trans., *Poetic Edda*, 30–62. In parts, words from Thorpe's translation have been replaced from more recent scholarly renditions. These changes are referenced.
2. Lönnroth, "Founding of Miðgarðr," in Acker and Larrington, 18, 21–22.

As in the first part of *Völuspá*, this part also contains kennings, a poetic phrase used in conjunction with or in place of the common name. For example, a kenning for blood is "wound-liquid."

MYTH SUMMARY: RAGNAROK

Ragnarok (the doom of the gods) opens with gifts being presented to the seeress by Odin in exchange for her prophetic visions.

> The War Father[3] gave her rings and necklaces,
> for useful discourse, and a divining spirit:
> wide and far she saw throughout every world.[4]

Odin (and the listening audience) were told that the coming of Ragnarok would be signaled by fratricide, punishment, and social collapse. Initially, it was ushered in by the death of Baldr and its consequences (stanzas 32–33). Baldr was Odin's son, who was invincible to everything but mistletoe. This stanza is a prophetic description of Loki's persuasion of Baldr's blind half-brother, Hod, to throw the lethal mistletoe grief-dart at Baldr.

> I saw Baldr all bloody,[5]
> Odin's son, his hidden fate.
> There stood grown up, high on the plain,
> slender and passing fair, the mistletoe.
>
> From that shrub was made, as to me it seemed,
> a grief-dart.[6] Hod shot it forth;
> Baldr's brother was quickly born:
> son of Odin began to kill one night old.[7]

In the lines that follow, the seeress described how she witnessed bloodthirsty men, perjurers, and seducers of other men's wives, all wading through sluggish streams.

> She there saw wading through the sluggish streams
> bloodthirsty men and perjurers,

---

3. War Father is a kenning for Odin.
4. Stanza 30.
5. The phrase "Baldr all bloody" comes from Boyer, "On the Composition," 126.
6. "Grief-dart" is from Larrington, trans., *Poetic Edda*, 8.
7. Woolf, "*Spaewife's Prophecy*," 29, stanzas 32-33.

and some who had lured women to love.[8]
There Nidhögg [NEE-thog][9] sucks the corpses of the dead;
the wolf tears men—do you understand yet, or not?[10]

Death and war predominate in the poem up through stanza fifty-six. As the battle raged, Odin was killed by the wolf Fenrir, Freyr by Surt; Thor and the Midgard-serpent killed each other. Odin is avenged by his son Vidar, and the world disappeared in fire (stanzas 51–5).

> Brothers shall fight, and slay each other;
> cousins shall violate kinship.
> Hard is it in the world, great whoredom,
> an axe age, a sword age, shields shall be cloven,
> a wind age, a wolf age, before the world sinks;
> no man will spare another....
>
> Then arises Frigg's[11] second grief,
> when Odin goes to fight with the wolf,
> and the bright slayer of Beli with Surt.
> Then Frigg's beloved will fall.
>
> Then comes the Victory-father's great son,
> Vidar, to fight with the deadly beast.[12]
> He with his hands will make his sword pierce to the heart of Loki's[13] son:
> then he avenges his father.
>
> Then comes the mighty son of Hlodyn:[14]
> Odin's son goes to fight the serpent;[15]
> in his rage will slay Midgard's-defender.[16]
> Nine feet will go Fiorgyn's[17] son,
> tired by the serpent, who feared no foe.

---

8. This line is adapted from Terry, trans., *Poems*, 4.
9. Nidhogg is a dragon who gnaws at the roots of the world tree, Yggdrasil.
10. Stanza 38.
11. "Frigg's" is from Larrington, trans., *Poetic Edda*, 10.
12. Odin's son is Vidar. He survives Ragnarok and kills Fenris, the Beast of Slaughter.
13. "Loki's son" is from Larrington, trans., *Poetic Edda*, 11.
14. Hlodyn is another name for Thor's mother (Larrington, trans., *Poetic Edda*, 334).
15. "Serpent" is from Larrington, trans., *Poetic Edda*, 11.
16. "Midgard's-defender" comes from Woolf, "*Spaewife's Prophecy,*" 32.
17. Another name for Thor's mother (Larrington, trans., *Poetic Edda*, 292).

All men will forsake their homes.[18]

Following the apocalypse, the earth was raised anew from the sea and some of the Æsir returned to live in peaceful bliss. In the final stanza, the sinister dragon Nidhogg was sighted as the seeress came out of her trance.

> She sees arise, a second time,
> earth from the ocean, ever green,
> waterfalls descending; the eagle flying over,
> which in the fell captures fish. . . .
>
> There shall be found again in the grass
> the wondrous golden game pieces,[19]
> which in days of old the ruler of the gods had possessed.
>
> Though unsown, the fields will flourish,[20]
> all evil will be amended; Baldr shall come;
> Hod and Baldr shall inhabit Hropt's glorious dwellings[21]
> —do you understand yet, or not?
>
> There comes the dark dragon flying,
> the glistening serpent comes from moonless mountains.
> Nidhogg, flying over the plain, in his wings
> he carries corpses. Now she will descend.[22]

COMMENTARY

Heroes were expected to have discernment. They were to be able to judge a situation and the character of the men and the women around them.[23] Norse myths gave wisdom to people as they were passed on by word of mouth. The preoccupation with prophecy in Ragnarok is an example of this transmission of wisdom, even though it describes a world overshadowed by pessimism and fate. The phrase, ". . . do you understand yet, or not?" which is repeated throughout the myth, underscores the acumen theme.

---

18. Stanzas 44, 51–53.
19. "Game pieces" is from Lönnroth, "Founding of Miðgarðr," 18.
20. The term "flourish" comes from Woolf, *Spaewife's Prophecy,* 33.
21. Hropt is an alternate name for Odin (Lindow, *Norse Mythology,* 185).
22. Stanzas 56, 58-62.
23. Constantakis, "Study Guide," n.p.

Völuspá Part 2, Ragnarok. Norse

Ragnarok communicates a moral degeneration for which the whole of humanity (including the listening audience) is held responsible. The myth demonstrates that this lapse into sin will lead to punishment and that the present state of the world is so corrupt that Ragnarok is inevitable.

In its entirety, the myth describes a cyclical view of history, beginning with the harmony of the earliest age, proceeding through a series of events towards a fragmented and inharmonious present, and reaching the great global catastrophe of Ragnarok. Although it appears that evil still lurks in the new world, suggested by the presence of Nidhogg, the myth concludes with the creation of a world full of life and harmony, as the one described in the beginning of the poem.

QUESTIONS FOR REFLECTION: THE HUMAN DIMENSION

1. What do or do not you find appealing or not appealing about the poem?

2. Might the myth *Ragnarok* have relevance today? If not, why not? If so, why?

3. Can there be value in knowing the future? Why or why not?

4. End of the world myths recount various views of time and history such as a linear view, culminating in either a paradisiacal or hellish end, or a cyclical view of history, where nothing is gained in a repetitive cycle of bliss and chaos. Given the presence of Nidhogg at the end, the poem presumes a view of history that repeats itself. How might this view of history impact your daily life? Do you find this view of history satisfactory?

QUESTIONS FOR REFLECTION: CRITICAL ANALYSIS

1. John Oswalt states, "The idea of a future when things will not be as they are now, plays no part in the myths. We do not find stories of utopian realms where the sun always shines and there is no war, and everyone eats simply by plucking grapes from a vine."[24] Do you agree

---

24. Oswalt, *Bible among the Myths*, 50.

with Oswalt? Support your answer. Does his view hold true for this myth? Why or why not?

2. Invoking and honoring ancestors is a universal human activity, performed in every known human culture. What functions might this activity serve within a culture?

3. Part of the purpose of kennings is to explore new ways of describing and understanding the world around us. War Father and grief-dart are two kennings quoted in the myth summary of *Ragnarok*. What effect does the new way of naming the object (the kenning) have on the context where it is used?

4. If you can obtain a full copy of *Ragnarok*, locate some central themes of this poem. Identify each theme with a quotation from the poem.

5. If you can obtain a full copy of *Ragnarok*, speculate on what might have been the functions of this myth for the original audience. Support your answers with quotations from the poem.

33

Afterlife. Persian
A Narrow Bridge

HISTORICAL AND THEMATIC OVERVIEW

ZOROASTRIANISM IS A RELIGION still practiced today that dates back at least twenty-five hundred years. The religion takes its name from an ancient Persian named Zoroaster (also known as Zarathustra). The traditional version of Zoroaster's biography places his birth at about 628 BCE and his death at around 551 BCE.[1] Some scholars studying the language in poems Zoroaster is said to have written place him at a much earlier time, perhaps around 1000 BCE or even as early as 1500 BCE.[2]

The single most important event in Zoroaster's life occurred at age thirty, when he is said to have received a revelation from the god Ahura Mazda.[3] Following this first revelation, he continued to have visions over the next ten years.[4] Zoroaster's visions, which evolved into an entire faith,

1. Olson, *Religious Documents*, 603.
2. Olson, *Religious Documents*, 603.
3. Cereti, "Myths, Legends, Eschatologies," 267.
4. The technique used to induce the revelation is described as transpiring after drinking a glass of water. Prior to his night visions, Zoroaster drinks the water, and the god Ahura Mazda is said to intermingle divine wisdom on the seer (Hultgard, "Ecstasy and Vision," 222). In one night vision, upon being presented in the celestial assembly, Zoroaster was no longer able to see his own shadow, due to the brilliance of the archangels that

were rejected in his native land (in what is now northern Iran), causing him to move to the province of Parthia (in today's northeastern Iran near the border with Turkmenistan).

There is evidence to suggest that Zoroaster was a priest who was well-versed in the religious traditions of his people.[5] It appears that from his visions he acquired a novel understanding of his traditional religious faith. This new religion retained many of the traditional beliefs and practices of its precursor.[6]

At the heart of Zoroastrianism is belief in the god Ahura Mazda, who is said to have created the world and all good things. A key characteristic of the religion is that of dualism, the idea that the world is divided between good and evil. The primary sacred text of Zoroastrianism is the Zend-Avesta. The Zend-Avesta comprises six main parts. One of those sections is called the *Vendidad*, from which the following myth concerning the afterlife is taken.

MYTH: PERSIAN AFTERLIFE[7]

> Zarathushtra said to Ahura Mazda: O Creator! Where will the rewards be decided? Where will they assemble and where will a man of the material world give account for his soul? Then Ahura-Mazda answered: After a man is dead, after he is departed, and gone, the wicked and evil-thinking demons rend him completely, in the third night, after the coming of the light of dawn. And when the victorious Mithra[8] places himself on the mountains with pure splendor. And the brilliant sun arises. Then, O holy Zarathustra, the demon called Vizaresha leads the bound soul, the sinful and wicked man, who worships demons, to the paths, which were created by Time, for both he who is godless and he who is holy, to the bridge Chinvat, created by Ahura Mazda. Here they interrogate the

---

encircled him. The ecstatic experience resulted in the seer's consciousness being entirely filled with the presence of God, having the feelings of belonging to the divine sphere. While the prophet was in the sacred assembly, the god Ahura Mazda instructed him in the doctrines and duties of the true religion (Noss, *Man's Religions*, 438).

5. Kreyenbroek and Munshi, *Living Zoroastrianism*, 4.

6. Kreyenbroek and Munshi, *Living Zoroastrianism*, 4.

7. This myth is adapted from Bleeck and Spiegel, *Avesta,* 141. The language has been updated.

8. Mithra is a pastoral deity who gives pastures to his worshippers, but he is also a military deity who destroys enemies of the faithful (Olson, *Religious Documents*, 607).

consciousness and the soul regarding the conduct practiced in the material world. Then she comes. The beautiful, strong, swift, and fair formed one, accompanied by dogs. She leads away the souls of the pure over the Hara, over the bridge Chinvat to the host of the heavenly Yazatas.[9] Vohu Manah[10] arises from his golden throne. Vohu Manah speaks: How have you come here, pure one, from the perishable world to the imperishable world? The pure souls go contented to the golden thrones of Ahura Mazda, of the Amesha Spentas, to the House of Song,[11] the dwelling of Ahura Mazda, the dwelling of the Amesha Spentas, the dwelling place of the pure.

COMMENTARY

These verses recount many features of Zoroastrian views of the afterlife. After death of the body, the soul makes an arduous journey, during which it encounters the Chinvat bridge that is guarded by dogs. The good and the wicked are differentiated from each other as they cross the bridge, as the path grows more narrow for the wicked person and wider for the righteous person.[12] The narrow path of the bridge causes the wicked to fall into hell, a dark pit of torment. The ethically righteous soul crosses the bridge safely to the House of Songs.

At the bridge, judgement transpires. Some accounts of the myth speak of a trial by three divine beings, while others say that the soul will be met by its alter ego—a beautiful young girl, if the person has been good, or an unpleasant hag, if it has not. Depending on the outcome of the judgment, the soul goes to heaven or hell, or to purgatory in case of an even balance between good and bad.[13] This seems to be what is being described at the Chinvat bridge in this text. "And there many adversaries wait, [such as] Eshm with bloody club, malevolently, and Astvihad, who swallows all creatures and is never sated. In the weighing, Rashn the just, who holds the

---

9. Yazatas are beings worthy of worship (Olson, *Religious Documents*, 618).

10. Vohu Mainyu (Good Thought) was one of the members of the Heptad, which are seven aspects of the Amesha Spentas (Holy Immortals). Amesha Spentas are emanations and aspects of Ahura Mazda (Olson, *Religious Documents*, 617–18).

11. The House of Song is a reference to Heaven (Olson, *Religious Documents*, 613).

12. Olson, *Religious Documents*, 626.

13. Kreyenbroek and Munshi, *Living Zoroastrianism*, 6.

balance for souls, never makes it dip to one side, neither for the just nor for the wicked, neither for a lord nor for the ruler of a land."[14]

QUESTIONS FOR REFLECTION: THE HUMAN DIMENSION

1. Speculation is widespread as to what the state beyond death might be like. Since the beginning of time, humans have tried to come to grips with the possibilities. People desire to know the fates of their deceased relatives and friends and the fate to which they too will eventually succumb. Does the Zoroastrian myth of the afterlife offer you a satisfying fate for the just and unjust? Why or why not?

2. People's daily decisions will undoubtedly be based, to some extent, upon their vision of what lies beyond death. In this view, death makes people better husbands, wives, parents, and friends. Do you agree with this view? If not, why? If so, exactly how might this work and how does it resonate with your own experience?

QUESTIONS FOR REFLECTION: CRITICAL ANALYSIS

1. If a key characteristic of Zoroastrianism is dualism—the idea that the world is divided between good and evil—find at least three examples of this feature in the texts above.

2. Some scholars contend that Zoroastrianism influenced Judaism and Christianity. In the texts above, can you find teachings similar to those in Judaism and Christianity?

---

14. *Menog-i Khrad*, ch. 2. As referenced in Olson, *Religious Documents*, 628–29.

34

The Moon and Death. Australian
The First Astronomers

HISTORICAL AND THEMATIC OVERVIEW

ABORIGINAL AUSTRALIAN CULTURES BELIEVED that the world was created by ancestral spirits during a creation period, which is called Dreaming or Dreamtime. It is thought that these spirits left symbols in creation, and by understanding these symbols, one could comprehend the meaning of life and the rules by which one must live. The symbols served as a sort of user manual for existence.

The night sky was one of the natural symbols carefully observed by the Aboriginal Australians. They possessed a complex understanding of the motions of celestial bodies and their correlation with terrestrial events, such as the changing of seasons and the emergence of particular food sources.[1] The Aboriginal Australian cultures are believed to be one of the oldest continuous cultures in the world. Since the night sky seems to have been of significant interest to them, it is sometimes suggested that these ancient people were the world's first astronomers.[2] For those living in Australia before the invention of streetlights, the night sky would have been a wonder to observe.

1. Norris and Hamacher, "Astronomy," 42, 44.
2. Norris and Hamacher, "Astronomy," 39.

It is hard to determine what ancient humans thought when they looked at the sky, for no records exist. However, the culture and worldview of the Aboriginal Australians, which has been passed down through legends, songs, myths, and dances for more than forty thousand years, can give us some insight into the way these earliest known astronomers viewed the skies. For example, the moon figures prominently in various Aboriginal Australian myths about the origin of death.

MYTH SUMMARY: BEFORE THE MOON[3]

Before there was any moon in the heavens, a man of the opossum totem died and was buried and shortly afterwards arose from his grave in the form of a boy. His people saw him rising and were very afraid and ran away. He followed them, shouting, "Do not be frightened, do not run away, or you will die forever. But I will die and will rise again in the sky." He subsequently grew into a man and died, reappearing as the moon, and since then he has continued to periodically die and come to life again. The people who ran away from the boy died. According to the myth, all people suffer the same fate.

MYTH SUMMARY: MOON AND POSSUM[4]

In this myth, Moon and Possum have a fight. Moon and Spotted Possum were once men. They quarreled, and Possum picked up a sharp wooden yam stick and knocked Moon down. After a while, Moon got up, grabbed the same yam stick and hit Possum, killing him. As he was dying, Possum spoke: "All the people who come after me, future generations, when they die, they'll die forever." But Moon said, "You should have let me say something first, because I will not die forever. I will die for a few days, but I will come back again in the shape of a new moon." Human beings die forever because Possum spoke first.

---

3. Myth summary from Spencer and Gillen, *Native Tribes,* 564.
4. Myth summary adapted from Venbrux, "Death and Resurrection," 31.

COMMENTARY

Like the two myths above, many Aboriginal Australian myths describe death as the consequence of human transgressions by the culture's earliest ancestors. The heroic ancestors had the chance to live eternally, but by speaking out of turn or through an act of foolishness, greed, or disobedience to an authority figure, immortality was lost forever for all subsequent generations. For the Aboriginal Australians, death was avoidable and was not perceived as being a natural event.

While these myths do not detail the afterlife beliefs of the Aboriginal Australians, Mircea Eliade stated that they believed in the eternal existence of the spirit following death.[5] Eliade went on to say that there are no moral issues involved in a person's spirit successfully reaching the abode of the dead and joining the other spirits. There is no punishment for sins. If there are any differences in a spirit's postmortem condition, it is in relation to the rituals a person performed and the religious knowledge he or she received and assimilated during his or her lifetime.

QUESTIONS FOR REFLECTION: THE HUMAN DIMENSION

1. Myths from various ancient societies, regarding the origin of death, reveal that many cultures view death as a consequence of disobedience to divine commandments or because of human transgression of the world's order. In these myths, death was not a necessary natural condition for humankind. Do you think death is natural or unnatural? Why or why not?
2. Why do you think people need an explanation for death?
3. While the myths in this chapter do not describe a chance for rebirth, where might a person go to find answers to death and possible solutions to the problem of death?
4. How do you feel about the Aboriginal Australians' view of the afterlife and the conditions for postmortem existence described by Eliade in the commentary section above?

---

5. Eliade, "Australian Religions," 248.

QUESTION FOR REFLECTION: CRITICAL ANALYSIS

Why do you think the Australian Aboriginals viewed the moon as an entity that was immortal?

35

Pele, Goddess of the Volcano. Hawaiian

Temper, Temper, Temper! Jealousy Causes Massive Lava Flows.

HISTORICAL AND THEMATIC OVERVIEW

POLYNESIA IS A WIDESPREAD group of geographically diverse islands in the central and south Pacific Ocean. With various cultures and political views, its people likely descended from Southeast Asian travelers arriving centuries ago on boats and rafts. These travelers brought with them legends and myths that they adapted to their new environment, including one about a minor goddess of fire. This minor goddess evolved in importance to become Pele the goddess of volcanoes, the goddess who creates and destroys unpredictably.[1]

Europeans came to Hawaii in the 1770s, led by Captain James Cook, who died there during his third exploration of the Pacific. Traditionally, Western history has told the story of his death in this way: Captain James Cook was an English explorer whose misunderstanding of Hawaiian religious rituals cost him his life. Cook was the first European to visit the Hawaiian Islands in 1778. With his dress and coloring, the Hawaiians believed

---

1. Nimmo, *Pele*, 2.

him to be one of their gods by the name of Lono. Cook took part in their temple worship and rituals, unknowingly confirming to the Hawaiians that he was indeed Lono. In their mythology, Lono was to ritually die and then leave them. Cook left, which was following the script of the myth, but then returned, which was a violation of the story. The islanders killed him to ensure that the storyline was followed.[2]

However, this view has been challenged. Scholarship by Gananath Obeyesekere and others has refuted that interpretation based on cultural observations and the journal of John Ledyard, an American eyewitness to Cook's death.[3] According to Ledyard's account, Cook's relations with the islanders had soured, in part due to Cook's lack of cultural sensitivity. He had chopped down a fence around a sacred burial ground to be used as firewood on his ship and offered two hatchets in return for the wood.[4] A series of poor decisions, including the attempted capture of a chief, led to the killing of Cook, who was stabbed in the back with one of his own iron daggers.[5] This eyewitness account of the story rejects the idea that the natives considered Cook a god and reveals both European bias and hubris. It posits that it was most likely Cook's lack of respect for the Hawaiian peoples and culture led to his death.

When Europeans arrived in 1778, they found a complex association of deities with Pele at the center. There was widespread veneration of Pele, from priests and priestesses performing rituals to appease her, to the ardent worshipers who lived close to the volcano.[6] Later the island was visited by Christian missionaries, and a number of Hawaiians converted to Christianity. Nevertheless, Pele was not forgotten, nor was worship of Pele discontinued. Pele remained a powerful goddess in the eyes of native Hawaiians because of her ongoing unpredictable eruptions that both created and destroyed. Even in modern times, Pele is a feature in Hawaii.

Other popular deities in Hawaii included the pig god Kampaua'a, a god of war and romance, and Maui, the trickster god and hero, who although short, had great powers and strength. He was said to be the one who provided humans with more light by slowing the sun's movement. The following myth explains the origin and activity of volcanoes.

2. "Polynesian Mythology," 4:842.
3. Obeyesekere, *Apotheosis of Captain Cook*, 3.
4. Sparks, *Life of John Ledyard*, 135–36.
5. Sparks, *Life of John Ledyard*, 148.
6. Nimmo, *Pele*, 2.

MYTH SUMMARY: PELE, GODDESS OF THE VOLCANO[7]

Pele, the goddess of fire, wind, and volcanoes, came to Hawaii from Tahiti. She had been banished from her homeland by her father because she had seduced her sister's husband. She visited various islands, but the floods came, so she moved on and eventually found a home in the volcano of Kilauea. Soon after, she traveled to another island and met a handsome young chief named Lohiau. They fell in love, but Pele was drawn away to fight some battles. She sent her younger sister Hi'iaka to bring Lohiau back to Kilauea. To assist her sister, Pele endowed Hi'iaka with magical powers. Hi'iaka arrived on the island and discovered that Lohiau had died of a broken heart longing for Pele. Hi'iaka invoked her magic to bring him back to life; however, this caused a delay. Pele, who was jealous and temperamental, imagined her sister had stolen Lohiau's love. In a fit of jealousy, Pele sent a stream of lava that killed Hi'iaka's closest friend, thinking that would punish her sister.

Eventually, Hi'iaka and Lohiau found their way back to Kilauea, where they learned of the death of Hi'iaka's friend. Hi'iaka turned to hug Lohiau in her grief, and Pele witnessed this embrace. In a rage, she poured forth more lava to kill Lohiau. But Hi'iaka's magical powers saved Lohiau. She restored him once again and returned with him to his home island. Pele was left behind, alone with her fiery rage in her volcano home.

COMMENTARY

The volcanoes of Hawaii are unpredictable and sometimes threatening. Pele represents a way to personify the volcanoes and to explain and come to terms with their unpredictable nature. Rage and explosiveness can occur in humans as well. Who among us has not encountered a temperamental man or woman who reminds us of Pele, who demonstrates rage against her family? The physical manifestation of lava contributes to the legend. Volcanoes produce hardened lava in the forms of long, thin volcanic glass referred to as Pele's hair and teardrop-shaped beads known as Pele's tears. An enraged, unstable goddess would surely produce such jet black obsidian tears.

One of the themes we see in Polynesian mythology is humans dealing with uncooperative or unfriendly gods.[8] Humans need to pacify the gods or

---

7. Myth summary from "Pele," 4:817–18.
8. "Polynesian Mythology," 4:843.

trick the gods so that the gods will provide food. This has historically been true with Pele, but nonetheless, Pele is revered for her beautiful destructive and creative abilities. In 2018, when the Kilauea volcano threatened thousands in Pahoa, Hawaii, the locals were resigned. Lokelani Puha said, "There's nothing to do when Pele makes up her mind but accept her will."[9] "My house was an offering for Pele," said Monica Devlin, age seventy-one. "I've been in her backyard for thirty years. In that time I learned that Pele created this island in all its stunning beauty. It's an awe-inspiring process of destruction and creation and I was lucky to glimpse it."[10]

This myth developed to explain the violence and creation of the volcanoes, and Pele became both feared and venerated. In the many myths about her, she is portrayed with a temper as turbulent as the fire in the volcanoes. In one such legend, the handsome young chief Kumukahi was playing sports. An old woman approached him to play as well; it was Pele in disguise. He ridiculed her. She became angry, chased him, and poured lava over him.[11] Such is the fate of those who cross Pele.

QUESTIONS FOR REFLECTION: THE HUMAN DIMENSION

1. How might the struggle against natural forces shape one's worldview?
2. Do you personally know someone like Pele? How can unpredictable behavior and volatility in humans be explained?
3. How can human volatility ever lead to positive personal growth?

QUESTIONS FOR REFLECTION: CRITICAL ANALYSIS

1. How do stories help people cope against the natural forces that might cause injury or death?
2. How do destruction and creation go hand in hand in this myth? In other situations? Provide an example.
3. What does Pele have in common with capricious gods and goddesses in other cultures?

---

9. Romero, "Madame Pele," n.p.
10. Romero, "Madame Pele," n.p.
11. Westervelt, *Hawaiian Legends*, 38.

4. How do other cultures pacify their gods and goddesses and to what ends?
5. Describe and comment on another historical example where a conquered people were misremembered in favor of the conquerors.

Bibliography

Anderson, John E. "Creation." In *The Lexham Bible Dictionary*. Edited by John D. Barry et al. Bellingham, WA: Lexham, 2016. Adobe EPUB.
Anton, Baeta. "The Power of the Word in the Maya Epic *Popol Vuh*." *Polish Journal of Arts and Culture* 14, no. 2 (2015) 7–21.
Arant, Patricia. "Folklore." In *Encyclopedia of Russian History*, edited by James R. Millar, 2:507–09. 4 vols. New York: Macmillan Reference, 2004.
Auerbach, Michal. "The Egyptian Creation Myth." In *Critical Survey of Mythology and Folklore: World Mythology*, 99. Ipswich, MA: Salem, 2013.
Bareja-Starzynska, Agata. "Mongolia." In *Countries, Greece to Philippines*, 464-72. Vol. 3 of *Worldmark Encyclopedia of Religious Practices*, 2nd ed., edited by Thomas Riggs. Farmington Hills, MI: Gale, 2015.
Barringer, Judith M. "Atalanta as Model: The Hunter and the Hunted." *Classical Antiquity* 15, no. 1 (April 1996) 48–76.
Beale, Gregory K. *The Book of Revelation: A Commentary on the Greek Text*. New International Greek Testament Commentary. Grand Rapids: Eerdmans, 1999.
Beaulieu, Marie-Claire Anne. "The Sea as a Two-Way Passage Between Life and Death in Greek Mythology." PhD diss., The University of Texas at Austin, 2008.
Belcher, Stephen. *African Myths of Origin*. London: Penguin, 2005.
Bender, Pat. Review of *Masterpieces of Classic Greek Drama*. *School Library Journal* 52, no. 5 (May 2006) 156.
Benson, Larry D., trans. *Sir Gawain and the Green Knight: A Close Verse Translation*. Edited by Daniel Donoghue. Medieval European Studies 13. Morgantown, WV: West Virginia University Press, 2012.
Bierlein, J. F. *Living Myths: How Myth Gives Meaning to Human Experience*. New York: Ballantine Publishing, 1999.
———. *Parallel Myths*. New York: Ballantine Wellspring, 1994.
Bleeck, Arthur Henry and Friedrich von Spiegel. *Avesta: The Religious Books of the Parsees: From Professor Spiegel's German Translation of the Original Manuscripts*. Hertford, UK: Austin, 1864. EBook.
Boussougou, Sosthène, and Karim Menacere. *The Impact of French on the African Vernacular Languages: For Better or for Worse? Gabon as a Case Study*. Newcastle, UK: Cambridge Scholars, 2015.
Bowen, Dorothy N. "Spiders in African Children's Stories." *Curriculum and Instruction Faculty and Staff Scholarship* 20, no. 10 (June 2004) 39–40.

Bibliography

Boyer, Régis. "On the Composition of Vǫluspá." In *The Edda: A Collection of Essays*, edited by R.J. Glendinning and Haraldur Bessason, 117–33. University of Manitoba Icelandic Studies 4. Winnipeg, Can.: University of Manitoba Press, 1983.

Brown, William P. "The Didactic Power of Metaphor in the Aphoristic Sayings of Proverbs." *Journal for the Study of the Old Testament* 29, no. 2 (December 2004) 133–54.

Bungard, Christopher. "Lies, Lyres, and Laughter: Surplus Potential in the Homeric Hymn to Hermes." *Arethusa* 44, no. 2 (Spring 2011) 143–65.

Carnagie, Julie L. et al., eds. "The Epic of Gilgamesh." In *World Religions Reference Library*, 5:61–72. 6 vols. Detroit: Gale, 2007.

Cereti, Carlo G. "Myths, Legends, Eschatologies." In *The Wiley Blackwell Companion to Zoroastrianism*, edited by Michael Stausberg and Yuhan Sohrab-Dinshaw Vevaina, 259–72. Wiley Blackwell Companions to Religion. Chichester, UK: John Wiley and Sons, 2015.

Chên, Ivan, trans. *The Book of Filial Duty: With the Twenty-Four Examples from the Chinese*. London: John Murray, 1908.

"Chinese Mythology." In *UXL Encyclopedia of World Mythology*, 2:232–41. 5 vols. Detroit: UXL, 2009.

Chinnery, John. "China." In *World Mythology: An Illustrated Guide*, edited by Roy Willis, 88–101. New York: Oxford University, 2006.

Colarusso, John, ed. and trans. *Nart Sagas from the Caucasus: Myths and Legends from the Circassians, Abazas, Abkhaz, and Ubykhs*. Princeton, NJ: Princeton University, 2002.

Collins, John J. "Introduction: Towards the Morphology of a Genre." *Semeia* 14 (1979) 1–20.

Constantakis, Sara, ed. "Aeneid: Virgil 19 BC." In *Epics for Students*, 2nd ed., 1–24. Detroit: Gale, 2011.

———. "A Study Guide for Anonymous's 'Poetic Edda.'" In *Epics for Students*, 2nd ed. Farmington Hills, MI: Gale, 2011. Kindle.

Cooper, Helen, ed. *Sir Gawain and The Green Knight*. Translated by Keith Harrison. New York: Oxford University, 2008.

"Cosmogony: The Origin of the World." In *Ancient Egypt 2675–332 B.C.E.*, edited by Edward I. Bleiberg et al., 1:187–90. Arts and Humanities through the Eras. Detroit: Gale, 2005.

"Creation Stories." In *UXL Encyclopedia of World Mythology*, 2:255–64. Detroit: UXL, 2009.

Crossley-Holland, Kevin. *The Norse Myths*. New York. Pantheon, 1980.

Dalley, Stephanie, trans. *Myths from Mesopotamia: Creation, the Flood, Gilgamesh and Others*. Rev. ed. Oxford World's Classics. Oxford: Oxford University, 2000.

Damrosch, David. *Buried Book: The Loss and Rediscovery of the Great Epic of Gilgamesh*. New York: Henry Holt and Company, 2006.

Dennett, Richard Edward. *Notes on the Folklore of the Fjort (French Congo)*. London: David Nutt, 1897.

Diodorus Siculus. *Books 2.35–4.58*. In *Library of History*, translated by C. H. Oldfather. 12 vols. Loeb Classical Library 303. Cambridge, MA: Harvard University, 1935.

Doty, William G. *Mythography: The Study of Myths and Rituals*. 2nd ed. Tuscaloosa, AL: University of Alabama Press, 2000.

Dowden, Ken. "The Amazons: Development and Functions." *Rheinisches Museum für Philologie, Neue Folge*, 140, no. 2 (1997) 97–128.

Bibliography

Driscoll, Sally, "Sedna, Goddess of the Sea." In *Critical Survey of Mythology and Folklore: World Mythology*. Ipswich, MA: Salem, 2013.

Dulles, Avery. "Symbol, Myth, and the Biblical Revelation." *Theological Studies* 27, no. 1 (February 1966) 1–26.

Dyce, Alexander. *Select Translations from the Greek of Quintus Smyrnaeus*. London: Baxter, 1821.

"Egyptian Mythology." In *UXL Encyclopedia of World Mythology*, 2:333–42. Detroit: UXL, 2009.

Eliade, Mircea. "Australian Religions: Part V: Death, Eschatology, and Some Conclusions." *History of Religions* 7, no. 3 (February 1968) 244–68.

Erdoes, Richard and Alfonzo Ortiz, eds. *American Indian Trickster Tales*. New York: Penguin, 1998.

Estés, Clarissa Pinkola. *Women Who Run with the Wolves*. New York: Ballantine, 1995.

Exum, Cheryl J. "Aspects of Symmetry and Balance in the Samson Saga." *Journal for the Study of the Old Testament* 6, no. 20 (June 1981) 3–29.

Finckenstein, Maria, ed. *Celebrating Inuit Art 1948–1970*. Toronto: Key Porter, 2000.

Finnegan, Ruth. *Oral Literature in Africa*. World Oral Literature Series 1. Cambridge, UK: Open Book, 2012.

Fletcher, David. *Myth Education: A Guide to Gods, Goddesses, and Other Supernatural Beings*. Fareham, UK: Onus, 2017.

Gaál, Balázs. "King Śibi in the East and the West: Following the Flight of a Suppliant Dove." *International Journal of the Classical Tradition* 24, no. 1 (April 2017) 1–34.

"Gabon." In *Africa*, edited by Melissa Sue Hill, 311–26. Vol. 2 of *Worldmark Encyclopedia of the Nations*, 14th ed. Farmington Hills, MI: Gale, 2017.

Garrett, John. *A Classic Dictionary of India*. Madras, India: Higgenbotham and Co., 1871.

Gentile, John S. "Shape-Shifter in the Green: Performing Sir Gawain and the Green Knight." *Storytelling, Self, Society* 10, no. 2 (2014) 220–43.

Gill, David W. *Doing Right: Practicing Ethical Principles*. Downers Grove, IL: InterVarsity, 2004.

Gimbutas, Marija. "Baba Yaga." In *Encyclopedia of Religion*, 2nd ed., edited by Lindsay Jones, 2:727. Detroit: Macmillan Reference, 2005.

Girardot, Norman J. "Chinese Religion: Mythic Themes." In *Encyclopedia of Religion*, 2nd ed., edited by Lindsay Jones, 3:1622–1629. Detroit: Macmillan Reference, 2005.

Glaser, Joseph. *Sir Gawain and the Green Knight Translated, with Notes*. Indianapolis: Hackett, 2011.

González, Ann. "The *Popol Vuh* for Children: Explicit and Implicit Ideological Agendas." *Children's Literature Association Quarterly* 39, no. 2 (Summer 2014) 216–33.

Gordley, Matthew E. *Teaching through Song in Antiquity: Didactic Hymnody Among Greeks, Romans, Jews, and Christians*. Wissenschaftliche Untersuchungen zum Neuen Testament 302. Tübingen, Germ.: Mohr Siebeck, 2011.

Grayson, James. *Myths and Legends from Korea*. New York: Routledge, 2001.

Greenfield, Jeanette. *The Return of Cultural Treasures*. 3rd ed. Cambridge, UK: Cambridge University Press, 2007.

Grottanelli, Cristiano. "Dragons." In *Encyclopedia of Religion*, 2nd ed., edited by Lindsay Jones, 4:2430–2434. Detroit: Macmillan Reference, 2005.

Gudorf, Christine E. *Comparative Religious Ethics: Everyday Decisions for Our Everyday Lives*. Minneapolis: Fortress, 2013.

Bibliography

Gunnell, Terry. "Eddic Performances and Eddic Audiences." In *A Handbook to Eddic Poetry Myths and Legends of Early Scandinavia*, edited by Carolyne Larrington et al., 92–113. Cambridge, UK: Cambridge University Press, 2016.

Harbus, Antonina. "Emotion and Narrative Empathy in Sir Gawain and the Green Knight." *English Studies* 97, no. 6 (June 2016) 594–607.

Hard, Robin and H. J. Rose. *The Routledge Handbook of Greek Mythology: Based on H. J. Rose's Handbook of Greek Mythology*. London: Routledge, 2004.

Heiden, Bruce. "Truth and Personal Agreement in Archaic Greek Poetry: The Homeric Hymn to Hermes." *Philosophy and Literature* 34, no. 2 (October 2010) 409–24.

"Hesiod." In *Encyclopedia of World Biography*, 2nd ed., 7:361–62. Detroit: Gale, 2004. EBook.

Hesiod and Homer. *Hesiod, the Homeric Hymns, and Homerica*. Translated by Hugh G. Evelyn-White. Loeb Classical Library 57. New York: Putnam's Sons, 1920.

Holm, David. "The Ancient Song of Doengving: A Zhuang Funeral Text from Donglan Guangxi." *Monumenta Serica* 49 (2001) 71–140.

Homer. *The Homeric Hymns*. Translated by Jules Cashford. London: Penguin, 2003.

———. *Homeric Hymns. Homeric Apocrypha. Lives of Homer*. Edited and translated by Martin L. West. Loeb Classical Library 496. Cambridge, MA: Harvard University Press, 2003.

———. *Iliad: Books 13–24*. Translated by A. T. Murray. Revised by William F. Wyatt. Loeb Classical Library 171. Cambridge, MA: Harvard University Press, 1925.

———. *The Odyssey*. Translated by Emily Wilson. New York: W.W. Norton, 2018.

Howard, Donald R. "Structure and Symmetry in Sir Gawain." *Speculum* 39, no. 3 (July 1964) 425–33.

Howard, Veena Rani. "Lessons from 'The Hawk and the Dove': Reflections on the *Mahābhārata*'s Animal Parables and Ethical Predicaments." *Sophia* 57, no. 1 (March 2018) 119–31.

Hultgard, Anders. "Ecstasy and Vision." In *Religious Ecstasy: Based on Papers Read at the Symposium on Religious Ecstasy Held at Åbo, Finland, on the 26th–28th of August 1981*, edited by Nils G. Holm, 218–25. Stockholm, Swed.: Almqvist & Wiksell International, 1982.

Hyde-Chambers, Frederick and Audrey Hyde-Chambers. *Tibetan Folk Tales*. Boulder, CO: Shambhala, 1981.

Jensen, Minna Skafte. "Performance." In *Companion to Ancient Epic*, edited by John Miles Foley, 45–54. Malden, MA: Blackwell, 2005.

Johnston, Sarah Iles. "Myth, Festival, and Poet: The Homeric Hymn to Hermes and Its Performative Context." *Classical Philology* 97, no. 2 (April 2002) 109–32.

Judson, Katherine Berry. *Myths and Legends of the Pacific Northwest*. Chicago: A.C. McClurg, 1916.

Kaeppler, Adrienne L. "Polynesian Religions: Mythic Themes." In *Encyclopedia of Religion*, 2nd ed., edited by Lindsay Jones, 11:7312–15. Detroit: Macmillan Reference, 2005.

Kamčevski, Danko. "Orality and Humour in *Sir Gawain and the Green Knight*." *Fabula* 54, no. 3-4 (November 2013) 263–74.

Kerven, Rosalind. *Viking Myths and Sagas: Retold from Ancient Norse Texts*. Morpeth, UK: Talking Stone, 2015.

King, Katherine Callen. *Ancient Epic*. Blackwell Introductions to the Classic World. Chichester, UK: John Wiley and Sons, 2009.

Bibliography

Kleivan, Inge. "Sedna." In *Encyclopedia of Religion*, 2nd ed., edited by Lindsay Jones, 12:8220–21. Detroit: Macmillan Reference, 2005.

Knapp, Keith N. "Reverent Caring: The Parent-Son Relationship in Early Medieval Tales of Filial Offspring." In *Filial Piety in Chinese Thought and History*, edited by Alan K.L. Chan and Sor-hoon Tan, 44–70. New York: RoutledgeCurzon, 2004.

Knipfer, Cody. "The Development of Xenia and Its Role in *The Odyssey*." *A Really Cool Blog*, November 27, 2012. http://www.reallycoolblog.com/the-development-of-xenia-and-its-role-in-the-odyssey/.

Korovessis, Despina. "Oedipus the King." In *Ancient Times to the Harlem Renaissance (Beginnings–1920s)*, edited by Joyce Moss, 301–12. Vol. 1 of *Literature and Its Times Supplement 1: Profiles of Notable Literary Works and the Historical Events that Influenced Them*. Detroit: Gale, 2003.

Kreyenbroek, Philip G., and Shehnaz Neville Munshi. *Living Zoroastrianism: Urban Parsis Speak About Their Religion*. Abingdon, UK: Routledge, 2001.

Larrington, Carolyne. *Norse Myths: A Guide to the Gods and Heroes*. London: Thames and Hudson, 2017.

———, trans. *The Poetic Edda*. Oxford: Oxford University Press, 2014.

Lauter, Paul and Richard Yarborough, eds. *The Heath Anthology of American Literature*. 2 vols. Lexington, MA: D.C. Heath and Company, 1994.

Leeming, David. "Tibetan Mythology." In *The Oxford Companion to World Mythology*. Oxford: Oxford University Press, 2005.

Lindow, John. *Norse Mythology: A Guide to the Gods, Heroes, Rituals, and Beliefs*. Oxford: Oxford University Press, 2002.

Long, Charles H. "Cosmogony." In *Encyclopedia of Religion*, 2nd ed., edited by Lindsay Jones, 3:1985–91. Detroit: Macmillan Reference, 2005.

Lönnroth, Lars. "The Founding of Miðgarðr (Vǫluspá 1–8)." In *The Poetic Edda: Essays on Old Norse Mythology*, 1–26. Routledge Medieval Casebooks, edited by Paul Acker and Carolyne Larrington. New York: Routledge, 2016.

Lorber, Judith. *Gender Inequality: Feminist Theories and Politics*. 4th ed. New York: Oxford University Press, 2010.

Lynch, Patricia Ann. "Navajo." In *Native American Mythology A to Z*, revised by Jeremy Roberts, 2nd ed., 75–76. Mythology A to Z. New York: Chelsea House, 2010.

Lysaght, Patricia. "Banshee." In *Encyclopedia of Death and the Human Experience*, edited by Clifton D. Bryant and Dennis L. Peck, 1:95–98. 2 vols. Thousand Oaks, CA: SAGE, 2009.

———. *The Banshee: The Irish Death-Messenger*. Dublin: O'Brien, 1986.

Maciver, Calum A. *Quintus Smyrnaeus' Posthomerica: Engaging Homer in Late Antiquity*. Mnemosyne Supplements 343. Leiden, Netherlands: Brill, 2012.

MacKillop, James. "Banshee." In *A Dictionary of Celtic Mythology*, 33–34. New York: Oxford University Press, 2004.

Madsen, Catherine. "Theological Reticence and Moral Radiance: Notes on Tolkien, Levinas, and Inuit Cosmology." *Mythlore* 32, no. 1 (Fall/Winter 2013) 113-28.

Magnusson, Magnus. "Introduction." In *The Return of Cultural Treasures*, by Jeanette Greenfield. 3rd ed. Cambridge, UK: Cambridge University Press, 2007.

Makarius, Laura. "The Myth of the Trickster: The Necessary Breaker of Taboos." In *Mythical Trickster Figures: Contours, Contexts, and Criticisms*, edited by William J. Hynes and William G. Doty, 66–86. Tuscaloosa, AL: University of Alabama Press, 1993.

Bibliography

Man, John. *Searching for the Amazons: The Real Warrior Women of the Ancient World.* New York: Pegasus, 2018.

Marco, Romani Mistretta. "Hermes the Craftsman: The Invention of the Lyre." *Gaia: Revue Interdisciplinaire Sur La Grèce Archaïque* 20, no. 1 (2017) 5–22.

Margeson, Robert W. "Structure and Meaning in 'Sir Gawain and the Green Knight.'" *Papers on Language and Literature* 13, no. 1 (January 1977) 16–24.

Marshall, Emily Zobel. "Anansi, Eshu, and Legba: Slave Resistance and the West African Trickster." In *Human Bondage in the Cultural Contact Zone: Transdisciplinary Perspectives on Slavery and Its Discourses*, edited by Raphael Hörmann and Gesa Mackenthun, 177–92. Cultural Encounters and the Discourses of Scholarship 2. New York: Waxmann, 2010.

Mathews, Kenneth A. *Genesis 1–11:26.* New American Commentary 1A. Nashville: Broadman and Holman, 1996.

Mayor, Adrienne. *The Amazons: Lives and Legends of Warrior Women across the Ancient World.* Princeton, NJ: Princeton University Press, 2014.

McKenzie, John L. *Myths and Realities: Studies in Biblical Theology.* London: Chapman, 1963. Reprint, Eugene, OR: Wipf and Stock, 2008.

Millman, Lawrence, ed. *A Kayak Full of Ghosts: Eskimo Tales.* Santa Barbara, CA: Capri, 1987.

Minchen, Elizabeth. *Homer and the Resources of Memory: Some Applications of Cognitive Theory to the* Iliad *and the* Odyssey. 1st ed. New York: Oxford University Press, 2001.

Morris, Richard. *Sir Gawayne and the Green Knight: An Alliterative Romance-Poem.* 2nd ed. London: Trübner and Co., 1869.

Moss, Joyce, and George Wilson. "Antigone." In *Ancient Times to the American and French Revolutions (Prehistory-1790s)*, 14–21. Vol. 1 of *Literature and Its Times: Profiles of Three Hundred Notable Literary Works and the Historical Events that Influenced Them.* Detroit: Gale, 1997.

Mphande, David Kapenyela. *Oral Literature and Moral Education Among the Lakeside Tonga of Northern Malawi: A Study of Tonga Culture in Northern Malawi.* Mzuzu, Malawi: Mzuni, 2014.

Mvé Ondo, Bonaventure. *Wisdom and Initiation in Gabon: A Philosophical Analysis of Fang Tales, Myths, and Legends.* Translated by James F. Barnes. Lanham, MD: Lexington, 2013.

Narayan, R. K. *The Mahabharata: A Shortened Modern Prose Version of the Indian Epic.* Chicago: University of Chicago Press, 2000.

Nassen-Bayer, and Kevin Stuart. "Mongol Creation Stories: Man, Mongol Tribes, the Natural World, and Mongol Deities." *Asian Folklore Studies* 51, no. 2 (1992) 323–34.

Netzley, Patricia D. "Creation Myths." In *The Greenhaven Encyclopedia of Ancient Egypt*, edited by Michael Berger, 94. Gale In Context: World History. San Diego: Greenhaven, 2003.

Niditch, Susan. *Oral World and Written Word: Ancient Israelite Literature.* Edited by Douglas A. Knight. Library of Ancient Israel. Louisville, KY: Westminster, 1996.

Nimmo, H. Arlo. *Pele, Volcano Goddess of Hawai'i: A History.* Jefferson, NC: McFarland, 2011.

Noble, Margaret E. and Ananda K. Coomaraswamy. *Myths of the Hindus and Buddhists.* New York: Henry Holt and Company, 1914.

Norris, Ray P. and Duane W. Hamacher. "The Astronomy of Aboriginal Australia." *Proceedings of the International Astronomical Union* 5 (2009) 39–47.

Bibliography

Noss, John B. *Man's Religions*. New York: Macmillan Company, 1956.
Obeyesekere, Gananath. *The Apotheosis of Captain Cook: European Mythmaking in the Pacific*. Princeton, NJ: Princeton University Press, 1997.
"The Odyssey." In *UXL Encyclopedia of World Mythology*, 4:778–84. Detroit: UXL, 2009.
Olson, Carl. *Religious Documents Explained*. Vol. 1 of *Sacred Texts Interpreted*. Santa Barbara, CA: ABC-CLIO, 2017.
Orchard, Andrew, ed. and trans. *The Elder Edda: Myths, Gods, and Heroes from the Viking World*. London: Penguin, 2013.
Osborne, Grant R. "Recent Trends in the Study of the Apocalypse." In *The Face of New Testament Studies: A Survey of Recent Research*, edited by Scot McKnight and Grant R. Osborne, 473–504. Grand Rapids: Baker Academic, 2004.
Oswalt, John N. *The Bible among the Myths*. Grand Rapids: Zondervan Academic, 2009.
Ovid. *Metamorphoses: Books 1–8*. Translated by Frank Justus Miller. Revised by G. P. Goold. Loeb Classical Library 42. Cambridge, MA. Harvard University Press, 1916.
Partridge, Christopher. *Introduction to World Religions*. Minneapolis: Fortress, 2005.
"Pele." In UXL Encyclopedia of World Mythology, 4:817–20. Gale in Context: World History. Detroit: UXL, 2009.
Pemberton, John, III. "Yoruba Religion." In *Encyclopedia of Religion*, 2nd ed., edited by Lindsay Jones, 14:9909–12. Detroit: Macmillan Reference, 2005.
Plato. *Statesman. Philebus. Ion*. Translated by Harold North Fowler and W. R. M. Lamb. Loeb Classical Library 164. Cambridge, MA: Harvard University Press, 1925.
"Polynesian Mythology." In *UXL Encyclopedia of World Mythology*, 4:837–45. Gale in Context: World History. Detroit, MI: UXL, 2009.
Quinn, Judy. "Dialogue with a Vǫlva: *Vǫluspá, Baldrs draumar* and *Hyndluljóð*." In *The Poetic Edda: Essays on Old Norse Mythology*, 245–74. Routledge Medieval Casebooks, edited by Paul Acker and Carolyne Larrington. New York: Routledge, 2016.
———. "Kennings and Other Forms of Figurative Language in Eddic Poetry." In *A Handbook to Eddic Poetry Myths and Legends of Early Scandinavia*, edited by Carolyne Larrington et al., 288–309. Cambridge: Cambridge University Press, 2016.
Quintus Smyrnaeus. *The Fall of Troy*. Edited and translated by Arthur S. Way. Loeb Classical Library, 19. New York: Macmillan Co., 1913.
———. *Posthomerica*. Edited and translated by Neil Hopkinson. Loeb Classical Library, 19. Cambridge, MA: Harvard University Press, 2018.
———. *The Trojan Epic: Posthomerica*. Edited and translated by Alan James. Baltimore, MD: Johns Hopkins University Press, 2007.
Radin, Paul. *A Study in American Indian Mythology: The Trickster*. New York: Schocken, 1972.
Raudvere, Catharina. "Vision, Ritual and Message. The Universe of Old Norse Mythology as Reflected in the Poem *Völuspá*." *Cosmos* 28 (2012) 77–96.
Rayor, Diane J. *The Homeric Hymns: A Translation, with Introduction and Notes*. Berkeley: University of California Press, 2004.
Ricketts, Mac Linscott. "The North American Indian Trickster." *History of Religions* 5, no. 2 (Winter 1966) 327–50.
———. "The Shaman and the Trickster." In *Mythical Trickster Figures: Contours, Contexts, and Criticisms*, edited by William J. Hynes and William G. Doty, 87–105. Tuscaloosa, AL: University of Alabama Press, 1993.

Bibliography

Romero, Simon. "Madame Pele, Hawaii's Goddess of Volcanoes, Awes Those Living in Lava's Path." *New York Times*, May 21, 2018. https://www.nytimes.com/2018/05/21/us/pele-hawaii-volcano.html.

Rosenberg, Donna. *World Mythology: An Anthology of the Great Myths and Epics.* Chicago: Contemporary, 1999.

Ryken, Leland, James C. Wilhoit, and Tremper Longman III, eds. *Dictionary of Biblical Imagery.* Downers Grove, IL: InterVarsity, 1998.

"Scarab." In *Encyclopedia of World Religions,* 975–76. Chicago: Encyclopaedia Britannica, 2006.

Schach, Paul. "Some Thoughts on *Völuspá*." In *Edda: A Collection of Essays,* 86–116. University of Manitoba Icelandic Studies 4, edited by Robert J. Glendinning and Bessason Haraldur. Manitoba, Can.: University of Manitoba Press, 1985.

Scielzo, Caroline. "An Analysis of Bába Yagá in Folklore and Fairy Tales." *American Journal of Psychoanalysis* 43, no. 2 (June 1983) 167–75.

Scodel, Ruth. "A Hidden God: Oedipus the King." In *Sophocles,* 58–72. Twayne's World Authors Series 731. Boston: Twayne, 1984.

"Sedna." In *UXL Encyclopedia of World Mythology,* 5:915–917. Detroit: UXL, 2009.

Sha, Heila. *Care and Ageing in North-West China.* Berlin: LIT Münster, 2018.

Sharma, Arvind. *Hindu Narratives on Human Rights.* Santa Barbara, CA: Praeger, 2010.

Smith, Helaine. *Masterpieces of Classic Greek Drama.* Westport, CT: Greenwood, 2005.

Smith, Pamela Colman. *Annancy Stories.* New York: Russell, 1899.

Somerville, Angus A. and R. Andrew McDonald. *The Vikings and Their Age.* Companions to Medieval Studies 1. Ontario, Can.: University of Toronto Press, 2013.

Sophocles. *The Antigone of Sophocles: An English Version.* Translated by Dudley Fitts and Robert Fitzgerald. New York: Harcourt, Brace and Company, 1939.

———. *Oedipus the King.* Translated by F. Storr. http://classics.mit.edu/Sophocles/oedipus.html.

———. *The Oedipus Trilogy: Oedipus the King, Oedipus at Colonus, Antigone.* Translated by F. Storr. First Avenue Classics. Minneapolis: Lerner, 2014.

"Sophocles." In *Encyclopedia of World Biography,* 2nd ed., 14:343-45. Detroit: Gale, 2004. EBook.

Sparks, Jared. *Life of John Ledyard, the American Traveller.* Boston: Little and Brown, 1847.

Spearing, A. C. *The Gawain-Poet: A Critical Study.* Cambridge, UK: Cambridge University Press, 1970.

Spencer, Baldwin and F. J. Gillen. *The Native Tribes of Central Australia.* New York: Macmillan and Company, 1898. Kindle.

Sproul, Barbara C. *Primal Myths.* New York: HarperCollins, 1991.

Stookey, Lorena Laura. *Thematic Guide to World Mythology.* Westport, CT: Greenwood, 2004.

Taube, Karl. *Aztec and Maya Myths.* Austin: University of Texas Press, 1994.

Tedlock, Dennis. *Popol Vuh: The Mayan Book of the Dawn of Life.* Translated by Dennis Tedlock. Rev. ed. New York: Simon and Schuster, 1996.

Terry, Patricia. trans. *Poems of the Elder Edda.* Philadelphia: University of Philadelphia Press, 1990.

Thorpe, Benjamin. *The Elder Eddas of Saemund Sigfusson.* New York: Norroena Society, 1906.

"Troy." In *Ancient Greece and Rome: An Encyclopedia for Students,* edited by Carroll Moulton, 4:110–111. New York: Charles Scribners and Sons, 1998.

Bibliography

Tzifopoulos, Yannis Z. "Hermes and Apollo at Onchestos in the 'Homeric Hymn to Hermes': The Poetics and Performance of Proverbial Communication." *Mnemosyne* 53 (2000) 148–63.

Vandiver, Elizabeth. *The Odyssey of Homer*. The Great Courses, Virginia, 1999. 12 audio lectures.

Vecsey, Christopher. "The Exception who Proves the Rules: Ananse the Akan Trickster." In *Mythical Trickster Figures. Contours, Contexts, and Criticisms*, edited by William J. Hynes and William G. Doty, 106–21. Tuscaloosa, AL: University of Alabama Press, 1993.

———. "Navajo Morals and Myths, Ethics and Ethicists." *Journal of Religious Ethics* 43, no. 1 (March 2015) 78–121.

Venbrux, Eric. "Death and Regeneration: The Moon in Australian Aboriginal Myths of the Origin of Death." In *New Perspectives on Myth: Proceedings of the Second Annual Conference of the International Association for Comparative Mythology, Ravenstein (the Netherlands), 19-21 August, 2008*, edited by Wim M.J. van Binsbergen and Eric Venbrux, 25–40. Haarlem, Neth.: Shikanda, 2013.

Vergados, Athanassios. *The "Homeric Hymn to Hermes": Introduction, Text and Commentary*, edited by Siegmar Döpp and Adolf Köhnken. Boston: De Gruyter, 2012.

Virgil. *Aeneid*. Translated by Sarah Ruden. New Haven, CT: Yale University Press, 2008.

"Virgil." In *Britannica Academic*. https://academic-eb-com.lcc.idm.oclc.org/levels/collegiate/article/Virgil/108776.

Walton, John H. *The NIV Application Commentary: Genesis*. NIV Application Commentary Series. Grand Rapids: Zondervan Academic, 2001.

Westervelt, W.D. *Hawaiian Legends of Volcanoes*. Boston: Ellis, 1916.

Whybray, R. Norman. *Introduction to the Pentateuch*. Grand Rapids: William B. Eerdmans, 1995.

Wiget, Andrew O. "Creation/Emergence Accounts." In *The Heath Anthology of American Literature*, edited by Paul Lauter and Richard Yarborough, 1:23–26. Lexington, MA: D.C. Heath and Company, 1994.

Wiget, Andrew O. and Daniel Heath Justice. "Native American Oral Literatures." In *The Heath Anthology of American Literature*, edited by Paul Lauter and Richard Yarborough, 1:20–23. Lexington, MA: D.C. Heath and Company, 1994.

Wolfson, Evelyn. *Inuit Mythology*. Berkeley Heights, NJ: Enslow, 2001.

Woolf, Judith. "*The Spaewife's Prophecy*: A Verse Translation of the Norse Poem *Völuspá* with Introduction and Notes." *Scandinavian-Canadian Studies* 24 (2017) 40–88.

Yeats, William Butler, ed. *Fairy and Folk Tales of the Irish Peasantry*. New York: Thomas Whittaker, 1888.

Yuan, Haiwang, Awang Kunga, and Bo Li. *Tibetan Folktales*. Santa Barbara, CA: ABC-CLIO, 2014.

Zuesse, Evan M. "African Religions: Mythic Themes." In *Encyclopedia of Religion*, 2nd edition, edited by Lindsay Jones, 1:91–102. Detroit: Macmillan Reference, 2005.

Index

Aboriginal, Australian, 185–87
Adlivun, 123
Aeaea, 101
Aeneas, 83–89
Aeneid, 81–90, 96
Aeolia, 101
Aeolus, 84, 101
Aeschylus, 51, 92
Africa, African, 5, 8, 57–60, 84, 116, 152–55
African mythology, 152, 154
afterlife, 171–88
Agamemnon, 98, 102
Ahura Mazda, 8, 181–83
Akan, 58
Amata, 87
Amazonian Warriors, 7, 33, 37
Anansi, 58–61
animals, treatment of, 60, 79–80, 109–11, 112–15, 120–23, 150, 154
Annancy, 58, 61
Antigone, 51, 54, 91–95
anxiety, 53, 56
Apache, 147
Aphrodite, 81, 144
apocalypse, 171, 178
Apollo, 40–43, 86, 89, 145
Arctic, 112, 120
Ares, 145
Artemis, 100, 145
Asante slaves, 58
Asian, 62, 163, 189
Atalanta, 33
Aten, 156
Athena, 84, 96, 99, 102, 145

Atlas, 145
Atum, 157

Baba Yaga, 13–17
Baffin Island, 120–21
banishment, 94
banshee, 18–21
beauty, 29, 34, 36, 75, 118–19, 192
blind, blindness, 34, 52, 54–56, 88, 93, 95, 97, 100, 176
Bön, 108, 163
Buddhism, 23, 108–9, 111, 163, 165
burial, 33, 36, 64, 93, 98, 190
Burqan Tenger, 164
Bwiti Fang, 117, 119

Caesar Augustus, 82
Calypso, 99, 101, 105
castrate, 145
Cerberus, 86
Ch'in dynasty, 22
chaos, 5, 8–9, 128, 137–38, 140–41, 143, 145, 152, 161, 179
character, 60–61, 119, 178
Charon, 86
Chenrezik, 109
Chi Li, 22–25
China, 22–23, 62, 160, 162–63
Chinese mythology, 22–23, 160–61
chorus, 53–54, 93
Christian, Christianity, 83, 171–72, 174–73, 184, 190
Cinderella, 118
Circe, 101
clay, 133, 153–54, 164, 168–69

205

Index

cleverness, 42, 46, 88, 105–6
colonialism, 116
coming of age, 43, 104–6
compassion, 24, 30, 80, 88, 109–11, 114, 119, 154–55
Confucianism, 23
Connolly, Thomas, 19–20
consequences, 57, 89, 123, 176
conservation, 112–13, 115
Cook, James, 189–90
cooperation, 36, 113, 123
Corinth, 53–54
coyote, 46–48, 149–50
creation, creation mythology, 1, 3–5, 8–9, 125–70, 173, 179, 185, 192
Creon, 52–55, 92–95
Cronus, 143–45
culture, 4–6, 36, 81–83, 116–17, 156, 162
Cupid, 84–85, 88

dactylic hexameter, 82, 97
death, 16–21, 28–31, 103, 113–14, 173–77, 181–88
defeat, 94
deformity, 153
deities, 156–58, 190
Demeter, 144
destruction, 192
didactic, 8, 43, 57, 59
Dido, 84–86, 88–89
Diné, 147, 150
Dionysus, 91
disability, *see blindness*
Discordia, 83
dishonesty, 42–44, 71–72
diversity, 148–51
divine judgment, 171–74, 182–84
doll, 13–17
dominance, 143–45
Dostoevsky, Fyodor, 12
dragon, 22–25, 145, 177–78
Dreamtime, 185
dualism, 162, 182–84
dung beetle, 158
duty, 65–67, 86–88

Eclogues, 81–82

egg, 5, 158–59, 161–62
Egypt, 156–59
elements, 157–58, 165–66
Elephantine, 157
Elysium, 86
emergence myth, 147–51
Emerson, Ralph Waldo, 96
Enkidu, 7, 28–31
epic, 82, 97
Epic of Gilgamesh, 26–31
Eros, 143
Estés, Clarissa Pinkola, 12
Eteocles, 92
etiology, 9, 64
Eurylochus, 101
Evander, 87

fairies, 19
family, 8, 13–17, 19–21, 24, 40–44, 64–67, 92–95, 96–97, 109–10, 112–15
Fang, 116–17, 119
fate, 54–56, 89, 144, 172, 174, 178, 184
Fates, 144
fertility, 5, 28–29, 138–39, 162
fiery skull, 15, 17
filial piety, 62–67
fire, 8, 14–15, 47–49, 57, 165–66, 173, 177, 189, 191
first man, 127, 129–30, 148–49
first woman, 149
fish, fishing, 49, 65, 112, 120, 122, 127–28
flood, 26, 28, 31, 149, 154–55, 158
foreknowledge, 55
forest, 30, 46, 109, 119
Freud, Sigmund, 51
friendship, 28, 30–31
future, 55, 89, 103, 131–32, 134, 136, 139, 171, 175, 179

Gabon, 118
Gaea, 143–45
Geb, 158
generosity, 79–80, 118–19
Genesis, 26, 125–30, 146
Genghis Kahn, 163
genitals, 144

206

Index

Georgics, 82
Gilgamesh, 7, 26–31
glory, 97, 103–6
gold, golden, 15, 65, 73, 104, 110, 117–16, 153–54, 165, 178, 183
good and evil, 153, 182, 184
Greece, 55, 82, 90–91, 94–96, 103
Greek mythology, 32–44, 51–56, 91–107, 142–46
Green Knight, 69–70, 72–75
Greenland, 120
grief, 21, 27–31, 169–70
growth, 29–30, 104, 151, 169–70, 191–92

hades, 42, 144–45, 172–73
Haemon, 93
hag, 13, 19, 183
happiness, 22, 79, 94, 103, 118
Hawaii, 189–92
Helen, 83
Heliopolis, 157
Hephaestus, 145
Hera, 81, 144–45
Hermes, 8–9, 39–44, 101, 145
Hermopolis, 157
hero, heroic, 6–9, 24–25, 33, 37, 46, 49, 61, 81–82, 84, 88, 109, 119, 136, 140, 178
Hesiod, 40, 142–45
homecoming, 96–97, 101–5
Homer, 39, 82, 97–98, 106
honor, 36, 39, 73–75, 89, 111
Hornung, Erik, 157–58
Horus, 158
hospitality, 98–101, 104–5
Hudson Bay, 112, 120
human responses to the supernatural world, 18–21, 65, 93, 96–97, 101, 116–18, 145, 186, 192
human suffering, 55, 65–67
hunting, 45, 109, 113, 120–21

Ife, 153
Iliad, 34, 82, 96–98, 103
immortality, 27–29, 31, 187
incest, 51–56, 143–45, 157–59
innocence, 57, 117–19

intellectualism, 55
intuition, 12–13, 16–17
Inuit, 112–13, 115, 120–24
Iraq, 27
Irish, 19–20
irony, 56, 95, 111
Ishtar, 28–29
Isis, 156, 158
Ismene, 54, 92, 94
Italy, 82, 84, 86
Ithaca, 96, 98, 101–2, 104
ivory, 117–18

jealousy, 191
Jefferson, Thomas, 96
Jocasta, 53–56
Juno, 84–87
Jupiter, 84–87

Kampauaʻa, 190
karma, 79
keening, 18–21
kenning, 140–41, 176, 180
Khepri, 157–59
kindness, 78–80, 103–4, 113, 115, 118–19
King Alcinous, 100, 104
King Arthur, 69–70, 73, 75
kleos, 103
Knights of the Round Table, 70–71, 73
Korean mythology, 63–64
Kublai Khan, 163
Kumukahi, 192

Lady Nart Sana, 32
Laius, 52–54
lama, 163–64
lament, 20–21
Latin, 87, 132
Latinus, King, 86–87
laundry, 14–17
lava, 191–92
Lavinia, 86–87
lawgiver, 94
Layard, Austen Henry, 27
Lohiau, 191
Loki, 139, 176–77
London, 26–27

Index

Lono, 190
loyalty, 73–74

Mahābhārata, 77, 79
mana, 169
Massa, 60
maturation, 13–17, 106, 151
Mayan mythology, 131–34
Memphis, 157
Menelaus, 83, 104
Mercury, 85
Merope, 53–54
Mesopotamian Valley, 27
metaphor, 3–4, 21, 173
Metis, 144
metis, 105
Mezentius, 89
Milton, John, 83, 96
mistreatment, 16, 117–18
Mnestheus, 85
Mongolia, Mongolian, 109, 163, 166
Moni-Mambu, 59
moon, 128, 137–39, 157–58, 161, 178, 186, 188
morality, 8, 57, 66, 73–74, 81–82, 88, 96, 117–18, 175–79, 187
mortality, 27–29, 30, 106, 166
Muses, 142–43
mythology, cultural characteristics, 22–23, 46, 57, 108–9, 125–26, 140, 152, 154, 160–61, 169, 191
mythology, defined, 1–4, 6–8, 8–10, 140

Native American mythology, 45–50, 147–51
Natural law, 93
nature, 9, 28, 30, 38, 45–47, 59, 112–13, 133, 148–50, 154, 169–70
Nausicäa, 99–100, 104
Navajo, 45, 145–51
Neb—er—tcher, 157
Nephthys, 158
Nestor, 104
Nigeria, 152
Nile River, 158
nine, 23–24, 64, 164–66
Nineveh, 27

Norse mythology, 135–41
Northwest Caucasian peoples, 32
Nun, 156–59
Nut, 156–59

Obatala, 152–54
obedience, 58, 62–64, 94, 118–19
Odin, 2, 137–40, 176–78
Odysseus, 83, 84, 88, 96, 97–107
Odyssey, 39, 77, 81, 82, 88, 96–97
Oedipal Complex, 51
Oedipus, 51–56, 92
Oedipus at Colonus, 91
ogress, 13
Ogun, 154
Olodumare, 152
Olokun, 153–54
oral cultures, oral tradition, 1, 5, 6–7, 11, 109, 136
Orisa, 152–55
orphan, 116–19
Orunmila, 153–54
Osiris, 156, 158

Pallas, 87
Pangu, 158–62
Papa, 167–69
Paradise Lost, 83
Pari, 63–64
Paris, 83–84
Pele, 189–92
Penelope, 98–99, 102, 104–5
Penthesileia, 7, 32–38
performance, 4–8, 47, 50, 139–40
Persephone, 144
Perses, 142
Persian mythology, 8, 181–83
Personal growth, 29–30, 104, 150–51, 169–70, 192
Phaeacians, 99, 10, 104–5
Poetic Edda, 136–38, 175–77
Poland, 12
Politeness, 118
Polybus, 53–54
Polynesia, 167–70
Polynices, 92–94
Polyphemus, 100–101, 104–5
Pontus, 143

Portuguese, 116
Poseidon, 97, 99, 100, 105, 144, 145
power, 8, 9, 24, 27, 28, 43, 46, 60, 79, 89, 94, 129, 133, 134, 138, 143–45, 150, 156, 158, 169, 190–91
pride, 82, 94–95, 100, 105
prophesy, 51–52, 54–56, 83, 84, 86, 92, 144, 153
protagonist, 94, 106
Purusha, 162
Pygmies, 116

Queen Arete, 100

Ra, 156, 157
Ragnarok, 136, 175–80
Rangi, 167–69
regret, 36, 87, 89
Republic of Benin, 152
reputation, 69, 74, 75
respect, 3, 17, 30, 46, 62, 89, 90, 113, 118, 119, 123, 150
Revelation, 171–74
reverence, reverent, 63, 66, 89
reversal of fortune, 52, 56
reward, 53, 109, 110, 114, 118, 123, 173, 182
Rhea, 144
Rig Veda, 79, 162
rite of passage, 44
ritual, 9–10, 16, 77, 93, 108, 12, 187, 189–90
Rome, 81–82, 84, 88–89
Russia, 12–13, 32, 163

Sanskrit, 77
scarab, 157, 158–59
Scheria, 99, 105
Scythia, 32, 33, 36, 37
Sedna, 120–24
seeress, 136, 137, 138, 139, 140, 176, 178
separation, 5, 167, 169
Sergestus, 85
Serpent, 5, 22, 23–24, 177, 178
Set, 158
Seven Against Thebes, 92
shaman, shamanistic, 45–46, 108, 121

Shu, 157–58
siblings, 44, 91–95, 159
Sir Gawain, 68–76
Slavery, 23, 58–60, 125, 147
Smith, George, 26
Sophocles, 51–53, 55, 91–92, 94–95
sorrow, 86–87, 89
Sparta, 83
Spenser, Edmund, 83
sphinx, 53–54
stepmother, 14–15, 65, 117–19
Styx, 86
subconscious, 16, 51
suffering, 52, 55, 66, 80, 92, 98, 123, 153
suicide, 54, 55, 87, 113
suitor, 98–105, 121–22
Sumerian, 27, 31
Sun god, 2, 101, 156
supremacy, 145, 152
symbol, symbolism, 3, 4–5, 16–17, 22, 69, 75, 93, 102, 119, 138, 158–59, 161–62, 173, 185

taboo, 121, 123–24, 134, 166
Tane-mahuta, 168–69
Tangaroa, 167–68
Taoism, 23, 162
Tartarus, 42, 86, 143–44
Tashi, 109–11
Tawhiri-mahuta, 168–69
Tchaikovsky, Peter, 12
Tefnut, 157–58
Telemachus, 98–99, 102, 104–6
The Ancient Song of Doengving, 63–64
The Faerie Queen, 83
The Twenty-four Exemplars of Filial Piety, 63
Theater of Dionysus, 91
Thebes, 52, 53, 92, 93
Theogony, 142, 143
Thor, 138–39, 177
Thrinacie, 101
Tibet, 108–9, 111
Tiresias, 52, 56, 93, 95, 101
Titans, 142–51
toga, 87
Tolstoy, Leo, 12

Index

tragedy, 55
trickster, 45–49, 57–61, 149, 190
Trojan horse, 83–84, 105
Trojan War, 33, 35, 83–84, 88, 96–97, 105
Tucca, 82
Tu-mata-uenga, 168
Turnas, 87

Udan, 163–64
underworld, 9, 41, 42, 86, 88, 93, 103, 123, 143–45, 147, 156
unfriendly, 170, 191
unity, 150, 169
Uranus, 143–44
Uruk, 27–28, 30–31
Utnapishtim, 28–29, 31

Varius, 82
Vasalisa, 12–17
Vendidad, 182
Venus, 81, 83, 84, 87
violence, violent, 19, 88, 99, 102, 157, 192
vipers, 118
Virgil, 81–83, 87–89, 96
volatility, 191–92
Volcano, 189–92
Völuspá, 135–41, 175–80
Vulcan, 87

war, 33–36, 82–84, 86–90, 92, 96–98, 100, 105, 132, 138, 177
water, 5, 19, 22, 49, 64, 117–19, 122, 126–27, 132, 149, 153–54, 157, 164–66, 167–68, 181
Water Monster, 149
wind, 19, 47, 65, 84, 101, 110, 122, 126, 139, 148–49, 168, 191
wisdom, 35, 94, 140–41, 149, 178
witch, 12–17, 75
women, status of, 23, 36, 37
words, power of, 13, 35, 59, 133–34
Works and Days, 143

Xenia, 98–99, 103–4, 106
Xenophobia, 37, 103
Xia, 22

Yang, 63, 161–62
Yeats, William Butler, 19
Yin, 161–62
Yoruba, 152, 154–55

Zend-Avesta, 182
Zeus, 35, 40–43, 81, 98–101, 103, 143–45
Zoroaster, 18–82
Zoroastrianism, 181–84

www.ingramcontent.com/pod-product-compliance
Lightning Source LLC
Chambersburg PA
CBHW070316230426
43663CB00011B/2149